CHRISTIANITY, THE OTHER, AND THE HOLOCAUST

Recent Titles in
Christianity and the Holocaust—Core Issues

CHRISTIANITY, THE OTHER, AND THE HOLOCAUST

Michael R. Steele

Contributions to the Study of Religion, Number 70
Christianity and the Holocaust—Core Issues
Carol Rittner and John K. Roth, Series Editors

GREENWOOD PRESS
Westport, Connecticut · London

Library of Congress Cataloging-in-Publication Data

Steele, Michael R.
  Christianity, the other, and the Holocaust / Michael R. Steele.
    p. cm. — (Contributions to the study of religion, ISSN 0196-7053 ; no. 70)
  Includes bibliographical references and index.
  ISBN 0–313–30645–1 (alk. paper)
  1. Holocaust (Christian theology) I. Title. II. Series
  BT93.S735 2003
  261.2—dc21   2002069604

British Library Cataloguing in Publication Data is available.

Library of Congress Catalog Card Number: 2002069604
ISBN: 0-313-30645-1
ISSN: 0196-7053

First published in 2003

Greenwood Press, 88 Post Road West, Westport, CT 06881
An imprint of Greenwood Publishing Group, Inc.
www.greenwood.com

Printed in the United States of America

The paper used in this book complies with the
Permanent Paper Standard issued by the National
Information Standards Organization (Z39.48-1984).

10 9 8 7 6 5 4 3 2 1

Copyright Acknowledgments

The author and publisher gratefully acknowledge permission to quote passages from
the following material:

Excerpts from Morton Irving Seiden, *The Paradox of Hate: A Study in Ritual Murder*
(New York: South Brunswick, 1967). Courtesy of Julien Yoseloff and Associated
University Presses.

Every reasonable effort has been made to trace the owners of copyrighted materials in
this book, but in some instances this has proven impossible. The author and publisher
will be glad to receive information leading to more complete acknowledgments in
subsequent printings of the book and in the meantime extend their apologies for any
omissions.

Contents

Dedicated to the memory of Harry James Cargas.

Series Foreword

The Holocaust did not end when the Allies liberated the Jewish survivors from Nazi Germany's killing centers and concentration camps in 1945. The consequences of that catastrophic event still shadow the world's moral, political, and religious life.

The "Christianity and the Holocaust—Core Issues" series explores Christian complicity, indifference, resistance, rescue, and other responses to the Holocaust. Concentrating on core issues such as the Christian roots of anti-Semitism, the roles played by Christian individuals and groups during the Holocaust, and the institutional reactions of Christians after Auschwitz, the series has an historical focus but addresses current concerns as well.

While many of the series' authors are well-known, established Holocaust scholars, the series also features young writers who will become leaders in the next generation of Holocaust scholarship. As all of the authors study the Holocaust's history, they also assess the Holocaust's impact on Christianity and its implications for the future of the Christian tradition.

In *Christianity, Tragedy, and Holocaust Literature*, an earlier book in this series, Michael R. Steele used his expertise as a literary scholar to show that views of tragedy formed largely by Christian thinking must be reconsidered and revised when the Holocaust is confronted. Steele now turns his attention to what might be called the tragedy of Christianity itself. In *Christianity, The Other, and The Holocaust*, a book destined to be as controversial as it is important, Steele contextualizes the Holocaust in provocative and disturbing ways. Not only was the Holocaust "implicit in the trajectory of Western culture and history," but Steele points specifically to Christianity when he adds that "Western Europe's Christian culture and civilization did not 'fail' or take a detour or collapse—indeed, they operated as they had been designed to do for centuries, achieving an unparalleled peak of efficiency in the genocide of human 'gardening' in the Nazi death camps."

Describing Christianity's long-standing tendency to marginalize and often to destroy those who were considered "Other," a tragic history that climaxed in the Holocaust, Steele's investigation is not revengeful, but it is unsparing, unrelenting, and, some readers may say, too little nuanced. Steele's critics are likely to object that his account makes things worse than they were, that it tars Christianity too much with a cultural brush, or that it overlooks the vast ways in which Christian traditions have helped to create civilization in positive ways, including those that have broken down walls of human separation and embraced persons who were outcasts. Critics will also argue that Steele has not done justice to significant developments in post-Holocaust Christianity, which include rejection of the triumphalism and supersessionism that led to much of the abuse that this book revisits.

Such reactions will have their place, but that place is not self-evident. Especially after Auschwitz, those criticisms will have to be earned. They have to be won by analysis and argument that take full account of Steele's case. More than that, Christian dissent that finds *Christianity, The Other, and The Holocaust* going "too far" will have credibility just to the extent that they are backed by Christian action that remains needed to redeem Christianity's integrity.

Carol Rittner and John K. Roth

Acknowledgments

I am deeply indebted to the following scholars and colleagues who helped me in the various stages of the preparation of this book. Father John T. Pawlikowski, Henry Giroux, James Waller, and Johnathan Shay made significant contributions, often on short notice. My Pacific University colleagues, Vernon Bates, Martha Rampton, Larry Lipin, Jeffrey Seward, Cheleen Mahar, and Jack Boas made highly pertinent suggestions for further investigation. They also made tremendous contributions in my life as respected colleagues who help make a small university a very special place. My English Department colleagues, Pauline Beard and Darlene Pagán, read chapters at crucial times and made significant contributions. Jennifer Nichols and Anna Goulden, close friends and students of the Holocaust, did likewise.

Very special thanks go to my longtime friend, the administrative assistant for the Humanities Division at Pacific, Norma Henry. Norma knows how to keep me up and running, well supplied with all the minutiae needed to write books, grade student essays, and attend meetings. I cherish our friendship, which goes back now ... no, let's not mention that. Virginia Adams, Alex Toth, Lois Martz, and Lynda Larremore of the Pacific University Harvey Scott Library have saved me from enough wasted time over the years to allow me to write another book. They are the true heroes of a well-run, productive university.

My friend and former student, Mike Larson, has in turn been an inspiration to me, with his keen dedication to Holocaust studies and the impact he has had on the lives of countless teachers and students in the states of Oregon and Washington. I wish him and his wife, Melissa, all the best as they go through life.

A new friend, Jill Neuwelt, had the onerous task of translating a particularly difficult Luther passage of German prose. She did this quickly and insightfully, and I apologize for any distress that his words may have caused her.

My friendship with the Reverend Charles Busch started with a phone call six years ago and continues to develop and flourish. He is an inspiration for me, the kind of person who shows us all how life can be lived without animosities, with a keen understanding of the need for mutual respect, with wisdom and charity. He has saved me from the slough of despond.

Martha Hauptman of Boston University helped me very quickly with a bibliographic query involving Elie Wiesel's works. One lost footnote can damage a book considerably, and she saved me from that particular indignity. Elie Wiesel himself, for me, goes beyond inspiration. There are no words for what he means to me. I am pleased to be able to dedicate this book to the memory of his long-time friend, Harry James Cargas, and equally pleased to know that we have mutual friends in Jim and Jill Langford.

Professor Wendy Whitworth of Cambridge University was very helpful in the long, tedious process whereby hundreds of scholars assembled at Oxford University in summer 2000 for an international conference. Dr. Darrel Fasching chaired the session at Oxford where my paper, based on this book, was presented. I had many good conversations with him while we were at Keble College and these remain indelibly imprinted in me. I hope this book will not disappoint him.

Dr. Geri Kern, child of two Holocaust survivors, a colleague whom I respect and admire deeply, has been a blessing as a co-worker with me recently. I wish her the very best and look forward to a fruitful collaboration for many years to come.

Once again, I must thank my dean at Pacific University, Tom Beck, who has been a beacon of hope for me in the administrative wilderness often occupied by faculty members. I am very thankful to him and my colleagues on the personnel committee, as well as the trustees of the university, for accepting my sabbatical proposal that helped me finish this project. Likewise, without the help of a generous Meyer Foundation Research Grant, this work would not have been completed.

Deep gratitude goes to my editors, Carol Rittner and John K. Roth, both of whom have been supportive and thoughtful in our dealings over the years. Like Charles Busch, they stand as beacons of hope for me. At Greenwood, Suzanne Staszak-Silva, Lynn Zelem, Barbara Jackson, and Jill-Marie McCormack kept me on task and provided timely and gentle information to my various inquiries. Thank you.

Finally, how does one thank a spouse for life itself? Gerianne Steele helped in untold ways, but especially with her quick research skills and constant affirmations. I do most sincerely hope to liberate our home from the piles of research materials that take up so much space. Thank you for each day, Geri.

This has been a massive undertaking. The flaws that will emerge have nothing whatsoever to do with the contributions from many people. I am solely responsible for them, and regret them, but hope that they will not measurably detract from the overall message.

Introduction

Most scholars over the years have seen the Holocaust as a terrible rupture in Western culture and civilization, an event that shattered all previously known moral categories. This is quite understandable, given the sheer enormity of the events and their location on a continent and in a century deemed by many to be a vast improvement over past human experiences. With the greatest of respect for these scholars, their work, and the sheer magnitude of the emotional and intellectual demands this subject makes on those who devote their lives to its study, my work seeks to reveal the degree to which the Holocaust, with its distinguishing features, is instead the culminating point of an intricate cultural process covering at least seventeen centuries. That is to say, Western Christianity's civilization and culture did not, in fact, "fail." Indeed, operating as they had been designed to do in order to produce religious, theological, and cultural uniformity on large numbers of people for those seventeen centuries, they achieved an unparalleled peak of efficiency in the death camps after centuries of brutal applications against The Other across the globe. During those centuries, all available technologies and cultural pressures and practices had been brought to bear against The Other, with large numbers of people directly involved and an even larger number doing nothing to help the afflicted victims. The Holocaust certainly continued that lamentable pattern.

Continuity marks the depredations practiced against the various groups constituting The Other from the early centuries of Christianity until today. First, there is the simple matter of separation, the identification of The Other as a group that is "not" Christian, initially the Jews, the Disconfirming Other. Then steps were taken against The Other, especially in the form of legal pressures or church directives that severely circumscribed the lives of The Other. Then dehumanization (although this is also an integral part of the initial perception of Otherness) acted out against The Other in deeds, social myths, language, and discourse. Having successfully dehumanized The Other, then came attempts at changing ("converting") them or forcing The Other to leave their current places of living, and failing that, destroying them. Of course, all this is supported by an impressive system of rewards for those entrusted with enacting the different phases, but for believers, these rewards include all members of the dominant religion. Jews have faced all this for many centuries.

Those involved in the study of the Holocaust are often asked what motivates them to work in this very disturbing area. Each person has his or her answer. In my case, it is personal. At one point in Alain Resnais's film, *Night and Fog,* we see a small group of children, following an adult male, nearing the train car that will take them to their deaths. The children are bundled up, but remain neat and well dressed. They shuffle along, then slow and come to a stop. A little boy turns and looks upward directly at the camera. In a film of incredible ugliness and brutality, it is this simple moment that haunts me the most whenever I see it. When that child turns and has his dark eyes and hair recorded for all of posterity, even as his short life is about to end, I see the countenance of my son when he was that child's age.

My son Matthew is adopted. He was abandoned by his birth parents, a loving act I believe, on the doorstep of an orphanage called The Park, in Santiago, Chile. He was found by one of the workers, probably within a day of his birth. When the worker bent over to pick up the little bundle, she was surprised by his small size. Matthew came to the orphanage weighing merely three pounds, three ounces. Seven months later, surviving several debilitating illnesses, and weighing barely more than ten pounds, he was flown to this country where he met his new family. Twenty-two years later, he is now a fine young man, with virtually no signs lingering from his difficult infancy, a fitting testimony to the sheer human drive to survive.

I see Matthew in the *Night and Fog* child because the two simply looked alike at a shared age. But there is now more of a resemblance, and a sense of urgency for me, one that emerged from the process of writing this book. It is likely that my son's Chilean lineage descends from the Mapuche tribes, the indigenous people who have lived in the vicinity of Santiago for many centuries. But for an accident of history, my son could have been one of the native peoples hounded to their deaths by the conquerors from Europe. Had he lived in Germany or Eastern Europe during Hitler's reign, his life might have resembled that of the child protagonist portrayed in Jerzy Kosinski's *The Painted Bird.* My son's presence in my life, my being a descendent of Spanish and Irish forebears, gives me an emotional connection to a past that I can only imagine, a past that no one would want to experience.

Having been a college professor since the mid-1970s, a teacher at the university level since 1967, and a publicly elected school board member in my community, I have been professionally and personally invested in education for virtually all my adult life. For more than two decades, I have taught classes at the graduate and undergraduate levels that discuss aspects of the Holocaust. In that span, the implications of the Holocaust for me in my professional and intellectual life have gradually become all-encompassing (my colleagues surely tire of my references to these implications in our various professional and departmental meetings). For instance, Walter Benjamin's declaration haunts my work: "There is no document of civilization which is not at the same time a document of barbarism."[1] College students constantly encounter documents of civilization, although I doubt that many of their instructors have heeded Benjamin's warning about barbarism. His insight has, in my case, given me pause on numerous occasions as I contemplate both what texts to select for a class and what to say about them. It is impossible for me to teach classes without some reference to the Holocaust and its cultural antecedents. David Svaldi, in his study of the U.S. slaughter of innocent Native Americans at Sand Creek, makes a point very similar to Benjamin's: "words evolved from centuries of conquest have been created for the purposes of conquest rather than the purposes of knowledge."[2] Edward Said, a pre-eminent cultural critic, contributes to this matter as well: "There is no discipline, no structure of knowledge, no institution or epistemology that can or has ever stood free of the various socio-cultural, historical, and political formations that give epochs their peculiar individuality."[3] Taken together—documents of civilization, words of conquest, barbarism, structures of knowledge, epistemology—these insights require a thoughtful, conscientious response to the professional task of teaching, and serious consideration to the matter of implementing an ideological critique of canonical texts. Stanley Aranowitz and Henry Giroux, in their study of postmodern education, argue, "We simply cannot retain the documents of the past twenty-five hundred years intact."[4] One can see from this perspective the massive nature of the project facing educators, especially if we take seriously the warning of Walter Benjamin, a Jewish voice coming from the genocidal abyss of mid-century Europe.

Parts of the final chapters for this book were written in the second week of September 2001. During that week, the world was reminded once again of the terrible depths of human evil as well as the sublime heights of human dignity and goodness. It has been a difficult task encountering time and time again in my research notes concepts and facts that are almost beyond one's capacity to comprehend. The thought kept crossing my mind that the people who perpetrated the atrocities in New York and Washington, D.C., most likely shared some of the characteristics of the motivations for evil suggested by Ervin Staub's impressive *The Roots of Evil*, published in 1992. I spent much time considering the likelihood that even more innocent people stand to suffer as the ripple effects of atrocity spread around the world. My sadness and grief over the prospects for humanity's future became almost overwhelming. My entire adult life has been lived as a pacifist; I have taught courses in the Peace and Conflict Studies program for twenty years. I have three male children and the talk of war following the atrocities has saddened me almost beyond expression. The many survivors of the Holocaust who have spoken in my classes over the decades have shared one common theme: hatred has no place in the human heart. But one can easily detect the drumbeats throbbing as hatred mounts, nearly an indiscriminate hatred. One truly fears the possible consequences.

I offer my most sincere regrets that this study is based largely on secondary texts rather than on primary sources. As its stands, the project took nearly five years. It strikes me that one lifetime is not enough to give the subject the attention to detail that it truly needs. I shall simply leave that to other scholars, should they choose to take up the challenge. There are impressive primary texts, to be sure, such as the Mayan Prophecy of Chilam Balam de Chumayel, which is discussed in Chapter 5. The secondary works also contain fragments from some primary documents, such as Crusaders' accounts, or those by their victims, or from the Inquisition. My sincere hope is that scholars from a wide variety of disciplines and areas of concentration will examine primary sources for their potential usefulness in Holocaust studies. I am sure that this project, if undertaken, will help shed important new light on this crucial field of study, especially insofar as cultural studies can augment the study of history.

1
Culture Studies, Christianity, and the Holocaust

"We have to refer to much more remote processes if we want to understand how we have been trapped in our own history."

—Michel Foucault

"There is no document of civilization which is not at the same time a document of barbarism."

—Walter Benjamin

Humanity is likely to spend the rest of its existence on earth without ever understanding fully all of the causes of the Holocaust, not to mention the event's countless ramifications and implications for virtually all aspects of life. Scholars serving in many disciplines around the world have already spent more than half a century attempting to bring to bear on this subject their precise instruments of study, and there is every likelihood that the effort will continue for the rest of the twenty-first century. We know more, much more than before, but, as many scholars point out, we have had to recognize that we do not understand more than before. No one person or team of scholars has the personal resources or luxury of time to grasp all of the details of the entire subject. Necessarily, we must be content with working within narrow disciplinary specialties, even as new documentation or theories from a variety of sources augment the public record. It is important to keep in mind that such disciplinary focus can color the results, at least in terms of a scholar's chosen emphasis.

This study proposes to employ the basic tenets and approaches of culture studies, which is a relatively new field, to the study of the Holocaust, specifically to matters related to Christianity's influence upon events, people, and places long before the Nazis' death camps scarred the earth. I undertake this effort not as a corrective to the work of others but as a way to provide new insights into the highly complex set of issues related to the creation of perpetrators and bystanders as seen in the Holocaust. Always kept in mind is Victoria Barnett's trenchant notion that bystanders are "simply somewhat more passive perpetrators."[1] Even though the Christian world has largely ignored the implications of the Holocaust for itself, it may be said that the "plausibility structure"[2] of that dominant worldview has begun to lose its integrity to a degree, perhaps partially because of its failures during the Holocaust. Christianity is less able to assert that it alone possesses the single transcendent truth, and is thereby more open to the kind of analysis that follows here, using a methodology that seeks to "take all signifying practice as its domain."[3] In *Unanswered Questions*, François Furet asks a question that is extremely pertinent: "How deeply is Christianity implicated in the formation of the preconditions for the genocide of the Jews?" The tentative answer proposed is that we can find significant elements that will recur and reappear from their inception shortly after the emergence of Christianity in Roman times up until today—and that these cultural phenomena are involved in the creation of perpetrators and bystanders. Furet also asks whether Christianity is "at all capable of changing its anti-Judaic attitudes without risking its very foundations?"[4] The answer to this, although not proffered in this study, is a good bit more complicated than it would seem, because the countless threads of the tapestry are so interwoven with the general culture we have come to inherit that it is extremely difficult to separate them. Furthermore, Christianity has had such an indelible influence on so many facets of life that do not appear at first glance to have any theological origins or underpinnings. Therefore, it is almost impossible to make a clear distinction between the sociological and the theological. In any case, this study proposes that in many instances to be investigated, we will find that Raul Hilberg's concept of the structural function of the "machinery of destruction" literally being "the organized community in one of its special roles"[5] is often the case being observed over these centuries.

Roger Bastide finds that Western culture "still remains profoundly steeped in the Christian culture of the past."[6] There are countless elements of this—the calendar, architecture, much literature, aspects of education, certain social behaviors, and often the way people think about each other. For example, no one would argue that anti-Semitism has not been operative in European history and culture over the course of many centuries, and that it often had devastating direct effects on many Jewish people. The indirect effects, those that impacted the inner sanctum of the human life, it may be surmised, most likely touched all Jewish lives in one way or another. Precisely how that past record of prejudice and hatred has had a cumulative impact on human beings and events today is difficult to measure and assess. Modern chaos theory may provide a useful perspective on the difficulties. An individual act of religious or racial hatred, impelled by institutional motivations, may be analogized to the single act of an insect's flapping its wings over the Gulf of Mexico. Chaos theorists have wondered about the relationship of that insect's flapping wings to the later development of a hurricane in the same area. In the human arena, then, how many anti-Semitic acts—seemingly small, individual flames of hatred—are required to ascend to the level of the all-consuming firestorm, the Shoah? The use of culture studies in this field of study enables us to perceive the possible relationship of individual and institutional acts of racial and religious prejudice and hatred as they mount up over the years and centuries. Thus, a field of action and a discursive arena is created, wherein humans, individually and in groups, develop (1) apathy with regard to the plight of victims or (2) active willingness to operate violently against them. Ervin Staub contends that even seemingly small, insignificant deeds can entangle an individual in a malevolent system, for example, by receiving incentives offered by the system.[7] In this regard, we might argue that promises of eternal life constitute some of the most powerful incentives known to humans. Identification with an imperial entity, which projects its power and success over entire continents and over many centuries, allows an oceanic feeling in the minds and hearts of devout believers of receiving alleged blessings of their God. Hyam Maccoby states the resulting case as succinctly as possible: Christianity provided the "model for the plan of exterminating the Jews."[8] This is not an easily assimilated concept, especially for the Christian faith community. Indeed, it is probably all but impossible to arrive at this conclusion from within the ideological, theological, conceptual, and mythic framework articulated by Christianity, a framework genuinely needed for the individual believer to avoid awareness of the "indelible wrongness of [European Christians] having all along been some of history's most pathological thieves and murderers."[9] Scholars of "contact" between Anglo-Europeans and the indigenous peoples of the Western hemisphere, however, continuously document the wrongness perpetrated and its implications. James Axtell observes, "to condemn every aggressive military, religious, or economic action in the past is to question some of the fundamentals of Western society, past and present."[10] Donald A. Wells offers insight when he notes that "not only is the citizen quite incapable of knowing what is happening, but he is indoctrinated to suspect his motives for wanting to know."[11] That is to say, if there is a possibility for the practicing of ideological critique, it is not easily available to those who could use it most profitably to overcome their own ignorance of the inhumane, violent system in which they are embroiled. This notion of not being able to suspect one's own motives hints at the carceral society, that is, a society in which virtually all denizens may be said to be imprisoned or self-imprisoned. The culture's normative pacification processes thus seek not only to proscribe social behavior but also one's inner thought processes, including self-awareness and self-assessments.

This study thus seeks to examine the sequence of events, covering some seventeen centuries, involving the treatment of The Other in the developing Christian West, with special regard to interrogating the cultural blueprint's linkages to the Shoah. Specifically, this involves the use of the theories of culture studies and discourse theory to investigate the ways in which Christianity has been involved in the social relationships of the phenomenon of power over The Other, how that power expresses and perpetuates itself, and how it manifested itself during the Holocaust. For this study, discourse is defined as the "socially produced groups of ideas or ways of thinking that can be tracked in individual texts or groups of texts."[12] Such a study is of crucial importance because Christianity has, for more than seventeen centuries, constituted the primary culture, or has been a major determinant of Western culture, by which hundreds of millions, perhaps billions, of believing Christians have had their most deeply held beliefs formulated. Scripture, scripture commentary, homilies, papal bulls, decretals, the arts, formal and domestic forms of education, government decrees, laws, and countless sermons, pamphlets, disputations, tracts, and books constitute the discourse within which those believing millions have lived. This discourse field provides the culture and the people within it "with 'taken-for-granted elements' of their 'practical knowledge,'" thus creating a "common sense" that "is rarely made explicit, and is often in fact unconscious, but it too is built upon a comprehensive foundation of ideological premises."[13] The human experience of culture is that it "is generated and experienced, becomes a determining, productive field through which social realities are constructed, experienced, and interpreted."[14] The tentative hope is that analysis of such factors will reveal the underlying cultural substrata and key examples of that culture in violent action against The Other over the centuries that then helped empower those who either actively perpetrated or passively acquiesced in the Holocaust.

What remains common to my concern with The Other and the Holocaust are Christianity and the master cultural narrative of triumphalism, supersessionism, and transcendence it has created and fostered in various ways over the centuries. In the cases examined, Christianity and its various agents largely defined the terms by which people were perceived to be either within or outside the circle of moral obligation, the latter by definition constituted The Other. It may be said that a Disconfirming Other denies the claims of the dominant culture's ultimate perception of the universe's reality, thereby, in the view of the dominant culture, taking "on the quality of evil as well as madness."[15] Such characterizations typified the experiences of many non-Christians, or those deemed to have denied Christianity's truth claims, scriptural interpretations, and worldviews. This could be done in a variety of ways: by demonizing a group, otherwise anathematizing them, or perceiving them as subhuman (lacking eternal souls), infidels, or heretics. In this regard, Regina Schwartz's study of monotheism and violence finds that "monotheism is a myth that grounds particular identity in universal transcendence ... a myth that forges identity antithetically—against the Other."[16] Her study cites telling examples of this identity myth involving universal transcendence both before the Common Era and after. These instances support the view that myths may "be acted upon as if they were real, in their capacity to set empirical events underway."[17] Such myths constitute "partial truths that emphasize specific versions of reality and conceal or overlook others." They are deeply "involved in relations of power, because they ensure that some accounts of reality count more than others."[18] It may also be said that myths function to conceal the problems encountered in interpreting a culture's value system.[19] The trajectory of violence against The Other, based largely on the claims to truth by this dominant religion, appeared to increase dramatically in the Common Era. It is significant to recognize that Israel was unable to operate as a military power after Rome achieved full prominence, subjecting the Jews in the process. Once allied with the power of Imperial Rome, the Christian religion, eventually becoming a cultural entity impacting virtually all other institutions in Western Europe, served to create and reward attitudes and behaviors that led to a long series of violent, repressive, and immiserating responses by Christians and Christianity practiced against The Other, which encompasses those who stand outside the Christian confession, either by geographical accident, race, religious tradition or chosen belief, or some other demarcating factor. The rewards and sanctions invoked resulted in a form of "coercive power" used by the society "to impose itself upon the reluctance of individuals."[20] A problematic cultural blueprint for handling people, beliefs, attitudes, and behaviors was created.[21] The sobering result of centuries of such cultural practices that Holocaust scholars must encounter is identified by Raul Hilberg: "The German Nazis ... did not discard the past; they built upon it."[22]

Coercive power is an issue of paramount importance, although the subtleties are not easily perceived or recorded. In his study of the sources of social power, Michael Mann distinguishes between "normative pacification" and "coercive pacification."[23] In practice the former appears most often to necessarily precede the latter. That is, it is difficult to envision a sudden eruption of coercive measures against a targeted minority group instituted through the various processes of political, legal, and enforcement jurisdictions unless there is a preexisting set of normative beliefs, claims, attitudes, behaviors, foundational documents. The ensuing cultural practices serve to motivate a wide variety of people in dominant positions to see the necessity of starting the complicated process to move to a coercive level of action. Indeed, as long as normative pacification is operating successfully, a state in which people have come to know their place and that of The Other in the scheme of things and think and act accordingly, then there is little reason to move to the level of coercive measures. In what Christianity set out to do in regulating the lives of the Disconfirming Other—the Jews—as well as the lives of those who might possibly associate with them, its own truth claims bore implications for behaviors that were difficult to monitor effectively. More coercive measures followed quickly when the religion had ready access to the legal and enforcement powers of the imperial government. It might be argued that the ability to create both normative and coercive pacification procedures is indicative of an advanced stage of hegemonic power in which a dominant group or alliance of groups "can exert 'total social authority' over other subordinate groups, not simply by coercion or by the direct imposition of ruling ideas, but by 'winning and shaping consent so that the power of the dominant classes appears both legitimate and natural.'"[24] Kiernan Ryan observes that this insidious process "incites ... induces ... seduces ... makes easier or more difficult; in the extreme it constrains or forbids absolutely."[25] Graeme Turner, making a point that also bears on the process of enculturation, finds that people "internalize ideology and thus are not easily made conscious of its presence or its effects; it is unconscious."[26] Not only is it unconscious, the masses of those involved in hegemonic domination need not support it actively.[27] Ervin Staub's study of evil and genocide finds that "shared cultural dispositions" lead people to "join rather than simply obey out of fear or respect."[28] The process is an insidious one and is not easily recognized or resisted by those involved. Discussing the Spanish Inquisition, Jaime Contreras states a point that must not be underestimated for its lasting power in the Christian West: in the Inquisition, each Spaniard, through an educational process, "became an impregnable fortress within himself [that] began with an analysis of one's own conscience and terminated in the conscience of one's neighbor." To take place, the individual "had to acquire a subtle inquisitorial sensibility for oneself in order to penetrate other peoples' minds."[29] I propose that a carceral process something like this has been a significant component of Christianity's dealings with its own adherents and, then, with The Other, certainly from the time of its ascendancy to imperial status under Constantine, and perhaps even before that, through history until today.

Given the nature of this process, its historical context and nearly invisible workings within the individual, and the near certainty that it also operated in other periods against other victims, we may justifiably wonder about the efficacy of resistance to the cultural forces operating upon individuals. That is, how might believing Christians, in their private lives or in their public functions, have come to realize that the religion's messages involving their belief commitments, their souls, their status for all eternity, and how they were to behave with regard to non-Christians were also operating invidiously against the welfare of those Other human beings, severely limiting their possibilities for enjoying fulfilling lives and self-actualization? The various inducements rewarding Christians were, and still are, extremely efficacious and empowering. Among other possibilities are claims to absolute, universal truth; the supersession of the validity of previous religious claims; a personally rewarding relationship with an ultimate being; the ability to read all of history as a vindication of one's religious community; and a certain social cohesiveness as one faithful member of an international organization of true believers that has dominated Europe and its world scene for nearly twenty centuries. Taken together, these inducements, this system of rewards, have proven to be a very effective mechanism to shape a wide variety of Christian behaviors, deeds, thoughts, and attitudes. To the contrary, from a culture studies perspective, Raymond Williams and E. P. Thompson, two British scholars who were crucial to the genesis of the discipline, believed that "human agency" was efficacious "against history and ideology" through "radical individual effort."[30] A strong case can be made that the range of potential choices became severely limited as Christianity consolidated its most central tenets of belief and demanded the total allegiance of its believers. A variety of powerful disincentives to radical freedom of thought operated from the earliest period. It will be instructive to look for instances of such radical effort in subsequent chapters. We will see that it is not impossible for a figure to overcome the appeals of the dominant culture, but not all of the dehumanizing elements will be rejected.

In light of these considerations, by any standard of measurement, the Christian West became very efficient over the centuries in eliminating the individual Christian's reluctance to execute the dominant religion's various mandates against The Other, whenever and wherever encountered. The result of its success over many centuries meant that The Other had to face, and live with, an

aggressive, anti-indigenous, self-imposing and dominant religion ... [in which] the church stuck to the idea of a single culture and defended Europe's monocentrism .... [W]hen it has been a question of the "other," she has regarded him as an enemy, a pagan, an infidel, Moor, Indian .... [I]n other words, they are *different*.... She has found it difficult to have any dialogue with these others .... [M]ost of the time she has engaged in subjection, suppression, domination.[31]

This study's use of culture studies as an approach does not explain the Shoah as a specifically Christian event, but analyzes it as one that had its sanctioning and conditioning in those culturally influenced historical antecedents that go far to account for (1) the apathy of bystanders, insofar as Christianity devised and put into execution a "moral universe" both excluding non-Christians and Others deemed to be beyond the pale, while also targeting them for a variety of sanctions, and (2) a preexisting moral framework supporting and empowering the willing executioners in the myriad details of their chosen work. This study examines key examples in which a Christian-influenced culture led to both the development of a certain kind of "knowledge" about The Other and subsequent structural and outright physical violence, based on a theology of sacred violence, practiced against The Other in a series of alarming preludes to the Holocaust. A crucial point is that each episode, after Christianity's rise to prominence under Emperor Constantine, used as a model for dealing with The Other the template established when the Jews were originally controlled by a variety of Christian constraints.

It may be argued that such a study fails to take into account the relative historical conditions, beliefs, and practices prevailing at a given time in the past, that we must not stand in judgment over people and practices using today's standards, and that to do so is to apply moral standards largely unknown at the prior time. Stephen Greenblatt, a Renaissance scholar, makes a point that is crucial for an understanding of the culture studies approach. In defending New Historicism against the critics of that field of study, Greenblatt argues for the need to study those cultural practices which are "directly in the way of coming to terms with [a] period's methods of regulating the body, its conscious and unconscious ways of defining and dealing with marginals and deviants, its mechanisms for the display of power and the expression of discontent" while avoiding the "absurdly restrictive boundaries" of the "disabling idea of causality."[32] This is perhaps best understood in terms of the chaos theory that seeks to engage factors that might otherwise escape one's notice, such as the butterfly's flapping wings.

Rupert Costo and Jeannette Costo, in their study of "crimes against humanity" in the Spanish mission activities in California, ask whether "cruelty (and therefore morality) [is] relative to the mortal judge, to the standards of the actors?"[33] Hyam Maccoby offers an insight that counters objections about historical apologetics: "We cannot understand a myth if we strip ourselves of the tools of moral evaluation. For the myths themselves are concerned with moral evaluation."[34] Furthermore, Maccoby argues that a culture is largely the creation of its own myths, "and once the myth has set and become established in the minds of the people, the outlines of the culture are determined."[35] Maccoby's point raises the haunting speculation that the demand for scholarly objectivity and moral relativity could itself be a self-preserving intellectual function of the dominant culture, a demand that ensures that a functional ideological critique cannot succeed, cannot be implemented. Jürgen Habermas helps account for this possibility, noting that an ideology may be perceived as a communication system "in which key semantic contents are sheltered from the light of critical examination."[36] Indeed, historian Francis Jennings argues that the "historian cannot wholly free himself [sic] from the outlook of his own cultural tradition."[37] Rupert Costo and Jeannette Costo go further—historical apologetics is "all part of an ideology of superiority and racism."[38] Eric Hobsbawm finds that events of this century have made us able to "tolerate the intolerable," that we have been "brainwashed into accepting barbarity."[39] One can only hope that, if this is indeed the case, we can resist the brainwashing successfully and thereby not be insensitive to the stupendous losses from the past, especially in light of the possibility that there are significant linkages to twentieth-century events.

It is obvious that there are cultural uniformities within the Christian universe that have survived from its inception and serve to bind together its many agents and believers, their dogmas and doctrines, as well as their acts over time. For instance, there is a certain uniformity across the centuries to Christianity's claims involving the universal truth of its message, or its incessant proselytizing and demands for conversions, its aggressiveness when encountering a new, different Other, and its consignment of various Others to both earthly and eternal hells. The Christian West, in the view of Ziauddin Sardar, arrogates to itself the *only* valid definition of reality and truth[40]; its claims to universal status, an "act of will and force," is directed against the "becoming of the Other."[41] Given these considerations, John Tomlinson raises the appropriate point: "at the root of [the] questions of culture lie enormously difficult problems to do with the nature of reason and the possibility of any rational social critique."[42] Echoing Michel Foucault, Tomlinson notes that modern academic disciplines govern the "control of discourse" and thereby "what counts as legitimate knowledge."[43] These disciplines grew steadily out of the developing university system of Western Europe that had obviously been deeply influenced by the cultural teachings and social and intellectual supremacy of Christianity. The very moral shape of the Christian West is a central feature, and supposed concern, of universities. This study argues that Christianity has perpetrated a ceaseless series of violent actions against The Other since its ascension to a position of preeminence with Imperial Rome. Given the centrality of this dominant religion, it should not be surprising that it has proven to be a very difficult task to ask the most probing of questions, to make certain assertions that place this culturally dominant force in a revealing critical light. When that critical light also involves the Holocaust, the issue becomes exceedingly difficult on a variety of levels, for example, psychological, cognitive, epistemological, and ethical. In her study of bystanders during the Holocaust, Victoria Barnett observes that the power of institutions "over the moral inhibitions of individuals is devastating."[44] Ervin Staub's examination of evil complements Barnett's work on bystanders; he finds that "ideological indoctrination made killing Jews the fulfillment of a 'higher ideal.'"[45] Francis Jennings—a scholar who has studied the history of the contact between early-modern Europeans and the indigenous peoples of North and South America—has suggested that "conquest aristocracies" typically "assume attitudes of great moral rectitude to divert attention from the abandonment" of their stated moral standards as they go about establishing illicit hegemonies. These attitudes become the accepted general view; eventually, the conquerors begin to believe their own rhetoric.[46] He also finds that "the ordering restraints of religion and law" repeatedly serve as the mechanisms for conquest and domination.[47] Jennings's work studied the period of Western Europe's initial contact with the people of the so-called New World. His claim may be seen as valid for many other episodes of Western European hegemonic behaviors, as will be seen in ensuing chapters.

To have a proper grasp of a culture studies approach to a subject, it is important to have a clear sense of the constituent elements of a culture. To that end, we may understand culture to be "a whole way of life, material, intellectual, and spiritual."[48] Ervin Staub finds culture to be composed of shared meanings, "shared rules, norms, values, customs, and life-styles." Culture, in his view, is "coded, maintained, and expressed in the 'products' of a group: its literature, art, rituals, the contents of its mass media, and the behavior of its members," resulting in shared "psychological reactions to culturally relevant events."[49] Anthropologist Clifford Geertz writes of the "traffic ... in significant symbols ... anything ... used to impose meaning upon experience ... to orient [oneself] within 'the ongoing course of experienced things,'" quoting John Dewey.[50] Geertz argues that human beings experience a vacuum between what their bodies tell them is needed and what they need "to know in order to function." People fill in this vacuum themselves, but with "information (or misinformation) provided by our culture." In an absolutely crucial insight, he thus argues, people themselves "are cultural artifacts."[51] Along these lines of inquiry, Graeme Turner, building on insights by Jacques Lacan, notes, "Just as we learn to speak in the language and customs of our culture, and are thus in a sense constructed through them ... so we are the subjects, not the authors, of cultural processes."[52] Furthermore, Turner notes that culture "is the site where meaning is generated and experienced, [and] becomes a determining, productive field through which social realities are constructed, experienced, and interpreted."[53] These are central observations for the purposes of both culture studies and this Holocaust study. In essence, culture perpetuates itself through humans by virtue of "living" within them, replicating itself in the course of human activity, and thus indelibly influencing the most intimate perceptions of Others. Humans serve as the hosts through which the culture is transmitted from one generation to the next, an observation that raises crucial questions about humans as free agents and the possibilities for resisting the mandates of the dominant culture in what Lee Patterson calls "the monolithic carceral society of the modern world, with its inescapable reproduction of itself within each individual."[54] This topic of human agency is discussed later. Any culture provides humans living within it ways of becoming involved and grasping meaning as perceived by that culture. But it is also the case that "we tend to live inside these maps [of meaning] as surely as we live in the 'real' world: they 'think' us as much as we 'think' them, and this in itself is quite 'natural.' ... It is through this process—a kind of inevitable reflex of all social life—that particular sets of social relations, particular ways of organizing the world appear to us as if they were universal and timeless."[55] Once normalized, it becomes increasingly difficult to bring to bear critical insights and perspectives. Foucault speaks of the struggle against the expression of power found in a

technique ... This form of power applies itself to immediate everyday life which categorizes the individual, marks him by his own individuality, attaches him to his own identity, imposes a law of truth on him which he must recognize and which others have to recognize in him. It is a form of power which makes individuals subjects ... a form of power which subjugates and makes subject to.[56]

With regard to culture and religion, Geertz asserts that the "holy bears within it everywhere a sense of intrinsic obligation: it not only encourages devotion, it demands it; it not only induces intellectual assent, it enforces emotional commitment."[57] In Christian Europe, Suzanne Langer notes, "the Church brought men daily (in some orders even hourly) to their knees, to enact if not contemplate their assent to the ultimate concepts."[58] Following from these points, the culture depicted in this study encompasses the myriad details of life as commonly lived—the views and attitudes deriving from the dominant religion, to be sure, but made operative in the countless decisions and choices comprising a human life. For The Other to be identified, defined, targeted, ignored, or acted upon legally, socially, militarily, economically, punitively, and so forth, involves a complex array of human beings functioning in various intricately arranged social and institutional structures in order to execute these tactics. Richard Rubenstein and John Roth, in *Approaches to Auschwitz*, assert that virtually all levels and components of German society were involved in the perpetration of the Holocaust.[59] Although specific individuals conceived, designed, and implemented a massive program of genocide that extended over a period of more than a decade, individuals on the margins were necessary to such a project. They included lawyers, judges, police personnel, bureaucrats, military personnel, engineers, draftsmen, civil servants, clerics, railway workers, construction personnel, journalists, educators, scientists, industrialists and the workers, neighbors, and families of all of the above. It is not likely that the remarkable degree of social and cultural uniformity required for such to happen came about in extremely short order. By the time the Germans of the Holocaust era were living and working, the Christian West had operated for seventeen centuries, during which it could impress upon its believers the significance of its message and views about The Other. Over that time, that message and those views could be said to have become, in the words of sociologist Peter Berger, "inevitable, part of the meaning of things."[60] Similar levels of active and passive support, enabled by a certain ideology and culture, were required. Starting with Christianity in the late Roman Empire, the crusades, the Inquisition and church actions against heretics, contact with the indigenous people in the Americas, and the subsequent slavery instituted in the United States are examined in this study. Finally, the Holocaust is discussed. The cultural processes at work for specific eras and episodes will be interrogated in detail. This is not an easy undertaking; it will be necessary to keep in mind, therefore, that the transcendent, universal truth claims of Christianity, as part of the "cultural self-concept of a people greatly influence ... the need to protect the collective psychological self."[61] Simultaneously, those who perceive themselves to be superior to those deemed to be "'natural' inferiors" will often be involved in ruthless behaviors that exacerbate "the barbarization latent between any confrontation between God and Devil."[62] Ironically, such barbarism easily becomes the handmaiden of civilization itself, in that the presence of civilization and its many human benefits is a necessary precondition to the existence and practice of one of humanity's most complex institutions—warfare. In other words, warfare in its various forms requires certain advanced, complex levels of human knowledge and skills, which are used in organizing and supporting large groups of people as they conduct the many intricacies of war.

There is little doubt that the moral, ontological, and eschatological claims of a religion constitute some of the most compelling life directives that human beings encounter in their cultures. In the various contentions of the Christian worldview, the experience of religion involves truth claims about one's soul and its status for virtually all of eternity. There is the promise of the possibility of a direct relationship for the true believer with his or her God, or identification with a powerful, universal corporate entity such as the Roman Catholic Church, or both. Early Christian apologists found that the Bible has "all truth ... contained in it, and all truth is Christian truth."[63] Such a claim admits of absolutely no pretenders or competitors. Adherence to certain normative beliefs, in thought and deed and in both public and private spheres, helps the believer achieve the promised ends. Given the process by which Christianity emerged from its parent religion, Judaism, and the consequent rejection of that parent religion and its believers—involving what Rubenstein and Roth have termed "religiously legitimated incitement to homicidal violence"[64]—the daily practice of various aspects of that rejection of Jews and Judaism became incumbent upon Christian believers over the centuries. It became an integral part of their daily lives, with some actively engaged in the process and many others abiding it.

Furthermore, this practice involved not only the ultimate truth claims of Christianity (the presence of the Messiah in human history, the role of Judaism in the Christian God's revealed plan, etc.) but also the enactment of that dominant religion's system of rewards and sanctions in motivating and controlling its believers. It is important to keep in mind, for the purposes of this study, that this religious motivation involved what theologian John Gager has identified as "ideological nihilation and conceptual liquidation"[65] of Judaism's basic tenets. Gager is speaking of the origins of anti-Semitism, but those attitudes have persisted to this day. Sadly, we have come to learn that the religious beliefs of the dominant religion have not been a guarantee against genocidal acts, much less the denigration and rejection of the tenets of religions deemed to be unacceptable or inferior. Indeed, greater "religiosity is frequently associated with greater prejudice."[66] The Servite priest John T. Pawlikowski refers to the "very serious distortion of Judaism central to Christian theology."[67] This distortion surely amounts to the "cultural misinformation" humans use in their lives to which Geertz refers, but it has been a widely experienced factor in the lives of believing Christians ever since Christianity completed, formalized, and enacted its estrangement from Judaism.

Such cultural misinformation, originally expressed in theological disputations during the period of Christianity's break from Judaism, eventually manifested in the Middle Ages as a wide variety of superstitious claims concerning Jews,[68] and continues in this century's treatment of Judaism as seen, for instance, in the clerical education most prospective pastors encounter, in mass-consumed entertainment,[69] and in increased hate crimes in the United States as recorded by the FBI.[70] Father Edward H. Flannery writes of "pathological anti-Semitism" (is this similar to Daniel Goldhagen's "exterminationist anti-Semitism"?), and notes its presence "in society as a source of infection that can contaminate the normal in times of stress."[71] If there is, as Robert E. Willis suggests, an evil essence to Christianity,[72] which surely contributes to the cultural misinformation Geertz mentions, the wonder then is that any goodness ever derived from it. Yet, it appears that much goodness has, indeed, been provided by the religion and its adherents throughout its existence in terms of consolation, social amelioration, and demands for justice, among other possibilities. But even this must be considered in light of the theological strings often attached and, certainly, of the simple fact that whatever goodness has come about is necessarily alloyed with centuries of the most troubling attitudes and behaviors as well as countless repulsive deeds often practiced on a massive scale. It is a rare Christian who, with Reverend Donald A. Wells, sees the possibility that "the Christian church is simply one more of the atavisms that need to be rooted out if man is to survive at all."[73]

"Violence is not only what we do to the Other. It is prior to that. Violence is the very construction of the Other."

—Regina M. Schwartz

Thus far, this study has engaged in a general discussion of culture and Christianity. Before turning the focus on specific eras and episodes within the Christian West, more specific considerations regarding culture and Christianity need to be established.

Initially, it is necessary to perceive the connectedness of the past to the present. Gerhard Falk, in *The Jew in Christian Theology*, asserts, "Every age and every society rests upon the culture base of all that preceded it."[74] There are, of course, those stunning moments, having evolved over time, that constitute what have come to be known as paradigm shifts. Indeed, the Holocaust may eventually come to be seen as having precipitated such a shift, but we are probably too close in time to see this with any clarity. It can be argued that Christianity itself constituted such a shift, if not in its earliest days before its separation from Judaism was completed, certainly when that process was finished. As the emergent religion came to enjoy imperial status and protection, and found itself in a position to enforce its exclusive view of the world, it replaced the relatively inclusive attitudes of pagan Rome. Michel Foucault sees Christianity's influence at this stage of its development as being one of spreading "new power relations throughout the ancient world."[75]

Hermann Doerris, in *Constantine and Religious Liberty*, insists that Christian intolerance differed significantly from the heathen form of intolerance it superseded. Because the latter simply insisted merely on the performance of certain ritual observances by those who did not subscribe to pagan forms of religion, it did not encroach upon the individual's free thinking. To the contrary, Christianity demanded that "the whole personal life ... be dedicated to God" and extended state jurisdiction to "souls and consciences"—a much more invasive approach to religious control over the lives of believers.[76] A new form of carceral state power emerged, based on the claimed ability to have knowledge of the individual's conscience and then direct it.[77] Doerris finds that "Christian intolerance" had specifically Christian origins. Scriptural mandates required the believing, practicing Christian to be "responsible for the welfare of his neighbor" and thus "the more must the Christian feel himself obligated to recall the erring from the path of destruction. One had to do something about the faith of others even if those imperiled resisted the measures taken on their behalf."[78] Obviously, Christianity created expectations for its believers to act out its claims of triumphalism and hegemonic attitudes by, in essence, having the faithful arrogating to themselves the privilege of judging the spiritual beliefs, values, and ideas of The Other, but especially Jews. As will be explored in greater detail, a pattern of behavior developed that reached its apotheosis in the Inquisition. This interventionist stance harbored implications that did not bode well for the fate of The Other during encounters with Christianity. Indeed, as Doerris points out, St. Augustine was one of the first to begin to justify the use of coercive tactics against The Other and that "force was justified on biblical grounds."[79] A seemingly innocuous beginning, this view of a holy, saintly man, but one that would make a significant contribution to the development of the theology of sacred violence in later centuries. The use of various forms of force would become the norm, initially and most importantly against the Jews, who were the rival believers. The Jews had to be formally differentiated from the emerging Church, then against other groups deemed to be leading spiritual lives unworthy of human belief, devotion, God—and ultimately unworthy of life itself. The implications of these early Christian stances became evident to Inquisition scholar Robert Ian Moore, who found that when victims are defined and fear sets in, instruments of persecution are set into motion. Moore then reaches the ominous conclusion: "In that case it becomes effectively impossible to distinguish between society and its agents."[80] Herein is found another early intimation of what has come to be known as the carceral society. Perhaps Blake's "mind-forg'd manacles" aptly describes a society in which virtually all denizens may be said to be imprisoned or self-imprisoned, either through coercive or normative pacification methods. This notion is not to excuse the depredations of the dominant group against The Other; it is to open up a consideration of the possibility for resisting the carceral forces operating around, within, and through the self. In any case, an emerging pattern of Christian exclusiveness, based on the private sense of what is spiritually meaningful, was empowered by the state apparatus of Rome in the fourth century C.E. and was characterized by hostility to anyone unwilling to convert to the dynamic, aggressive young religion. Knowing that The Other is anathema spiritually for the Christian faithful, we should attend seriously to Donald A. Wells's observation regarding "the preoccupation of religion with sin, predestination, Devil, Hell, and dire divine punishment contribut[ing] to the likelihood that such religion will promote paranoia."[81]

The underlying belief system for this scriptural-based exclusiveness, in the view of Marcel Simon, was "driven into the minds of believers and shaped their entire way of thinking ... [and] was reinforced day by day."[82] Writing at the start of World War II, John Westbury-Jones asserted that Christianity united with Imperial Rome as the only two powers ever to claim "absolute dominion" over mankind. In seeking to achieve this total dominion, after more than two centuries of struggle to establish an independent identity, the religion's innate aggressiveness precluded tolerance for The Other.[83] Indeed, in the case of Jews, for them to be perceived as a "criminally guilty people" became an element of the organization of the Church.[84] Eventually, united with imperial strength and beliefs, a reversal of fortune for the Church invited an outcome that would reverberate through the remaining centuries. In Westbury-Jones's view, "the Empire ... conquered the Church."[85] Invested with immense temporal power for at least a millennium to follow, Christianity would use every weapon at its disposal to make life difficult for the non-Christians under its control. Although chiefly targeting Jews, it eventually targeted many Others, human beings who had lived for eons with no knowledge of the existence of either Jewish or Christian religions. Christianity claimed the absolute right to rule over Others, their bodies and souls, and to condemn their religious insights as inferior, superseded, sinful, damaging, satanic, and invalid. The eventual culmination of this complex of theological attitudes meant that "anyone who believed in an erroneous religion must also be the product of an inferior culture,"[86] a position that would condemn millions of The Other in the New World, for instance, to lives of brutal misery in the midst of European-inspired genocidal projects and actions.

The supporting attitudes manifested in human and institutional actions in a variety of ways, but also had to permeate the consciousness of the humans entrusted with executing the directives, as well as that of the people who were only indirectly related to the religious imperium. For the life experiences of Jews, Christian triumphalism, claims to dominion, and actual political control led to "anti-Jewish behaviors tending to become more widespread and more frequent over time."[87] As Ervin Staub assures us, people will kill for a higher cause,[88] and the potent combination of imperial political power with the promises of eternal rewards for faithful Christians provided fertile inspirational and motivational grounds for such acts. Here we find the beginnings of the "Just World" hypothesis, in which the efforts expended to achieve the promised ends are supported by the view that the victims have earned their misery by virtue of their perceived faults, even though these faults have been defined by the dominant religion. Rigid adherence to belief in a Just World seriously erodes the true believer's empathetic ability to project into the world of the victim. Instead, allegiance to the dominant group's imposition of social restrictions on the rejected minority is emphasized.[89] Armed with multiple legal, social, and military weapons to use against The Other, and intent upon achieving "the realization of its ideological blueprint,"[90] those operating in the service of a Just World have the ability to broaden their potential circle of victims to impressively extensive dimensions.[91] Thus, even as Christianity exacted its measures against an increasingly helpless Jewish population, there were groups of Others in other places of the world, creating and living out their own social and cultural realities, who were already unwittingly in the target line of an expansionist, aggressively missionizing religion that would eventually come to state its self-declared rights to the bodies, souls, and property of all the people in the entire world. In the words of theologian Robert MacAfee Brown, the emerging theology of violence to be used against these Others was supported by traditional "orthodoxies ... perilously close to affirming God as executioner."[92]

2
Christianity as Rome's Chosen Religion

"The attribution of divinity to Jesus has had serious consequences for non-Western cultures."

—Ziauddin Sardar

In *Modernity and the Holocaust*, Zygmunt Bauman makes the case that modern genocide, indeed, modern culture and the work of the modern state, is little else than a "gardening" operation[1]: "viewing the society it rules as an object of designing, cultivating, and weed poisoning"[2]; "separating and setting apart useful elements destined to live and thrive, from harmful and morbid ones, which ought to be exterminated."[3] This is a useful observation, although I shall argue that there are clear antecedents to those manifested by the modern state and in modern culture. The weeding operation began long before the age of modernity. There is another side to gardening; Alan Davies has inverted the gardening image in *Infected Christianity: A Study of Modern Racism*, arguing, "Once the Jewishness of Jesus has been diluted ... Christianity is easily captured by nationalism and racism and, once captured, is not so easily rescued from their snares, for the roots of these alien weeds are deeply embedded in the soil of Western civilization, where eradication is not an easy task."[4] It might be said that the weeds of which he speaks, once having taken root, over time virtually become the garden, protected from eradication by the removal of competing entities. As suggested earlier, gardening, in Bauman's sense of the word, has been practiced for many centuries, from the theologically inspired gardening from the Roman era until today, a constant process that has attempted to remove the Disconfirming Other either through conversion, removal, or death.

That Davies cites racism as a problem within the Christian *weltanschauung* is a matter not to be discounted for the purposes of this study. Although Nazi Germany's anti-Semitism was a biologically based racism, as opposed to a strictly religious racism or prejudice, it was Christianity that began to define itself early in racial terms, providing a theological precedent that would contribute culturally to later genocidal developments. Hans Kohn notes that Christianity's self-perception as a "nation, a people, a race" helped lead to a "bond of blood" becoming a "bond of spirituality."[5] This bond entailed a developing sense of superiority for the in-group, the emerging religion, and was most likely accompanied by vestiges of Imperial Roman attitudes. I do not believe that this use of race is cognate with later notions of race, especially as they evolved in the nineteenth century. But they were nevertheless an aspect of the circle of moral obligation and helped stamp the template that would be used in later centuries. As the "Christian race" swept across the globe, it encountered Other races not previously known in the Christian sense of the word and its particularly dogmatic scheme of things. As this cultural pattern emerged, it replaced the former pagan attitude toward Jews, which merely held them to be "strange, stubborn, impious, and rebellious." The emerging Christian image of the Jew would take on the following elements over time: Jews were "avaricious usurers, unscrupulous traders, possessors of uniquely ugly and unhealthy physical traits, impenitent deicides, [and] refusers of redemption."[6]

Certainly one of the most significant turning points in the world's history took place in the fourth century C.E. when Christianity became aligned with Imperial Rome under Constantine. This convergence of the twain would prove to have disastrous consequences for non-Christians in later centuries, not the least being the Jews in Europe in the twentieth century. Having previously eschewed violence in general as well as service in the Roman military, the alignment of the emerging religion and its truth claims with the power, structure, and morality informed by *realpolitik* of the Roman state apparatus proved to be a potent cultural and ideological mix. A train of events began that would see an aggressive, absolutist Church united with a variety of political entities over the centuries to have its way morally, politically, socially, and legally when it saw fit. It proved ironic that Constantine provided this opportunity for believers in Jesus Christ because of his willingness to use horrific forms of violence to pursue his personal agenda, or reasons of state. Murdering his son, Crispus, and boiling to death his wife, Fausta, are a few of his political murders.[7] As a harbinger of future moral concerns, it is significant that these murders took place two years after he elevated Christianity to the status of state religion in 324 C.E. Equally revealing is that Constantine viewed Judaism as a religion guilty of despicable parricides.[8] Revealed here is the early result of a religion's willingness to become a partner in power with a state apparatus that had no qualms about operating in an utterly brutal fashion. Constantine, who also had particularly negative views of Judaism, complemented the Church's views.

Robert Ian Moore, discussing the dynamic complex of forces that operated in the Spanish Inquisition a thousand years later, makes an observation that is useful for understanding the Roman period under consideration: "deliberate and socially sanctioned violence began to be directed, through established governmental, judicial, and social institutions, against groups defined by general characteristics such as race, religion, or way of life; and that membership of such groups in itself came to be regarded as justifying these attacks."[9] Although obviously not totally descriptive of the Roman era, Moore's point is significant because it need not be isolated to the Inquisition. Indeed, blaming the victim in this manner started long before the Inquisition wrought its terror. As Moore also points out, it was Constantine who insisted that the benefits received for believing in Christianity did not include "heretics and schismatics [who] shall not only be alien from these privileges but be bound and subjugated to various compulsory public services."[10] Such views constitute the initial stages of a wide range of eventual measures sponsored by Christianity that legally destroyed competing belief systems.[11] Indeed, the "national community" that was Rome, subsequent to Constantine, was defined by the taking of the Christian sacraments.[12] The powerful appeals of religion, in this case, a fledgling national religion, allied with the immense temporal power of the state, combined to create a gardening operation of impressive dimensions. It would have deadly reiterations in later centuries. We know today of the horrible pressures faced by the victims of Nazi Germany's legal revolution. We can only conjecture about the social, psychological, and personal trauma of the legal destruction experienced in Imperial Roman times by the people who held views and participated in religious traditions and practices contrary to the accepted dogma of Christianity. What were the public and private articulations of being theologically, socially, and legally anathematized? How did people express their views to each other about the victims known to them? Were friendships shattered? Were marriages and families ruined? Did devastated people, much of the social meaning in their lives denied, turn to suicide as an escape, or simply try to live in diminished circumstances?

Prior to Constantine, and lacking dominant status, Christianity had valued and sought religious toleration instead of persecution. Within fifty years after ascending to the status of an imperial state religion, it became "the persecutor of every other form of religious expression"[13] and began the long process by which it "justified conquest by evangelization" through the imperial ideology with which it allied itself.[14] Several factors contributed to this process. On one hand, Christianity made universal claims regarding its message, function, and role in human affairs; regarded its truth claims as the only valid truth claims, replacing those of the parent religion; and interpreted the will of its God through historical events, some of which it initiated and controlled. An early example of this is found in the view of the Bishop of Lyon, later canonized as St. Irenaeus, that there could be no salvation outside the one, true Church.[15] This particular viewpoint would be reiterated and emphasized by later papal authority. David Olster observes that the alliance of Christianity with the Roman Empire provided the religion with "a religio-political rhetoric called triumphalism" rooted in three themes: "victory demonstrated divine power, ... divine favor guaranteed victory, and ... the emperor [was] the empire's mediator for, and personal recipient of, divine favor."[16] Matters of religious doctrine became questions of "power within the framework of Roman imperial government."[17] Averil

Cameron, with reference to Michel Foucault and Michael Mann, notes that Christianity thus has operated as a "totalizing discourse" with "transcendent ideological power in human history."[18]

It did not take very long before anti-Jewish attitudes manifested in literature. The earliest examples of Christian-influenced literature that rejected Jews are found in the first years of the third century. The North African Tertullian penned *Aduersus Iudaeos.* Similar works appeared by Cyprian and Lactantius, the *Collection of Testimonies* and *Diuinae Institutiones,* respectively. A few decades later in Italy, Novatian wrote a pastoral letter warning his congregants against observing Jewish practices. Such warnings were repeated by Zeno of Verona and Ambrose in Milan.[19]

A good example of the results of such totalizing discourse is found in fourth-century Spain. After a long period of tolerance and acceptance of local religious customs, an imperial decree declared the confiscation of all lands used—even unwittingly—for "prohibited worship." Notably, this decree would have been read, with appropriate fanfare and solemnity, in the most crowded of public places. Ramsay Macmullen's *Christianizing the Roman Empire* lists the kind of state-sponsored language regarding prohibited religious activity to which the citizens hearing this would have been exposed: "madness, contamination, poison, perfidy, monstrousness, polluted contagion." Macmullen is aware of how the perspective of the state's approved religion could circulate among the people of the empire even though far removed from the center of imperial splendor:

What items of experience were people talking about and passing on to their neighbors? What impinged on a person's settled universe of ideas, disturbing it and preparing him to question his previous beliefs and even abandon them? What made news? The most likely items on the religious page concerned Christian holy men, miracles, exorcisms, healings, wonderful things. They concerned the emperor's laws read aloud in the town center, declaring all but Christian views to be entirely tolerable. They were oratorical displays in cathedrals for both everyday folk and the upper classes. For the latter alone, new publication of any ideologically aggressive sort likely to attract attention was Christian. The prevailing close social and economic relations did not allow non-Christian people to shut out this noise of Christian exuberance, this din of defeat.[20]

Macmullen asks the appropriate question: What made news in the lives of these people? We may add, what ideas motivated them? What issues did they attend to? What did they ignore? Did they feel empathy for those who were the targets of imperial wrath and restrictions? Or did the changes in social life just pass them by, never engendering attention on their part? What accommodations did they make in their personal relationships? What did they say of these matters in the privacy of their homes? Did their children perceive difficulties in the lives of those known to them and ask about problems? If so, what did the parents tell their children? Were people able to converse freely with their anathematized neighbors or not? Did they feel a sense of coercion, or did they simply go along with events? What differences did any of this make for them?

Rome, for its part, obviously provided a splendid platform for Christianity to use to broadcast its message. Especially now that it was based on the twin pillars of Roman law and military organization, strength, and presence throughout the Empire, that is, the ability to project Roman power and law across much of Europe, northern Africa, and eastern Asia. This change of fortune provided Christianity a quantum leap in its ability to persuade or coerce non-Christians to convert and to execute a variety of punitive measures against Jews and Judaism and, later, other infidels and heretics. Keeping in mind the crucial point that these practices became a template for the kinds of controls to be exercised against The Other in a variety of ways in later centuries, it is highly instructive to consider the legislative specifics that impacted the lives of Jews either in the empire or, later, under the influence and control of Christianity:

Christianity created ghettos for Jews, prohibited mixed marriages, and prohibited Jews from serving their communities as judges. [21]

Rome barred intermarriage, removed Jews from the army, prohibited construction of new synagogues, barred Jews from serving in administrative and municipal positions, rewarded conversions to Christianity, forbade Jewish parents to disinherit children who converted, decreed the death penalty for those who attacked Jewish apostates, decreed the death penalty for intermarriage (also loss of property or exile), forced Jews to obey Roman law instead of Jewish law, disallowed synagogues taxation rights of Jews, forbade circumcision unless of one's son, and denied the study of the Mishna in synagogues.[22]

The Theodosian Code stipulated death by burning for any Jew who assailed an apostate Jew.[23]

Both before and after the demise of the Roman Empire, Orthodox and Catholic Church councils continued the pressures already instituted against the Jews: Christians are not to eat unleavened bread sent to them by Jews, are not to be friendly with Jews, are not to use medicines prescribed by Jews, are not to bathe with Jews, no Jews are to own Christian slaves, no Christians are to rest on Saturday—but work, Christians are not to accept gifts from Jews, nor celebrate holidays with them.

The Catholic synod in Elvira in 306 C.E. declared no intermarriage; Jews could not bless a field owned by a Christian. The 465 C.E. synod in Vennes, France, mandated that clergy not eat with Jews, and this mandate was extended to laymen in 517 C.E. The Narbonne synod in France did not allow Christians to stay in a house with a Jew. The synod of Macon in 581 C.E. prohibited Jews from being in the streets during Holy Week, and mandated that Jews must pay attention to the wishes of Christian clerics. Jews must not sit in the presence of such clerics unless permitted. Jews could not be judges or tax collectors over Christians. Jews could not own Christian slaves, which greatly reduced access to farming by Jews.

The 633 C.E. synod in Toledo kept converted Jews from having any dealings with Jews, including relatives. The 681 C.E. synod of Toledo led to the Visigothic Code of Law. Old laws were renewed. Jews were not to insult the Trinity; Jews were not to withdraw themselves, sons, or male servants from baptism or conversion; Jews were not to celebrate Passover in their traditional manner, nor celebrate their Sabbath or festivals; Jews must stay away from work on Sunday; Jews were not permitted to make distinctions among foods; Jews were not to advise relatives; Jews were not to attack Christianity nor defend their sect; Jews were not to emigrate to apostate again; Jews were not to read books rejected by Christianity; their slaves were freed if they converted to Christianity; no Jewish landlord was allowed over Christian serfs; and Jews new to a country had to identify themselves to the local bishop, who could require them to appear before him on certain days.

The 694 C.E. synod of Toledo added that the king could make Jews into slaves, and their children could be removed after the seventh year and married to Christians.[24] The synod of Toulouse in 883 C.E. ruled and "the emperor confirmed that on every Christmas, Good Friday and Ascension Day a Jew was to be given a powerful slap in the face in front of the church door." The slapped Jew was to "shout three times: 'It is just that Jews must bend their neck under the beatings of Christians, as they are unwilling to submit to Christ.'"[25]

The 1209 C.E. synod of Avignon forced Jews to work on Sunday. Jews were prohibited from eating meat on Christian holidays. They were prohibited from taking usurious interest and had to return it to those from whom they had received it. The Fourth Lateran Council of 1215 C.E. declared that Jews had to wear different clothes from those of Christians, as a way of giving a clear sign so sexual intercourse could be avoided.[26]

Bernhard Blumenkranz lists church councils that promulgated anti-Jewish canons, including "Albi (1204), Apt (1365), Arles (1263 and 1275), Avignon (1209 and 1326), Béziers (1241), Bourges (1276), Chateau-Gontier (1231), Lavaur (1368), Lyon (1245), Montpellier (1195 and 1258), Narbonne (1227), Pont-Audemer (1256 and 1279), Rouen (1231), Tours (1236), Valence (1248)." In the three-quarters of a century after 1195, forty church councils were convened; seventeen of them took the trouble to pass anti-Jewish resolutions.[27] Christianity's authorities thereby expressed significant interest in controlling the lives of the Disconfirming Other, both in their midst and beyond, over many centuries.

Once allied with the state apparatus, Christianity did not tarry in making life as difficult as possible for the Jews in its midst. Building upon past success, it continued to do so long after the collapse of the Roman Empire. The laws, rescripts, and edicts, some executed locally, others taking effect across the empire, impacted and invaded even the most intimate details and functions of life and constructed obstacles that made normal human relations with and for Jews virtually impossible. The structure and complexity of Roman governance meant that the promulgation of the laws involved a wide array of officials as they moved the paperwork along: The emperor, possibly a complainant, the *praefecti praetorio*, departmental heads at court such as "the Master of Offices ... the Comes of the sacred Largesses ... the Comes of the Private Property ... the Comes and Master of the Two Services ... the 'Comes of the East' to name a few."[28] Laws were edited, recorded in a register, and, later, deposited in archives after codification and manuscript transmission.

This brief account offers a clear sense of the large number of government personnel involved, prefiguring the legislative and bureaucratic complexity and precision of Germany some 1,500 years later, as well as other powerful political and religious bodies that operated against The Other. Such restrictions on the activities and lives of Jews echo down through the centuries. Most laws were enacted as a form of normative pacification, as opposed to coercive pacification. Coercion was later practiced against Jews, resonating in the Crusades, within Luther's lifetime, in Spain and elsewhere during the Inquisition, and into the Third Reich, among other lamentable episodes involving sacred violence. Thus an implicit ideology emerged, one lacking overt reference to theological justifications and rationales, but one that nevertheless came to be experienced as the norm by practicing Christians. Newly empowered in the secular sphere, Christianity in Roman times thus set out on a course that would alter the lives of virtually every human being who would ever come under its sway in the centuries ahead. Although it may be argued that it did not do this without often seriously compromising its message of love and charity for all, Christianity nonetheless made universal proclamations of truth while also offering vituperative condemnations of The Other.

One of the most significant vestiges of the Roman-Christian past is the change in practice allowing Christian males to serve in the Roman army. In the first two centuries of the Common Era, the church's theology was pacifistic.[29] The first record of a Christian entering the Roman army is dated 173 C.E., although no written support from Christian authorities existed for the faithful to participate in warfare between the years 100–313 C.E.[30] Origen, who lived during this period, took the position that Christians cannot kill, even in self-defense,[31] an essential feature of classic pacifism. Tertullian argued that a soldier could not be a Church member and that a soldier who converted to Christianity was bound to leave the military.[32] In "De Idolatria," Tertullian made the point that a Christian should not take an oath to the supreme leader of the Roman army and also one to serve Jesus Christ.[33] This position would be mirrored in the twentieth century in Hitler's demands for singular obedience and allegiance. In the next three-quarters of a century, perhaps another six followers of Christ followed in the martial path of the single military pioneer.[34] St. Cyprian, Bishop of Carthage in the middle of the third century C.E., admonished that the guiltless are not permitted to put even the guilty to death,[35] a perspective that kept Christian magistrates of the day from decreeing death penalties.[36] At the end of the fourth century, St. Basil had mandated that a soldier "with unclean hands abstain from communion for three years."[37] With Constantine's triumph over Maxentius, however, according to Adolf Harnack, the Christian God was revealed to be the "God of war and victory";[38] accordingly, pacifism was eventually all but lost as one of the options for the "lay person's expression of Christian ethical life."[39] Indeed, after a decree of the Council of Arles in 313 C.E., Christians could be excommunicated if they attempted to *leave* the Roman military. At about this same time, Eusebius of Caesarea, a theologian and historian, reflected these changes when he did not censure imperial troops who had committed atrocities during war, preferring to see them as divine agents for Christian justice in repaying the earlier sufferings endured by believers.[40] He saw Christians as members of a nation "beginning in heaven, warring for God and Christ against the devil."[41] By the time of Theodosius II, in 416 C.E., *only* Christians could serve in the Roman military,[42] a development signifying a stunning reversal of Church teaching and practice within the passing of a single century, clearly indicating the nature and depth of the changes taking place within the Christian community as it came to terms with the implications of becoming an integral institutional and bureaucratic part of a military empire. This change would prove to be truly momentous because it contributed significantly to hardening forever the results of the Church's negative stance against The Other. It provided only a narrow range of responses to The Other, primarily hostile ones, with physical violence always an option. Outside the military realm, the newly hardened values were present in other realms. Christian masters were encouraged to enforce religious conformity among their domestics by means of a good beating, with heavier beatings to follow if necessary.[43] Christian courts commonly used torture, as opposed to Rabbinic courts, which took care to offer "special protection to the poor, weak, and dispossessed."[44] Ramsay Macmullen notes that Christian courts did very little to abolish gladiatorial contests. Indeed, amidst signs of greater cultural focus on God's undoubted ability to inflict a wide variety of tormenting, painful acts, "Christian zeal was directed over all of daily life .... threats and torture, the stake and the block, spread over many new categories of offense."[45] In these instances, a developing cultural pattern, one that enveloped many facets of the lives of both Christians and non-Christians at the time, eventually led to a certain disregard for the avoidance of violence. All but lost to the world was the earlier Christian's refusal to offer blind obedience to any human superior,[46] a perspective that would have been a critical option for people to have had available during the evil of Nazi Germany. Also lost were other directives. For example, the fourteenth *Canon of Hippolytus* contained a directive to early Christians that would have been a powerful counterweight to prevailing norms in the Holocaust. Regarding a Christian soldier and the act of killing, according to Jean-Michel Hornus, this canon advised, "Neither the pretext of patriotic duty nor the theory of obedience to a superior could absolve him of responsibility."[47] Eventually, Augustine would remove the option of violence only for the clergy; in his view, non-clergy could kill out of duty, but not malice.[48] The Augustinian duty to kill would include extending Christian dominion over all souls that came under its control in later centuries. Reverend Donald A. Wells records a twentieth-century echo of Augustine's ancient concern. Applying to be a chaplain in the U.S. military during World War II, Wells was denied on the grounds that he refused to sign a non-pacifist pledge.[49] The complete obedience of believing Christians to powerful figures, such as the Pope, or to the state, came to be seen as a prime virtue. Martin Luther made obedience to the state a virtual requirement for devout believers, and it became an ominous portent for later events in Germany. Thus embracing martial roles and values, Christianity succumbed to the empire, and the emerging religion was infected with reasons of state.[50] This being the case, in the view of Jacob Neusner, Eusebius's writings provided Christianity a fully expressed ideology for a "world-conquering Christian civilization,"[51] which is precisely what transpired as subsequent centuries unfolded. The result of these changes very early in the history of Christianity forever altered the range of possible options available to individuals as they negotiated the difficult social and psychological terrain that involved sorting out the claims of the state versus the claims of a higher authority. We also find the diminishment of the individual's conscience in favor of serving and following the institutional dictate.

Elie Wiesel stated, "In the beginning there was the Holocaust. We must therefore start all over again."[52] A focus on the period during which Christianity evolved the theology of violence that would come to permeate its culture puts us very close to a beginning that must be examined critically for its legacy. Robert Jay Lifton, in *Nazi Doctors*, theorizes that German physicians involved in the death factories practiced what Lifton calls "doubling" and "derealization" in order to function with minimal psychological distress,[53] which Lifton sees as part of the "universal proclivity toward constructing good motives while participating in evil behavior."[54] Lifton defines doubling as the partition of the self into "two functioning wholes," with one of the partial selves serving as the whole self.[55] Thus, Nazi German physicians, having sworn the Hippocratic Oath, could zealously throw themselves into the daily tasks involving mass murder found at Auschwitz. Derealization, according to Lifton, divests the self "from the actuality of what one is part of, not experiencing it as 'real.'"[56] Added to this is a feeling of powerlessness, that one is merely a very small part of a much larger functioning unit.[57] Taken together, these make the perpetrator's assignment more easily rendered. The gardening project spoken of by Zygmunt Bauman becomes an easier task, if not altogether enjoyable in every case. It appears that the inaction of bystanders, those who are apparently not so morally compromised (in terms of a professional oath prescribing one's behavior) as were the Nazi doctors, may also be said to be facilitated by doubling. The Nazi doctors were faced with making their circle of moral and professional obligation slightly smaller by rejecting Jews. But Christians had been doing precisely that, reducing the number of human beings eligible for their moral concern, for many centuries before the Nazi doctors functioned in the state's euthanasia program and death camps. Given the Christian mandate to love, the faithful were faced with meeting this command while also functioning as agents of their God in aggressively punishing their God's alleged enemies, or in bystanding as their God's righteous wrath was levied against The Other. Lifton's analysis of this phenomenon becomes all the more intriguing when we also consider his notion that doubling could be associated with transcendence, akin to the sense one has upon

entering a religious order.[58] We will see that the empowering cultural apparatus functioning over the centuries to anathematize Jews lent itself readily to reactions against different Others whenever encountered—Muslims, indigenous
people in the New World, Africans, heretics, lepers, gays, witches, and others
deemed to be beyond the pale.

Contrary to Lifton's "divided-self" notion of perpetrating evil is James E.
Waller's insightful "unitary-self" concept. For Waller, "the primary, and only,
self or psychological constellation *is* fundamentally altered as a result of the
power of potent social forces generated by the situation or organization."[59]
Waller cites several studies dealing with "the foot-in-the-door" phenomenon,
"the tendency for people who have first agreed to a small request to comply later
with a larger request."[60] Similar to Ervin Staub's position, Waller concludes that
harming "victims can become 'normal' behavior."[61]

Both theories offer relevant possibilities, although from the perspective of this
study, Lifton's argument clearly gives a significant degree of personal choice to
the individual in a situation involving atrocity. Waller's account, which is somewhat closer to the approach taken in this study, more accurately reflects the impact on the individual, the self, of much larger social forces. Indeed, "impact"
may miss the point; culture actually does much to create, inform, and sustain
the self that operates in a social setting. Waller's unitary-self theory sees the individual as, in essence, neither inherently good nor evil: "We become that to
which we are exposed."[62] If that larger entity is itself evil in its views and practices, the devastating human results should not be altogether surprising.

It is perhaps useful to combine the two views of the personality. Rather than
an either-or situation, it might be said that the unitary self *is* a divided self. That
is, the single self is culturally disposed to function in seemingly antithetical ways,
loving and caring for those within the self's circle of moral obligation while hat-
ing and vilifying those who are not. Western Christianity's culture creates
human selves who can function in apparently contradictory fashion: practicing
Christian love in certain cases, but perfectly capable of executing the theology
of violence against The Other when required or expected to do so. There is one
self—the Western Christian self—that rewards both kinds of behaviors. A transcendent hierarchy of values privileges the soul and the afterlife over the body,
the life lived on earth. This is an especially powerful concept when the believer
operates against The Other with the strong, perhaps even absolute, assurance of
one's own righteousness and salvation. The cultural discourse of Christianity
both mandated and empowered believers to "save" The Other, either through
conversion or destruction, as will be seen in lamentable detail in subsequent
chapters. The seemingly disparate behaviors of the two selves are united by the
command to serve one's God, whose representatives on earth, the authorities of
the Christian church, asks of the deity's believers to love fellow Christians even
as they go about destroying Others—Jews, Native Americans, Africans. Doing
so results in the activation of *both* the various forms of love and its opposite,
the varieties of hate. Ervin Staub's assessment of doubling tends to support this

latter view. People, he claims, "tend toward integration."[63] It seems likely that one of the functions of the Christian religion is to provide the necessary psychological and spiritual tools for such integration; otherwise, the tasks asked of its adherents could prove to be too psychologically difficult. Similarly, Nazi perpetrators and the countless bystanders to the various processes of the Holocaust could find in Nazi Germany an integrating state mechanism, perhaps akin to early Christian integration with the Imperial Roman state mechanism, resulting in a highly efficacious cultural situation.

These issues necessarily involve the implications of what it means to be involved in a culture. In other words, what does it mean to give one's assent to a belief system, an ideology? Doing so is, generally, not a conscious decision, even though it entails virtually any thought the believer may have, any attitude, any behavior. In the focus—a dominant religion operating across twenty centuries—of this study individuals are not readily able to ascertain whether that institution or its culture is morally compromised, or evil in its essence and many functions. Individuals are not inclined to perform the ideological critique that could determine such status. There is much evidence available to the believer that his or her involvement is benign, thus producing positive, good, moral results. Perpetrating evil acts, or bystanding, will have a vast, rationalized support system. This was true for the Nazi German perpetrators, who enjoyed the benefits of a strong supporting social system—a culture, in the terms of this study.

Aside from the momentous changes for Christians discussed above, the example of St. John Chrysostom is a particular case that highlights the emerging views and attitudes of the dominant culture. His writings and speeches incessantly attacked Jews as well as Judaisers, the nominal Christians who were simultaneously observing some elements of Jewish and Christian law and rituals. Prior to the early Church councils and the harshness of popular figures such as Chrysostom, Christians and Jews did coexist and fraternize in normal ways, but this changed as the pressures mounted against continued normal relations.[64] Marcel Simon finds Chrysostom to be an extreme case but by no means a unique case in the first few centuries after Christ.[65] His attitudes were reflected everywhere in early Church writings, but reading Chrysostom's venomous attacks today is nevertheless a shocking experience. At the time, however, his sermons were very public events, delivered in a setting in which his pulpit was located in the center of the church's nave, with his listeners pressing close upon him, "like crowds around a soap-box orator." Christians of the fourth century C.E. were accustomed to dramatic performances in church services that rivaled what they liked in theatre. Chrysostom's close proximity to his audience allowed him to have an advantage in working up an emotional appeal,[66] to the point where he grew hoarse from his exhortations.[67]

A brief review of Chrysostom's rhetoric will, perhaps, give insight into the appeals being made to his homilies' listeners. In his eight *Homilies Against the Jews*, apparently delivered in Antioch in 386–387 C.E., he accused the Jews as sons of God who had become like dogs, in language that echoes the Theodosian

Code's reference to Jews as a "feral sect."[68] Chrysostom orated that they always resist the Holy Spirit; they are stiff-necked; they are senseless beasts; they are voracious, gluttonous, drunken, beasts fit only for slaughter; they are carnal even when fasting, an insult to God. Their synagogue is a brothel, a wild beasts' den; "they behave no better than pigs or goats."[69] They are enemies of the truth; their temples are dens for thieves; God will exact his vengeance against them.[70] Jews are like balky farm animals, or are more dangerous than wolves; they are vipers; they are filled with sexual lust; they are rude, insolent, treacherous, hypocritical, greedy; they are godless and consort with demons; they are proud of having killed Christ.[71] Jews kill and eat their own children.[72] Chrysostom vilified Jews in this manner to impress upon Judaizers the depth of their own perfidy, as a way to intimidate them back into the Christian fold.[73] Part of the appeal was that turning away from Judaism would strengthen the Church, but he also appealed to the Christian's self-interest: those saved from such Judaizing evil would gather at the final judgment and help preserve those from possible perdition who had deterred them from Judaizing.[74]

Chrysostom's rhetoric was matched by his contemporary, Jerome, a Christian saint whose monastery was located in Bethlehem. According to Frederic Cople Jaher, at about the same time that Chrysostom's hurtful words were stirring his congregants against Jews and Judaizers in Antioch, St. Jerome "anticipated modern anti-Semitic propaganda" by prophesying "the emergence of an infernal Jewish conspiracy for global dominion." The good saint argued that the Jews would produce the Antichrist in the year 407, who would then turn his evil powers on the task of persecuting "the people of Christ." According to St. Jerome, Jews accept Lucifer's deputy as their Messiah, a figure who will lead his followers in a defeat of Rome, returning Israel to its former glory, only to be, in turn, crushed "in the apocalyptic fulfillment of Christianity."[75]

In Chrysostom's invective against Jews, Hyam Maccoby sees an ominous prefiguration of Hitler's language seventeen centuries later.[76] Most striking in this regard is Chrysostom's claim, in the eighth *Homily*, to be meeting his duty in ministering to his congregation as a physician does to his patient, to provide medicine to avoid further infection.[77] This is a clear harbinger of the ubiquitous medical and biological references larded throughout Hitler's speeches and writing. Chrysostom's language itself recalls that of Claudius from a century earlier; he saw Jews as a plague upon the world.[78] A quarter of a century after Chrysostom's *Homilies* were delivered, Christians in Antioch seized the synagogues of the city. Although it is difficult to establish a direct cause and effect relationship, one scholar thinks it not unlikely that his inflammatory language had some residual effect on believing Christians, and probably did result in a "distorted view of Judaism,"[79] a mild condemnation, to be sure. Whether this conjecture is true or not, we necessarily can wonder about the reception of these vile accusations on the part of Chrysostom's listeners. Were they disturbed on behalf of Jews known to them? Did they disagree with their priest, who would eventually become a saint in the eyes of the Christian Church? Or did they go about their lives with little regard for the fate of their neighbors? Did they bother to check Chrysostom's claims against their personal experiences? Did Chrysostom somehow speak to their deep inner needs?

Keeping in mind that a major culture is in the process of being created, one that will persist largely unchanged in certain respects for many centuries, Chrysostom articulated a point of view in his fourth *Homily* that would be heard again in the twentieth century, in Germany, after World War II. Professor of New Testament Theology and accused war criminal Gerhard Kittell[80] reiterated Chrysostom's assertion: "What is done in accordance with God's will is the best of all things even if it seems to be bad .... Suppose someone slays another in accordance with God's will. This slaying is better than any loving-kindness .... To spare the other's life would be more unholy than any slaying. For it is God's will ... that makes the same actions good or bad."[81] Chrysostom's sentiments reverberate through the centuries, and Christians would spend much time executing their sense of God's will against The Other in precisely this fashion. Countless attacks against Jews became "part of the pre-conscious fear-system of the people."[82] Repulsive, violent beliefs arose and subsequent actions struck innumerable victims, sanctioned and supported by the dominant religion. Marcel Simon makes the point that virulent attitudes like Chrysostom's were not isolated to the hierarchy of the Church, nor were the Church's august figures the only source of information for believers. He finds strident anti-Judaism prominently displayed in the liturgy, although he believes that its anti-Jewish sentiments were not uniformly spread throughout the liturgical year, clustering instead around certain holy observances.

Although Jews and Christians had formerly been able to live in relative peace together for decades, it is perhaps not coincidental that at the very time that St. John Chrysostom was fomenting against Jews in 388 C.E. a synagogue in the Mesopotamian city of Callinicum was burned by Christians at the urging of the local bishop. The city's administrators notified the emperor, Theodosius, who ordered that the bishop must indemnify the victims and rebuild the synagogue from his own resources. The arsonists were to receive blows as punishment. St. Ambrose, bishop of Milan, intervened on behalf of the local bishop, avowing the legitimacy of putting synagogues to the torch. Laws forbidding such acts were bad laws, to be disobeyed as one's Christian duty—a clear example of the kind of choice the Christian individual must make between obeying the alleged dictates of one's God or living in accordance with the laws of the state. St. Ambrose supported his argument by invoking God as the source of approval for the destruction of the Jewish places of worship. Theodosius, excommunicated by Ambrose,[83] eventually revoked his initial ruling,[84] providing an early precedent for the kind of influence that the Church could bring to bear against government and government officials. As happened in the twentieth century, it became apparent that a state's legal system could be brought to bear against Jews, with no semblance of neutrality, thus ensuring that "they should exist in misery, [with] a precarious status, a diminished existence ... once chosen, but now condemned."[85]

We can only surmise about the nature of the difficulties that Jews faced in their lives, their human fulfillment stymied, their hopes diminished, and their beliefs ridiculed.

Other acts of violence against Jews were repeated elsewhere in areas under Christian control. The first recorded expulsion occurred in 414 C.E. in Alexandria, mobs attacked Jews, confiscated their property, and then expelled them from the city. The spectre of a charge of ritual murder allegedly committed by Jews led to a mob's attacking Jews living in Innestar, Syria in 415.[86] A synagogue in Magona in Minorca was burned in 418, and bands of *illuminati*, "brigand monks," roamed Palestine for forty years burning synagogues and killing Jews.[87] A mob of Christians attacked Jews in Chrysostom's Antioch in 405.[88] Such incidents, combined with the restrictions stipulated by the councils and synods and invective emanating from church pulpits throughout Christendom, give some indication that the attitudes inculcated by Christianity's proclamations were taking root and shaping human behaviors. Contrary to Simon's own sense that anti-Jewish pronouncements clustered at key times in the liturgical calendar is his perspective that "Anti-Jewish polemic ... was ... driven into the minds of the believers and shaped their entire way of thinking. Being thus reinforced day by day, anti-Jewish sentiments hardened" in the minds of Christian believers.[89] Jean Juster traces anti-Jewish practices among the Visigothic heirs to Roman practices: King Sisebut (616–620 C.E.) initiated policies that forced Jews to leave or convert. This was the first such expulsion involving Jews of an entire Christian country. A quarter century later, King Chintila expressed his desire that only Christians live in the kingdom. King Recceswinth, at the Ninth Council of Toledo, used the opportunity to call Jews infectious pests. Punishments for Jews included confiscation of their property, whippings, and shaving their heads. King Erwig, who saw Jews as a corrupting plague, required priests to make Jews listen to the oral reading of laws.[90]

Decrees, sermons, attitudes, and behaviors would not cease when the familiar world of Roman-controlled Europe passed into oblivion. At best, a long period of relative quiescence ensued. But attitudes and behaviors persisted throughout Christendom, perhaps just below the level of human consciousness. Emerging on frightening occasions over the following centuries to cause shock and despair, to destroy property and countless lives, such incidents reinforced the mind-set for later perpetrators as well as the bystanders of atrocity.

3

The Crusades

"Where a blessing fails, a good thick stick will succeed. Now we shall raise princes and prelates against you; and … a mighty number will die by the sword …. [Y]ou will all of you be reduced to servitude. Thus force will prevail where gentle persuasion has failed to do so."
—St. Dominic, 1209 Albigensian Crusade

"Kill them all, for God knows His own!"
—attributed to Arnald-Amalric, at the Béziers massacre

The implications of the Christian acceptance of military roles and views within the Roman Empire, as well as those of the theological position of Christian believers as "soldiers of Christ," came to full fruition in several crusades initially motivated by Pope Urban II in his appeal of 1095. Having achieved status as an "imperial ecumenism," offering its version of civilization along with subjugation, conditions and an ideology existed in which there was "no room for dissent, minorities, heterodoxy, or discrepant positions in a state designed for a religious goal."[1] Augustine's doctrine of *cognite intrare* (compel them to enter)[2], manifested as a demand for orthodox belief, led to what came to be termed "constructive persecution," that moment when Christian ideology turned into military practice based on the devout "We" operating violently against the obstinate "They."[3] After a lengthy period of seeming quiescence, during which normative pacification largely characterized social and cultural practices, Christianity began to assert itself more coercively in its efforts to impose itself in places far from its own centers of cultural, political, and spiritual power. Innocent IV asserted the papacy's "divinely instituted Petrine mandate," which conferred responsibility for all souls, including infidels, upon the pope.[4] Myths operating at the center of the Christian faith had reached a volatile new stage, one in which they were being "acted upon as if they were real, in their capacity to set empirical events underway."[5] The empirical events discussed in this chapter constitute the early examples of Christianity's "relentless conquest of one region of the earth after another."[6] As Ziauddin Sardar explains, Christianity, as an "exoteric religion," possessed a "reified and deified belief" system that sufficed to explain all aspects of reality, making it fully capable of "serving as a complete system of values and beliefs" for a society.[7] Such beliefs include claims regarding Christianity's truth, its rights of dominion, transcendence, and superiority over all forms of Otherness. In essence, the crusades provide the first examples of the large-scale extension of power of the Christian master narrative, thus creating the opening gambit of the Christian West's ideology and practice of world domination.[8] Proving ominous, Ervin Staub argued in his study of evil and genocide that "once a culture evolves aggressive characteristics, *aggression can become a way of life.*"[9] Based on self-proclaimed notions of innate superiority, religious and secular leaders of the Christian West, beginning in earnest with the crusades, "legitimated and dignified the conquest, dispossession, and enslavement of non-Christian peoples throughout the non-European world."[10] As Peter Berger notes, the encounter with the Disconfirming Other's denial of the supposed ultimate reality of the universe "takes on the quality of evil as well as madness"[11]—ample warrant for the ensuing violence that would shatter the lives of hundreds of thousands of innocent people. The trajectory of such conquests and attempted conquests, beginning with the crusades, maintained itself or expanded as Western Europeans moved inexorably across and around the globe from the late twelfth century until, roughly, the end of World War I. Then colonial empires began to break up, especially in the second half of the twentieth century.

From a viewpoint centuries later, the beginnings of European hegemony found in the Christian faith "an exceptional role as imperial ideology ... the official ideology for imperial expansion."[12] Sardar appropriately notes that the West's "universalizing principle" declares its way as the universal way, an intentional "act of will and force"[13] often directed explosively against The Other. It goes without saying that individual humans, both privately and in a wide variety of groups, constitute the chief instrument through which such acts of will and force are executed. In so doing, human beings necessarily encounter their culture's ideology, imbibe it, and are in turn constituted by it; Henry Giroux finds that ideology "inserts individuals into social relations, for which they merely serve as props."[14] Even if true, this does not absolve humans of responsibility for their actions taken under the influence of a culture and its empowering ideology. There is always a possibility for an individual to resist, to exercise what amounts to an ideological critique; there is always a moment when a human could take a different path, one not sanctioned by the dominant ideology. Leonardo Boff asks the appropriate question in this regard: "To what extent does culture promote liberation, consolidate oppression, hinder a defiant conscientization, and foster or impede life and freedom?"[15] Individuals in a position to promote the supposed benefits of the dominant culture have not addressed Boff's question adequately, in my view. Most humans living under the influence of the dominant religion and its culture seem to have little or no interest in the lives and freedom of The Other, or in the impact the culture has had on the lives of The Other. Indeed, the mere recognition of the culture and its ideology could provide a significant starting point for an individual's critical awareness of his or her actions. A successful ideology nevertheless provides powerful incentives to counteract this possibility for conscious awareness and resistance, leaving an "ideological imprint upon the psyche itself."[16] Such imprints might provide most of the features of the cultural world surrounding us, offering, as Alan Davies notes, the psychological-political context "nurtured within the consciousness of Western Christendom since 1099."[17] Indeed, historians have argued that the crusades influenced virtually every aspect of Europe's subsequent intellectual and cultural phenomena, involving virtually all European countries and impacting almost all areas of life.[18] The incentives offered to the soldiers of the Church were extremely seductive; combined with the social pressures of large group interactions, it is not surprising that few people found the inner strength and personal fortitude to resist successfully.

The case of the crusades offers a clear, explicit example of this process at work. The highest clerical authorities assured crusaders of the spiritual significance of their involvement. The crusaders received countless assurances that they were serving the purposes of their God, and in so doing, they would save their souls for all of eternity, their sins forgiven. In addition to such spiritual blandishments, there were powerful mundane enticements to offset the obvious drawbacks facing the warriors. Crusaders were given the right to claim property in perpetuity in the conquered areas.[19] Crusaders went berserk in defeated cities, killing innocents wantonly, raping, and pillaging. Zoé Oldenbourg notes that the papacy was aware of the atrocities during the Albigensian Crusade.[20] Booty could be so extensive that experience eventually taught the crusading leaders to quickly inventory and protect it with armed guards so that God's glory and future good works would be guaranteed.[21] Crusaders who killed a Jew in meeting their crusade vows were assured of absolution for their sins.[22] Following the first three expeditions, perhaps the ultimate in motivation came from the emerging view that successful crusading efforts would help bring about the Second Coming and the Day of Judgment.[23] Earthly military successes against The Other contributed to eschatological developments claimed by the faithful, thus providing a prime example of the complex interplay between a culture's structure of myth and empirical events.

In his study of ideology and warfare, James Turner Johnson cites Roland Bainton's four characteristics of holy war: a holy cause, God's direction and help, godly crusaders and ungodly enemies, and unsparing persecution.[24] The crusades obviously qualify in all regards, perhaps in a paradigmatic way. Building upon precedents established in the Roman period, Christianity had arrogated to itself the claim of being the single, uniquely truthful religion for all time, for all peoples. Even though it shared the Holy Land with other religions as a site of holy places, religious and secular leaders in Europe alike viewed the commanding presence of Christian influence, indeed, hegemony, as a necessity. The secular leaders often responded readily to papal calls for involvement, operating at a time when the Roman Catholic Church commanded a degree of official respect that would only diminish as the Reformation spread across Europe. The role of the pope as the vicar of Christ, God's deputy on earth, was not to be doubted. Crusader victories, as we shall see, were invariably interpreted as evidence of God's approval, support, and even intervention on behalf of the crusading venture. Crusaders, adorned with images of the crucifix, were seen as sainted personages, their sins absolved, their lives possibly forfeit in the endeavor but their souls saved for all eternity. Those who stood to suffer from the crusaders' enmity—heretics, Jews, Muslims, even lepers—were, by definition, outside the Christian circle of moral obligation. They were described in every vile way possible in sermons and other religious and secular modes across Europe and treated accordingly. Guibert of Nogent specifically identified Jews as the enemies of God.[25] Jews and other enemies of the crusaders and their God were "therefore outside the protection of the moral law applicable to that god's devotees."[26] The crusaders, upon actually encountering The Other as they met the obligations of their crusading vows, refrained not at all in the violent expressions of their pent-up animosities. Mass atrocities were often inflicted on women, children, and the elderly. In sum, the holy wars were "only one expression of a wider concept, that of sacred violence" that "requires as a premise the conviction that God and his intentions for mankind are intimately associated with the well-being of a political structure here on earth," which perceives itself to be threatened.[27]

An apparent offshoot of Augustinian-influenced Just War theory, Jonathan Riley-Smith's "moral theology of violence,"[28] the holy wars known as the crusades had numerous iterations in which various Others were targeted. Eight major crusades and numerous minor expeditions involving Christianity's *gladium spirituale* were sent to the Holy Land and other points east from the late eleventh century until the fourteenth century. Crusades were also declared against Others in the Iberian peninsula, Germany, Greece, northern Africa, the Baltic region, Finland, Poland, Flanders, Aragon, Bosnia, Italy, Bohemia, and Russia; these thrusts were ongoing through the sixteenth century.[29] It is significant for the purposes of this study that at any time during these crusades, both major and minor, Jews anywhere in the vicinity of the combatants could be assailed,[30] often on a scale of violence and horror never before experienced.[31] Léon Poliakov asserts that accounts of popular outbursts against Jews are absent until the eleventh century,[32] which is when the crusades were institutionalized.

A crusading army, like any army, requires significant levels of support. Aside from the actual soldiers, there would be servants, grooms, smiths, cooks, armorers, and women.[33] Also, civilians followed the crusading excursions in large numbers. Hundreds of thousands of participants, both civilian and military, from all stages and conditions of life, with the full involvement of their societies, governments, and religious brethren, operated across many thousands of miles of terrain and seas, ongoing across six centuries. Mass groups of people were both directly and indirectly involved in the various stages of theorizing, preaching, designing, supporting, and implementing sacred violence against The Other. As seen in the case of early Christian pressures against the Jews in their midst, we may also justifiably ask about the nature of the public's reaction to the events engulfing the world. According to Jonathan Riley-Smith, the crusaders' contemporaries supported the projects with alacrity.[34] Writing about the soldiers of Christ, Adolf Harnack points out the extreme difficulty faced by the faithful believers in rejecting war supposedly waged on behalf of their God.[35] Nevertheless, couldn't any individual see the difference between the abstract allegiance to a theological stance and the direct experience of seeing fellow human beings, perhaps one's neighbors, being attacked, tortured, and slaughtered wholesale? Accounts from the age indicate a bimodal response. Jews and Christians in Europe lived near each other, although typically in separate living quarters, on fairly amicable terms. In the centuries just prior to the crusades, contacts between Jews and Christians, with relations ranging from cordial to tense, were extensive.[36] Despite a real possibility for peaceful relations, Jews found themselves facing a mounting progression of anti-Jewish acts, practices, and atrocities. As crusading armies (and even larger contingents of unruly camp followers in the wake of the armies during the early crusades) advanced throughout areas of Europe toward their primary objective in the Holy Land, they were urged on by crusading slogans that posited "destruction of Jews and Judaism as a core objective of the crusading mission."[37] Along the way, the sheer weight of the fervor of the masses mitigated against intervention by local authorities as lepers and Jews faced slaughter. Léon Poliakov records massacres of Jews perpetrated by "formless mobs" at the time of the First Crusade. Other massacres were caused by "outbreaks of popular fanaticism" as "multitudes inconsolable for the offense to the living God rushed to slaughter" hapless Jews, including eight hundred in a single atrocity at Worms.[38] Jews were often burned indiscriminately; 160 died in the flames of a large pit near the royal castle of Chinon in Tours and Parisian Jews faced attacks that served to benefit the French king financially. The failed Shepherd's Crusade, denied the ultimate earthly goal of reaching Jerusalem— where it was considered sacrilegious for Jews to reside[39]—made sure that local Jews were attacked throughout Languedoc, with massacres and forced baptisms receiving the support of the locals.[40] The frustrated Shepherds also violated Jewish synagogues, destroying holy books and seizing goods.[41] Not all the violence was of the ad hoc variety; Jews of Cologne and Mainz faced planned, coordinated military actions conducted systematically by crusaders. A Jewish account of the Mainz action records the crusaders, upon finding an open gate, asserting, "All this the Crucified has done for us, so that we might avenge his blood upon the Jews."[42] After the First Crusade, travel for Jews on the roads of Europe became considerably more dangerous.[43] Poliakov argues that Europeans of this time "killed Jews first and hated them afterward," and that animosity toward Jews fed on the very massacres it provoked.[44]

An appreciation of the difficulties The Other faced during the crusades is evident. No Jew was safe, to be sure, but lepers, pagans, heretics, and Muslims also felt the wrath of righteous believers under the tremendous emotional sway of the preaching, popular songs, and mob frenzies that impelled the crusades. Scholars suggest that no European Christian alive at this time escaped hearing these appeals. Pope Urban II's xenophobic rhetoric set the initial tone. While there were some moments and incidents in which victims received some solace and protection from authorities or neighbors, far more often they were trapped and slaughtered, or made captive and converted, or committed suicide. No widespread organized support emerged to help protect the persecuted; avenues of escape were rare. The oppressors could rely on centuries of a theology of violence and potent promises of eternal glory. Those involved in the dominant culture had many reasons and incentives to behave the way they did; they had very few disincentives.

Chief among the increasing problems faced by Europe's Jews was the matter of forced conversions. The stark alternative was death, either at the hands of Christians or by suicide. Conversionist discourse was ubiquitous within Christian realms. In addition to incessant ecclesiastical and scriptural demands for conversion, Jews were faced with conversions under the particular cruelties of the duress of force. Indeed, the possibility of a successful conversion experience involving individuals or a group actually sanctified the use of violence. Such force could be applied not only to hasten the desired conversion process, in the opinion of Pope Innocent III, but also to coerce continued obedience to the church when converts were evincing doubts about their new spiritual condition.[45] Pope Clement IV in 1267 added capital punishment for Jewish converts who relapsed.[46] In another example, the Council of Vienne in 1311 ordered chairs established in universities in Rome, Paris, Oxford, Bologna, and Salamanca to study foreign languages, as a way to enhance the Church's efforts for the propagation of Christianity among non-Christians.[47] Jews had to live in the daily presence of private and institutional pressures within the culture to force their conversion. Compelling evidence exists that "conquest and the spreading of Christianity were very closely linked" and that the crusade "as a war of conversion seems to have been deeply rooted"[48] in the culture. Under these conditions, it would be virtually impossible to find a crusader, perhaps even a European Christian, who would have had significant doubts about this cultural mandate for conversion, at least in principle. The sacred violence used to put the conversion mandate into execution against Jews and slaughter of Others might have proven to be a disturbing experience to some of the bystanders, but broadly speaking, it seems that very few stepped forward in conscience to make a concerted protest against the enabling ideology of a war of conversion. Cistercian monks, however, were an exception.[49] Prior to Urban's preaching of the First Crusade, at the time of Leo IX and Gregory VII, some Catholic thinkers had returned to a consideration of matters—the degree to which "armed force was consonant with Christianity."[50] One Cistercian, the abbot Isaac of Etoile, wrote in protest of the military religious orders that had emerged during the early crusades. With considerable prescience, he observed that the members of these orders "consider that they have every right to attack anyone not confessing Christ's name ... but we do insist that what they are doing can be an occasion of many future evils."[51] Needless to say, although this issue had apparently been resolved in favor of a just use of violence against

The Other centuries earlier, the faithful seem to have managed once again to resolve any remaining doubts in the decades leading up to Urban's call, thereby contributing to the crusade's enabling set of attitudes and beliefs. Other objections may have been registered against certain details related to the waging of the crusade effort, *but, notably, not against the conversionist ideology itself.* For instance, the *Collectio de Scandalis Ecclesiae* recorded the clergy's severe dislike of the tithes on their income to support the crusades.[52] Papal control of the crusading army became a significant friction point by 1227; the practice of granting general absolutions, without an accompanying penance, developed into a popular subject for troubadours critical of the crusades.[53] Franciscan Roger Bacon in 1268 (in a preview of events in North America and Spain three centuries later) opposed crusading as a tool for converting infidels on the grounds that it did not facilitate conversion; rather it obstructed it.[54] Despite such critical concerns, the broad thrust of Christianity's claims to universality and uniqueness somewhat predictably resulted in its stance of "universal aggressiveness."[55] Ziauddin Sardar states the case succinctly: "Christianity's universal mission [was] the total subjugation of all [O]thers in the name of God and salvation through Jesus."[56] Pope Gregory VII, later canonized as a saint of the Church, exemplified this attitude, and helped set the tone for later popes, when he charged, "Cursed be the man who holds back his sword from shedding blood."[57] With attitudes like this emanating from the highest possible earthly source for the spiritual guidance of the devout faithful, the distance Christianity has traveled from the precepts of the Prince of Peace is manifestly clear. The papal echoes in Nazi rhetoric are also obvious in these lyrics from a Hitler Youth song:

> *When Jewish blood spurts from the knife,*
>
> *Then everything is fine.*[58]

To achieve the goal of subjugation, as stated by Sardar, an impassioned act of preaching by Pope Urban II at Clermont in November 1095 echoed this sense of Christian mission and master narrative in his effort to create crusading fervor. In attendance were many bishops, other clerics, and princes from other areas of the surrounding Gaul as well as Germany. Addressing the Frenchmen in the large audience, Urban assured them that they had been "singled out by God and ... are loved by him." He praised their country and its people who "are set apart from all other peoples by the location of your country, by your Catholic faith." He spoke solemnly of "the melancholy reasons" and "distressing news" that had come to him from Jerusalem: of the Persians—actually, Seljuk Turks—"an alien people, a race completely foreign to God ... [of] a spirit that broke faith with God, [who had] invaded Christian territory and devastated this territory." Following this "discourse of racist xenophobia,"[59] he catalogued the many repulsive charges against these people: circumcisions of Christians, the defiling of altars, torturing and eviscerating Christians, floggings, decapitations, rapes. Having inflamed his listeners, the pope then cried out: "Who is to revenge all this

.... You are the people upon whom God has bestowed glory in arms, greatness of spirit, bodily agility, and ... courage to humble ... those who resist you." Note that Urban's call for revenge exceeds the Just War limitations expounded centuries earlier by Augustine, another good indication of the moral and cultural distance traveled by Christianity in the intervening centuries. Simply stated, Urban was calling for "the extirpation of the infidel rather than his conversion."[60] He recalled the glories of Charlemagne, "who destroyed pagan kingdoms and planted the holy church in their territories." Note the echo of Zygmunt Bauman's sense of the political project of "gardening" in the pope's rhetoric. Urban told his rapt listeners that they should, above all else, be especially outraged that the Holy Sepulcher "is in the hands of these unclean people." To enhance the nature of his appeal, the pope reminded his audience that the Christian God promised life everlasting should the faithful have to leave all behind in the service of the Lord. Then he urged them to put aside their internecine feuding, so they may better focus their energies on the common enemy whose presence in the Holy Land constituted a defilement so egregious that it would require a holy war. His final appeal was once again to these valiant warriors, upon whom "God has bestowed glory in arms ... more than on any other nation." He promised them the full remission of their sins and unfading glory in the heavenly kingdom. In its enthusiastic response, the enraptured audience members spoke as with one fevered voice: "God wills it! God wills it!"[61]

With his preaching, Urban was breaking new ground in instigating a crusade. Later popes would be able to improve upon this by relying upon the centralized authority and bureaucracy of the church to disseminate papal bulls and encyclicals.[62] From the fall of 1095 to the summer of 1096, Urban toured through western and southern France in an effort to use his office to impress the necessity of the crusading spirit upon locals. He targeted large urban areas with abundant churches—Limoges, Poitiers, Angers, Tours, Saintes, Bordeaux—but rural areas were not ignored, with monks serving as the primary motivators there. As the crusading fervor grew, leaving little of Europe uninvolved, tens of thousands of incipient crusaders—nobility and commoners, including those mired in poverty, the aged and the infirm—gathered and began their dangerous treks to the Holy Land.[63] The composition of the various groups covered men and women from every social class and occupation. Very few Europeans escaped hearing any of the Church's powerful appeals in their lifetimes.[64] A list of passengers on a 1250 crusaders' ship, for example, reveals that 75 percent of those aboard were commoners.[65]

Urban's preaching, supported widely by his clerical underlings using letters called *excitatoria*,[66] perhaps worked better than anyone might have anticipated, because one result was the "exhilaration and frenzy of the masses."[67] Indeed, Urban's rhetoric seems to have resulted in popular excesses against Jews, thus indicating that papal control over events it had precipitated had been lost. The Christian outbursts against Jews in 1096 provided an ominous portent of later atrocities by introducing, for the first time, "large-scale massacres of Jews into

European reality."[68] Robert Chazan adds that the papacy not only lost control of the masses and the military, but also the ideology that motivated the crusaders,[69] a very significant matter for the purposes of this study. With a specific though somewhat remote military objective, the Church could not maintain rigid control over the actions and beliefs of its faithful, partially because they were grounded in fertile cultural soil cultivated assiduously from the time of Constantine and Augustine. The supporting theology of violence spoke powerfully to the many European Christians who put aside their normal lives in order to avenge the crimes alleged by the pope and his ministers against The Other. Inflamed by language from the highest possible earthly source, and urged on by clerics using model sermons, manuals of themes, and collections of exempla,[70] a discourse providing for a remarkable personal theological relationship to the greatest powers of the universe, tens of thousands of devout Christians could not restrain themselves from turning on the Jews in their midst or those unfortunates encountered on the crusaders' way to the Holy Land. Destructive forces, which must be said to have been implicit in the theology of violence all along, were unleashed. Léon Poliakov notes that each crusade brought with it terrible violence upon those Jews within striking distance of the Christian faithful.[71] A good example of this kind of popular support is found in the reaction of the people of Venice, assembled in the basilica of St. Mark's, to hear Pope Innocent III's appeal to join the Fourth Crusade. Following the celebration of Mass, a French spokesman addressed the Venetians, urging them to join the French barons in their effort to regain Jerusalem, to "avenge the injury done to Our Lord!" The assembled host then cried out, "We consent! We consent!"[72]—an echo of the earlier "God wills it!" response to Urban. To support their fervor, collection boxes were placed in all churches, as a way to raise funds to help offset the crusading expenses incurred by indigent knights.[73]

The frenzy often described when the crusaders went into action seems to have reached an apotheosis in their capture of Jerusalem in 1099. Pope Gregory VII would not have been disappointed; Urban's rhetoric wrought the following, as narrated by Raymond of Aguilers:

Wonderful things were to be seen. Numbers of the Saracens were beheaded.... Others were shot with arrows, or forced to jump from the towers; others were tortured for several days, then burned with flames. In the streets were seen piles of heads and hands and feet. One rode about everywhere amid the corpses of men and horses. In the temple of Solomon, the horses waded in blood up to their knees, nay, up to the bridle. It was a just and marvelous judgment of God, that this place should be filled with the blood of unbelievers.[74]

Indeed, the language of violence had changed, perhaps a function of doubling and derealization. St. Bernard argued that crusaders killing on behalf of Christ was *not* homicide but malecide, "the extermination of injustice rather than of the unjust, and therefore desirable." According to the good saint, for a crusader "to kill a pagan is to win glory since it gives glory to Christ."[75] Robert Lifton's concept of doubling was captured precisely in the Hospitallers, one of the military religious orders that emerged during the crusades. Its function was a "twofold vocation, to nurse and to fight"[76]—a chilling portent of the horrific actions of later Nazi medical personnel during the Holocaust. Finally, attend closely to the enormous implications of Lifton's thought that doubling "may well be an important psychological mechanism for individuals living within any criminal sub-culture." He then uses a Mafia capo as an example: equally capable of ordering a killing and of being a solicitous, loving husband and parent.[77] The example is an obvious one; there are many, many mundane examples found in the events described in this present study. We cannot help but wonder about the criminality of the perpetrating culture.

Much of the foregoing has a certain disconcerting resemblance to events in the twentieth century. The illiterate European masses encountered in the Church's power a virtual police state, an early form of the modern carceral state. The Church commanded virtually all the most significant means of communications needed to convince them to do its bidding. Via its particular brand of the theology of violence, little personal discretionary room was left for thinking and acting contrary to the prevailing norms. All the while the Church provided impressive promises of various rewards for those involved. Ervin Staub notes that medieval popes referred to Germany as "*terra obedientiae.*"[78] The Albigensian Crusade initiated the practice of having a priest and two "good" laymen in each parish searching diligently for heretics.[79] An early sign of the collaboration between those in power with private citizens, The Other was sought out, watched, known, identified, and operated against. Once The Other had been accused and subsequently faced official sanctions and proceedings, it was still possible for a mob to intervene, seize, and then execute the victims.[80] As Victoria Barnett observes, there was "widespread complicity" of ordinary people in the Holocaust, which, in her view, "is not an anomaly ... [for] the potential for such evil exists in us all."[81] Such complicitous behavior and potential had significant antecedents and conditions during the crusades, with its series of violent outbursts that most likely killed millions over several centuries.[82] Perhaps the most significant lesson to be drawn from the crusades is one that will echo from those centuries until today: Victoria Barnett's assertion that institutions have devastating influence over the moral inhibitions of individuals.[83] A further insight is that institutions can also create moral climates in which people see nothing wrong in executing the worst depravities against innocent Others. Contemporary concern over human evil indicates that humans, behaving in the culturally approved way as "righteous conformists," will execute evil acts upon cognition, rather than emotion, "if raised in an ideology that teaches them that people of another religion, color, or ethnic group are bad."[84] The crusaders may have never reached this cognitive level in their response to The Other, but they clearly acted out the papacy's recommended sacred violence. Both in militarily organized ways and in ad hoc mob actions, they acted on extensive Church teachings that declared that Others were unworthy of life.

4

The Inquisition

"We cannot indict a whole civilization, a whole continent, a whole era of human activity."

—Alan Lawson Maycock

"To ignore the question of human responsibility would make all history meaningless."

—George G. Coulton

Prior only to the Holocaust, the series of events beginning in the twelfth century and collectively known as the Inquisition served as one of the chief examples of the kind of terror and inhumanity that an oppressive religious institution allied with an obedient state machinery could inflict on The Other, in this case primarily Jews and heretics. The eventual goal was the achievement of "religious unity" through the "extirpation of Jewish heresy."[1] It is significant for the purposes of this study that the word heresy derives from the Greek word denoting "choice"—briefly, proscribed ways of thinking, behaving, and worshipping in the unceasing efforts of Christianity to define and enforce rigid standards of theological uniformity. In formal operation for several centuries, the Inquisition ceased to operate as recently as the nineteenth century (although the Holy Office still exists). Inflicting its torments on the minds and bodies of people both in central and western Europe and the Americas, the Inquisition seems to have taken on a mythic reputation, the proportions of which perhaps surpass the statistics for its murdered victims. Nevertheless, it is, to this point in history, the key example of carceral methods imposed as coercive pacification on entire populations and reflects a violent activation of crucial possibilities within the Christian culture of Western Europe. Robert Ian Moore, in his influential study of "the persecuting society," finds that "part of the character of European society" is the process whereby an enemy of society, a contaminant, is defined and then "held liable to pursuit, denunciation and interrogation, to exclusion from the community, deprivation of civil rights and the loss of property" as well as of life.[2] Moore sees that the attempt to impose a "high culture" and "a dominant elite across the breadth of Latin Christendom" required "the ruthless elimination" of rivals, Judaism being the chief of these.[3] For the purposes of this study, Moore's assertion of this being an element of the "character of European society" may be said to be analogous to my use of the term "culture." This is another way of perceiving the depth to which the elements of culture permeate a society and the people within it.

Jean-Pierre DeDieu believes that the primary goal of the Inquisition was to contribute to the public good and intimidate the multitude. In essence, according to DeDieu, the Inquisition may be thought of as an enormous teaching machine,[4] as Virgilio Pinto Crespo says, dealing with "the education of conscience through a process of moral coercion."[5] Fernando de los Rios, writing of religion and the state in sixteenth-century Spain, notes that the Inquisition worked to impact the conscience and terrorize dissent.[6] Echoing these points is Inquisitor Francisco Pena, speaking in 1578, who said of the Inquisition that its "main purpose ... is not to save the soul of the accused but to achieve the public good and put fear into others."[7] As mentioned earlier, each Spaniard, for instance, "became an impregnable fortress within himself"—each was driven to examine his own conscience as rigorously as possible. But it did not stop there; the examination necessarily included the interrogation of the conscience of Others, including one's neighbors.[8] If this process succeeds in affecting the thoughts and behaviors of the target population, achieving theological, intellectual, and cultural uniformity and hegemony, including the bystanders to the Inquisition's many forms of sacred violence, then "a Christian form of self-discipline" has been achieved, making further "external force secondary or unnecessary."[9] Using terms described earlier, such a process reveals a period of intensive coercive pacification that gradually becomes normative pacification, thus succeeding in imposing a carceral state on those so encultured. As T. J. Jackson Lears argues, no active commitment is required by "subordinates" to maintain such a state of hegemony once achieved; it is thereafter protected by the potential for coercion.[10] When the process is completed, if it ever is, the culture's population is seemingly in a stable condition, with potentially threatening dissonances and disconfirmations neutralized, converted, or destroyed. Ziauddin Sardar speaks of "hegemonic panopticism," a state of centralized surveillance and control,[11] which is an apt assessment of the process and end result of the Inquisition, although the fully expressed centralized feature would be internalized in the individual human psyche, the quintessential carceral condition. Because the Inquisition persisted over several centuries, we may surmise that total uniformity and hegemony, a final solution to the culture's religious discontents, was never fully achieved. Humans somehow found the inner means to resist the cultural pressures and attempted to live and believe as they wished. However, we must not minimize the psychological, emotional, and intellectual stresses experienced by millions of Europeans over several centuries.

The few who did resist the pressures successfully did it despite the vigorous efforts of the Church while it was near the peak of its power. Very early in its history, the Church exercised its power against heterodoxy as a crime against the ecclesiastical community. Under Christianized Roman emperors, heterodoxy "became a crime against the Empire." Imperial legislation moved against secret meetings held by heretics and "condemned those who failed to denounce heretics."[12] Based thus on Roman legal practices that had helped to form the Christianized empire,[13] the struggle began in earnest in the twelfth century, not insignificantly overlapping the early period of the crusades, with Church officials apparently having realized that they would need to exercise formal Church authority against The Other near its European power centers as well as in the distant Holy Land. Pope Lucius III created the "founding charter" of the Inquisition with his decretal, *Ad abolendam*,[14] which initiated an episcopal inquisition in 1184. Although it seems to have languished at first, it was energized by a bull from Innocent III in 1199 and further prompting from the Lateran Council in 1215. Shortly after the release of Pope Lucius's decretal, Jews were burned in 1189 after the coronation of England's Richard I. In 1190, the entire community of Jews in York was killed.[15] Jews had been disarmed, by law, in England in 1181,[16] leaving them virtually helpless before their antagonists; this situation would be duplicated eight centuries later in Europe. "Synodal witnesses" were commissioned to report heretical matters to the bishops. The Council of Toulouse created teams of two laymen and a parish priest in all parishes in 1229 for the purpose of spying out any and all breaches of Church doctrines.[17] Gregory IX took these early initiatives to a new level in 1233 when he made the Inquisition "an instrument of terrorization" and created a cadre of Church officials formally charged with Inquisitorial powers. Not responsible to local bishops, this revolutionary advancement gave Church officials virtually unlimited discretionary powers.[18] Innocent IV advanced Gregory's changes with his bull in 1252, *Ad Extirpanda*, which proposed the complete subservience of civil power to the Inquisition. This proposal, surprisingly, had a counterpart in the United States in 1966–1967. It charged the state with the destruction of heresy as its primary task. We see here the culmination to this point of the potential for malignant Church and state collaboration, as initially formed in the Roman era, for the purpose of controlling behaviors, minds, and beliefs. Cecil Roth's study of the Inquisition confirms this perception when he observes that the "conception that dissent should be punished by force was indeed almost as old as Christianity itself."[19]

Five provisions in Innocent's bull did much to shape the Inquisition's future: confessions to be extracted by torture; the death penalty by burning; a police force to assist Inquisitors; a crusade preached against Italian heretics, with the same system of eternal rewards as for other crusades; and confiscation of a heretic's property extended to the accused person's heirs. Edward Burman's study of the Inquisition finds that Innocent's proposals eventually led to the implementation of a police state in Italy.[20] It did not take long for the initial delineations of the Inquisition to be seen. Death by fire was perceived as the norm by 1231;[21] by 1288, thirteen Jews had been burned to death in an *auto de fé* (Portuguese for an "act of faith") in Troyes, France.[22] Eventually, the Inquisition developed a highly complex apparatus, including "preaching, confession, the Catechism, ecclesiastical courts [and] lay tribunals."[23] The Council of Narbonne in 1235 forced Jews to wear a yellow patch,[24] yet another of the many times that Jews faced this particular indignity. By 1248–1249, a detailed manual for the questions to be used by Inquisitors had been developed, and the bureaucratization of the Inquisition could be seen in the presence of scribes, notaries, priests, local laymen, and bishops to record and witness the proceedings.

Even with a massive bureaucracy, the leaders of the Church nevertheless managed to show vestiges of moral and spiritual sensitivity for certain Inquisition personnel. Popes were concerned with the presence of the Inquisition's priests at scenes of torture. As if in recognition of a doubling dilemma, Popes Alexander IV and Urban IV, in 1260 and 1262, respectively, issued rulings that allowed the priests serving the Inquisition to be present at torture but then be able to "dispense" each other for the "irregularity" committed in viewing the scene[25] of disturbing sacred violence. John A. O'Brien, a theology professor at the University of Notre Dame, offers revealing details in his study of the Inquisition about one of those Kafkaesque instruments of torture that later priests would have seen in use:

The visitor to the Horniman Museum in southeast London finds his attention drawn to an unusual exhibit: a steel torture-chair that comes from Cuenca, a city about midway between Valencia and Madrid. It includes a moveable seat, with pinion and rack, manacles for feet and hands and, most unusual of all, a skeleton-helmet with screws to put pressure on the top of the head, to pierce the ears and to torture the nose and chin.

In addition, there is a gag for the mouth with rack-action for forcing the mouth open and dragging forward the tongue, screw-forceps for extracting toenails, single and double thumbscrews, and various other padlocks, buckles, chains, keys and turnscrews. Excavated with the chair was a steel whip, having eight thongs, each of which ends in a blade. Engraved on the mouth-gag are the words "Santo Oficio Caballero"—the noble Holy Office, namely the Inquisition, and the date 1676. What a monument to the Roman Congregation in charge of the Inquisition.[26]

An instrument of this intricate complexity would have a history of its own, an evolution perhaps, based on meticulous trial and error testing and experience in the field. The era's best technology would have been applied; perhaps as with the case of the crematoria at Auschwitz, it could have involved the seventeenth-century version of blueprints, a competitive bidding process, possibly competitive design testing. Skilled workers and craftsmen would have been involved in the construction process. This process may have taken place quite publicly, or it might have been done in secret. In either case, the creation of the torture instrument would have necessarily involved numerous individuals from the inception of the idea through production and its actual use for inflicting agony in The Other. A certain social context would be involved, one in which the larger culture would have been operative. Perhaps no one involved questioned what they were doing as they made the various features of the torture chair. Even the priests most likely would have been expected to offer a solemn blessing on be-half of the chair and its mission. The culture that supported sacred violence surely would have provided sufficient motivation for those involved to be able to see their work as crucially important in the Inquisition's work, and that they were participating in a project for the saving of souls and the greater glorifica-tion of God. Noting all of this, we can see why the Church would have been con-cerned for the priests who administered the Inquisition, because their work placed them in close proximity to their victims as the instruments of torture took The Other beyond the limits of psychological endurance and physical pain. In light of all this, we can wonder if this ominous instrument ever raised any doubts or concerns in the minds of those involved in its production and use. We see the Church showing clear evidence of humane concern for some human be-ings—those involved in the perpetration of the Inquisition—yet apparently that concern did not extend to the victims.

In other aspects of the Inquisition, secular town government officials were in-volved in the execution of verdicts concerning destruction or confiscation of property, much as government bureaucrats in Germany helped execute the Nuremberg laws. Females as young as twelve and males age fourteen were re-quired to swear an oath before the Inquisitors. Husbands were required to tes-tify against wives, as were children against parents. Testimony was accepted from sources not admissible in other courts—"heretics, criminals, accomplices, and young children."[27] Application of the Inquisition's mandate involved many ter-ror tactics. Robert Ian Moore finds that persecution became "habitual" under these conditions, a permanent condition in Christian Europe. Moreover, the vi-olence was no longer isolated to strike against individuals. Instead, "deliberate and socially sanctioned violence began to be directed, *through established gov-ernmental, judicial, and social institutions,* against groups of people defined by general characteristics such as race, religion, or way of life; and that member-ship of such groups in itself came to be regarded as justifying these attacks."[28] Significant elements of coercive pacification were practiced against the masses, as well as the elite, as the Inquisition inserted its cultural preferences in the minds and behaviors of much of the population of Europe. We can only wonder about the long-term results of that set of practices.

It is important to remember that the Inquisition "followed and expressed deeply rooted popular sentiments; it did not create or formulate them."[29] Not coincidentally, numerous accounts record the presence of massive crowds to watch the imposition of the Inquisition's sentences. Jaime Contreras asserts that millions of people assisted the Inquisition in watching and listening for hereti-cal offenses.[30] Mob violence could break out as popular beliefs and prejudices inflamed people. Angel Alcalá and Benzion Netanyahu both find that these out-bursts were rooted in the most deeply held desires of the masses.[31] In some cases, the masses[32] took matters into their own hands to kill heretics. Arthur Stanley Turberville records mob killings in 1076 at Cambrai, in 1114 at Strasbourg, in 1144 at Liege, and in 1163 at Cologne.[33] One unruly mob took the initiative to burn heretics out of their concern that the clerics involved were going to be lenient.[34] Similarly, a mob in Spain deflected its attention away from hanging *conversos* in a public display of fanaticism long enough to hack to death a constable who had attempted to help the hapless victims.[35] The gruesome theatre of the *auto de fé* remained a popular sight for the masses of people; thousands could be expected to witness these events, even when they included the sight of exhumed corpses being put to the torch. Edward Peters finds that widespread killings, such as the atrocities committed in Northern France against the Cathari, revealed "the continuing willingness of the laity to take the most severe steps against heresy without much concern for the heretics' conversion and salvation."[36] Not only was there little such concern, in 1665, 450,000 *maravedis* were spent in Spain on entertainment arranged around these spectacles.[37] This level of public involvement suggests haunting implications for the roles of ideology and culture. We know that sermons delivered by priests and friars did much to turn congregants against Jews.[38] Jews were seen as human disasters, but good could be done to the Jew if he was destroyed.[39] Based on Psalm 95, Jews were perceived to be constitutionally evil.[40] Ziauddin Sardar notes that the Christian perspective makes it virtually impossible to "become fully human" unless Jesus is seen as God,[41] a crucial point for supporting the atrocities of the perpetrators and the passivity of bystanders. Seen in countless instances of genocide, this was especially important in any consideration of the Holocaust. As with the highly suspect Jews, converts to Christianity were not at all immune to fanatical suspicions and allegations. Relapsed converts in thirteenth-century Italy faced the prospect of a fiery death at the stake. As was the case in many places, Jews were also required to wear a yellow badge. Jews were not allowed to build new synagogues; indeed, New Christians (converts) stood to benefit from the sales of synagogues to buy necessities.[42] In Spain, the Marranos, or converts, faced tremendous hostility in the person of Marcos García in 1449. García operated in Toledo and was not averse to misusing scripture to support his racist views in his attacks on the Marranos. His views, reflected in an anti-Marrano tract sent to the Roman curia, echo the Nazi rhetoric of the Nuremberg laws:

All converts who belong to the Jewish race or those who have descended from it—that is, who were born as Jews, or are sons, grandsons, great-grandsons, or great-great-grandsons of Jews who were baptized ... including those [converts] who descended newly and recently from that most evil and damned stock, are presumed, according to the testimonies of the Scriptures, to be infidels and suspect of the faith. From which follows that the vice of infidelity is not presumed to be purged until the fourth generation.[43]

According to Netanyahu, García's thought is based on three considerations that will seem familiar to modern consciousness: a theory of Jews as a race, a belief in a Jewish conspiracy, and genocide as a solution to the nagging problems represented by the conversos.[44] In sum, Ervin Staub makes a key point when he observes that it is necessary for "guilt-free massacres" to be based on "the denial of humanity to the victim." Under these conditions, murder becomes a service to humanity.[45] Hitler's speeches, private musings, and writings reflect the same kind of thinking. In "Religion and the Legitimation of Violence," Christopher G. Ellison and John P. Bartkowski note that "religious rhetoric" is often involved to provide "meaning and purpose, thus *sacralizing* violence by linking it with matters of ultimate concern."[46] This is a common pattern found in the motivating factors supporting sacred violence.

The Inquisition's services to humanity in Spain alone impacted hundreds of thousands of lives directly, and, indirectly, many more, if not all, under the great power and influence of the Church. One Inquisition official estimated the number of heretics killed by fire from its inception until 1808 reached 31,912, with another 17,659 burned in effigy, and 291,450 "reconciled *de vehementi*" to the satisfaction of the Inquisitors. Amador de los Rios, a Catholic historian, reported on the statistics from 1484 until 1525: 28,450 people burned to death, 16,520 burned in effigy, and 303,847 penanced.[47] Figures, however, do not reach this order of magnitude in more recent scholarly discussions, for example, in Edward Peters's *Inquisition*.

In addition to the deaths caused by the Inquisition, hundreds of thousands of Jews were forced into conversions,[48] a condition viewed in Karl F. Morrison's study of conversion as "subversive of self."[49] Statistics cited above are for Spain. Living in the New World, however, did not provide protection from the Inquisition. The latter part of the sixteenth century saw increasing activity from the Holy Office as Judaizers, Protestants from England and Ireland, Calvinists from France, and indigenous people faced the wrath of the Inquisition in Mexico. One victim was the governor of the province of New Leon, who died with his mother and three sisters. In twenty-five years, 879 trials were conducted by the Inquisition in Mexico, and a somewhat smaller number in Peru.[50]

In the Inquisition's self-proclaimed service to humanity, we find stunning examples of unbelievable cruelties. Elkan Adler, writing nearly a century ago, offers an example in which an Inquisition functionary, a notary, extracted testimony from a fifteen-year-old girl against her mother by locking her in a room, stripping her naked, and "scourging" her until, broken, she agreed. Adler also includes a victim for an *auto de fé* being brought to the site for his execution in a chair because his feet had already been burned to the bone.[51] In 1222, a student at Oxford was burned at the stake for having converted to Judaism, a crime against the state. Relapsed heretics, given lighter punishment than death by fire, had their tongues torn out[52] although Pope Nicholas IV specified burning at the stake for relapsed converts.[53] Some victims were thrown into pits filled with snakes, or were buried alive, or eaten to death by rodents.[54] Pope Martin V, disgusted by the Fraticelli (followers of St. Francis), ordered a village called Magnalata "leveled and every resident slain."[55] Similarly, Lidice, Czechoslovakia, was eradicated following the death of Reinhard Heydrich in 1492. Cecil Roth's study of the Spanish Inquisition includes a reference to a pregnant woman being dragged to the stake to meet her death. He also notes that the costs of imprisonment for those accused, being interrogated, or incarcerated were paid for by the victims themselves, similar to the Nazi practice of charging Jews for the train fare to the death camps, with children, of course, receiving a thoughtful half price rate. In one case from Italy, an accused nun was imprisoned from 1699 until her acquittal and release in 1703, although her heirs were faced with repayment of the costs incurred by the nun until 1872.[56]

The rabble at the time of the Inquisition could become frantically involved over what might seem ridiculous allegations and prejudices, but such had already haunted the Jewish experience as the Disconfirming Other for a millennium or more. For instance, in 1410 Jews in Segovia were accused of torturing a consecrated communion Host as part of their supposed customs. A "confession" came about from the Jewish physician to the recently deceased king. Along with several others caught in this web of suspicion, he was hung, drawn, and quartered.[57] Conrad of Marburg, a zealous Inquisitor in thirteenth-century Germany, used the simple expedient of burning anyone who claimed to be innocent of his charges.[58] Jews could be attacked for suspicions involving missing persons, or contaminated wells, or epidemics. They were accused of crucifying Christian children and wax images of Jesus.[59] On the day Columbus set off on his voyage to eventually encounter the indigenes of North America and extend the culture and power of Western Europe to new dimensions, some Jews faced a charge of crucifying a Christian child, after ripping out his heart. The stated purpose for this crime was to counteract the power of the Inquisition and to drive Christians into insanity and death. Jews, including *conversos,* suffered grotesque deaths over this allegation. A father and son had their flesh torn off with hot pincers before they were burned to death. Six *conversos* were strangled and then burned. A Jew in Avilon was stoned to death by a mob as retribution for the story of the murdered Christian child.[60] A century earlier, a riot in Seville led to no fewer than twenty thousand Jews converting out of fear for their lives; thousands of Jewish men chose death, and their children and wives were sent into slavery.[61] On the other hand, a Christian could be extended a pardon for killing a Jew.[62] With clear ramifications for events in the mid-twentieth century, Léon Poliakov traced the spurious "Protocols of the Elder of Zion" to the twelfth century.[63] The sacred texts of Jews were viewed with enough suspicion that the Inquisition could become involved. Jewish books could be confiscated;[64] copies of the Talmud were burned in Paris and Rome in 1244 following papal orders to investigate it for its heretical status.[65] Angel Alcalá makes an important point, in light of the foregoing: we must take into consideration the "receptive mood of the audience ... which may be created by acute popular hatreds."[66] Perceiving and understanding the sources of popular hatreds are paramount. Certainly, one of the chief sources is the larger culture of Western European Christianity, informed by the theology of sacred violence that had developed in virulent ways and articulated with the greatest vehemence since the fourth century of the Common Era. The hatred was aimed at anyone or any institution that did not adhere to Church dogmas and truth claims. Indeed, one of the deans of Inquisition scholarship, Henry C. Lea, found that clerics were given the scope needed "to excite abhorrence and stimulate popular passions."[67]

Priests had delivered countless sermons to millions of Christians with various admonitions seeking "to purify the land from the pollution of Judaism."[68] J.H. Elliott, writing of Imperial Spain, notes that Jews were seen as "the most noxious" of impurities.[69] Nicolas Davidson, writing about the Inquisition and society, found that the mere presence of Jews among Christians came to be seen as "damaging and dangerous." Church officials insisted on the position that "the entire Jewish people is the enemy of Christian blood";[70] note well this reference to Christian blood. Previewing subsequent Nazi attitudes, beliefs, and practices, Christians at the time of the Inquisition held that a child born of a Jewess and a Christian father "puts Christian blood in eternal damnation."[71] To bring greater glory to the Christian God, Jews had to be reformed and punished. In yet another echo of Nazi beliefs and rhetoric, they were to be treated legally in order to dispossess them of their goods so that they could be returned to those from whom they had stolen them.[72] Pope Paul IV (1555–1559), one of Europe's leading authorities at the time, unwittingly but ominously previewing later events involving Jews in the twentieth century, solemnly proclaimed, "We want to see the whole lot burned."[73] We must ask about those who heard the pope's exclamation. Did he say this in the presence of his cardinals? Visiting dignitaries? Did his staff hear this? Were officials of the Inquisition present? Did they see this as a desirable objective and act accordingly? Did this papal wish empower those in a position to light the kindling under the feet of Jews? Did the attitudes supporting the pope's statement penetrate to the consciousness of the clergy and their parishioners? It is interesting that Pope Paul IV would have been near the center of the Vatican's power at the very time that Las Casas and Sepulveda were debating the merits of inhumane treatment of Native Americans in 1551, a debate that this pope might not have understood. Christians had been hearing similar viewpoints for centuries; sermons had been delivered from countless pulpits by priests and friars, and had affected whole populations.[74] Such rhetoric recalls the venomous theology of Chrysostom, a clear precursor to the theology of sacred violence that developed in later centuries. Heretics were not immune from this kind of invective in the service of sacred violence. For instance, Hoffman Nickerson reported that Pope Innocent II found heretics to be "a scourge, a pestilence, filth, an ulcer infecting society, a savage beast, a wolf in sheep's clothing, a fox that destroys the Lord's vine."[75] In Spain, Father Ferrán Martínez, much like Chrysostom one thousand years earlier, appeared and haunted the lives of Jews. A Castilian priest, his low birth limited his prospects within the Church. He nevertheless enjoyed a close rapport with the common people he served, showing a strong "ability to move, guide and control them." Basically, Martínez sought the complete elimination of Jews—incorrigible criminals in his eyes—from Spanish life and used his pulpit in inflammatory ways to achieve that end. He relied on the ubiquitous presence of anti-Semitic rhetoric in Church literature to make his point.[76] Using the pulpit as well as his authority as a diocesan judge, Martínez issued orders for the expulsion of Jews in 1378, although the Spanish king, Enrique II, opposed his attacks. With the unexpected death of the king in 1379, the priest was able to assert himself as a judge overseeing Jewish legal disputes with Christians. He eventually began an operation to convert Moorish slaves of Jews, knowing that this would, by law, strip them away from their owners.[77] King Juan I intervened, but Martínez then moved against synagogues while claiming that Christians could kill or injure Jews with little fear of legal retribution. After further conflict between the crown and the priest, Juan I also died, leaving only a minor son as heir. Seeing his chance, in 1390 Martínez ordered the destruction of synagogues, within three hours, in dioceses he claimed to control. Once again, he faced opposition from the crown's regents. Ultimately, he defiantly claimed responsibility for the destruction of two synagogues.[78] Riots in Seville in April 1391 were the culmination of his vituperation. Netanyahu speaks of a "long social evolution" in Castille, beginning with an outbreak of violence against Jews in 1109 and spanning nearly three hundred years of sacred violence against The Other.[79] Martínez faced stern opposition from government authorities, and seems not to have enjoyed widespread support from the upper classes. Although a very different scenario from the violence against Jews centuries later in Nazi Germany, Martínez did succeed in arousing the masses and relied upon the explicit anti-Semitism found within the Church. The result was the expulsion of Jews from Spain in 1492. Cecil Roth estimates that as many as fifty thousand Jews were victimized following one of Martínez's violent sermons.[80]

Less than a century after Martínez's destructive activities in Spain, another inquisitorial individual likewise devastated the lives of Jews elsewhere in Europe. St. John of Capistrano, a grim but effective orator who attracted audiences as large as 100,000, impacted the lives of large numbers of people in Italy, Germany, Silesia, and Poland with his incessant verbal attacks on Jews. He menaced government officials who sought to protect Jews and fought to have special privileges for Jews, as he saw it, nullified. He raised the specter of ritual murder in Silesia, which led to trials to accuse and convict Jews, who were then destroyed in the grisly public rituals of the *auto de fé*.[81] Once again, we see a revered saint of the Church wielding immense power over large numbers of people in the practice of sacred violence directed against The Other, and another lamentable episode of a culture's sacrality replacing morality.[82]

We need to consider the impact, over time, of having large numbers of impressionable, typically unsophisticated people listening to respected authority figures speaking in terms of hatred in a context where disagreement is not valued and where there is virtually no opportunity for different perspectives to manifest. The tentacles of the Inquisition reached all places and levels of society. Richard Kieckhefer notes that the dean of the Theological Faculty at Cologne, Jacob Hochstraten, was an inquisitor; Jacob Sprenger, a professor of Theology at Cologne, was a papal inquisitor.[83] The theological faculty of the University of Paris, in the fourteenth century, increasingly took upon themselves the duties of advising the Inquisition's prosecutors as they moved against heretics.[84] We can only wonder about the impact inquisitors might have had on the life of the mind for faculty and students at a university. What would their presence have meant for what we now recognize as "academic freedom"? In point of fact, there is little resemblance between academic institutions at the time of the Inquisition and today, not the least reason being the absence of the heavy hand of the Church weighing against the intellectual pursuits of the faculty and students. But at the time, the presence of the Church's influence was an accepted fact of life, although there were early rumblings portending later revolutionary events. Still, the scholars in the universities were being educated in conditions that did not permit them to think beyond certain intellectual and cultural limits; this acquired culture would then be transmitted to others over many generations and centuries. The Church's pressure placed on Galileo is well known; also instructive is the Inquisition's death sentence for Giordano Bruno, who was burned at the stake for revealing Copernicus's De Revolutionibus in a 1584 sermon.[85] Ervin Staub finds that children readily learn from "aggressive scripts" that serve as ideological blueprints for aggressive behavior[86] and it may be argued that such cultural blueprints abounded throughout the period covering the several centuries when the Inquisition was at the service of the dominant European religion. Alan Lawson Maycock noted in his early study of the Inquisition that the Church "was unquestioned; she was part of the atmosphere which everybody breathed."[87] He observes that the dominant characteristic of medieval society was its "unity of culture," with the Church serving as the "corporate conscience" of Europe.[88] Along these lines, Herbert S. Klein notes that in Spain, the Catholic Church existed as "the prime arbiter" of the social and intellectual life of the people, determining "the moral basis of society" and "the limits of [their] intellectual world view."[89] Given these conditions, it is not surprising that few people were able to overcome the normative facts of cultural life, that individuals might come to feel that they lived "freely" even though residing in a state of terror, and that bystanding in the presence of public mass executions and other Inquisitorial proceedings came to be an acceptable aspect of life.

An account by Guillelmi Pelisso (William Pelhisson), contained in Zoé Oldenbourg's Massacre at Montségur, reveals interesting, significant facets of the Inquisition's mentality at work. An incident took place during the Albigensian Crusade against the Cathari in Languedoc, involving a Dominican bishop, Raymond du Fauga. On August 4, 1235, the feast day of St. Dominic, founder of the order given his name, the bishop had just completed celebrating a solemn Mass in honor of the newly declared saint in the city of Toulouse. The bishop was washing his hands following Mass, preparing to enter the refectory for a meal with his fellow Dominicans, when he received word that an elderly lady had just received the Cathar sacrament, the consolamentum. She was the mother-in-law of Peytavi Borsier, who in the eyes of the Inquisition was a person known to be friendly with Cathari heretics. The bishop quickly gathered the prior of the local convent and several of his monks. They marched to the old lady's address, where he found her bedridden and near death. She was not fully cognizant of the scene around her. The bishop introduced himself, but she apparently thought he was the local Cathar bishop. Du Fauga began Inquisitorial questioning of the old woman, to confirm the allegations of her heretical beliefs. Before long, he had what he needed; he then introduced himself properly and asked her to abjure her heretical beliefs. She refused to recant, in front of many witnesses, including Pelisso, so the bishop had no other recourse but to turn her over to the local magistrate for final adjudication. "Summary judgment was passed on the old woman," who, unable to walk, was then taken in her bed to a spacious area known as the Count's Field, where she was promptly burned to death. The bishop and monks then returned to the refectory, where they blessed the food that awaited them since their meal's interruption, but also gave thanks to God and St. Dominic before falling "cheerfully upon the food set before them."[90]

An excellent example of the behaviors involved with Robert Lifton's sense of doubling, this incident also reveals Ervin Staub's concerns over "the reversal of morality" in which "killing can be seen as good, right, and desirable." Staub finds that "perpetrators of evil often intend to make people suffer but see their actions as necessary or serving a higher good."[91] The bishop, having just celebrated a solemn Mass on a day reserved to honor the saintly founder of his religious order, almost immediately implemented the theology of sacred violence. He appears to behave duplicitously with the old woman, recognizing her confusion as to his true identity, but nonetheless questioning her in such a fashion that her revelations were forthcoming without the usual Inquisitorial pressure and use of terror tactics. Not content with allowing nature to take its expected course in her approaching death, the bishop exercises his influence with the secular authority to ensure her immediate demise. Using the Count's Field makes certain that the local public would see her death for the dire warning of the Inquisition's justice that it was. We must wonder about the reaction of those who viewed her miserable death. Many of the citizens of Toulouse might have been part of her spiritual cohort. Would the irony of the situation have registered with those in attendance? Did children watch in rapt fascination? What might their parents have had to say to them about the event? Then, for the priests, business proceeded as usual—a phenomenon not unknown during the Shoah—as these devout religious figures leave their Inquisitorial roles and give thanks to their God for the meal provided, even as the flames and smoke signifying the old woman's horrible death linger over the Count's Field nearby. We may justifiably ask if there is much of a gap between one function and the other, between the inquisitor's role and that of the priest's, the bishop's. The bishop would surely not see himself as performing an evil act; indeed, he would have an entire theology and a massive cultural infrastructure to support him in his work, to offer explicit rewards for his work. He could facilitate the old woman's death and then give thanks to God, pray, and enjoy a hearty meal with no pangs of conscience, no doubts, no regrets other than for the soul he would see as having been lost. In his cultural world, he has not been party to a murder; his recently washed hands would have remained clean, holy. In Zygmunt Bauman's terminology, Bishop du Fauga has merely been gardening, removing an unwanted weed from God's garden on earth. In Staub's terms, the bishop has rendered an important service to the world to which he ministers. Furthermore, this incident also supports the contention that perpetrators of violence need to execute a "reversal of morality" and an abandonment of any "feelings of responsibility for the welfare of the victims."[92] Hyam Maccoby makes a similar point, pertinent throughout considerations of this chapter and the next, regarding the sacred slaying: "Some good consequence will be seen to flow from the slaying: a city will be founded, or a nation will be inaugurated ... a famine will be stayed ... or a threatening enemy will be defeated."[93]

It is perhaps surprising but nevertheless a fact that the shadow of the Inquisition lingers over the lives of people today, and not merely in a list of censored books kept in Rome or the continued existence of the Holy Office. A chief example comes from a Jesuit priest, Maurice Bévenot, who wrote a series of essays dealing with "The Inquisition and its Antecedents" appearing in the *Heythrop Journal* in four issues published in 1966 and 1967. For Bévenot, a "Catholic State" must take as its primary function the elimination of anything that threatens the truth as perceived by the Church. We must wonder what a Catholic State is precisely. A government run by confirmed Catholics? A country with a large majority of Catholics? Both of these? A government where there is a religious test and no chance for an opposing religion or sect to have its members elected? I do not think, based on his own words, that Bévenot is writing with the Vatican in mind as a Catholic State. Whatever the case, this Catholic State has a responsibility toward its citizens to "protect them from harm"—as do all states. If the state recognizes that the Catholic Church possesses the truth, then "is it not its duty to prevent the dissemination of error" because injuring the soul is far graver than anything suffered by the body? The Catholic Church, in Bévenot's opinion, has an inherent right to ask for assistance from the secular state's force structure to help the Church achieve its goals. Basically, the Church can ask for a state's security forces—the police, the military, the judiciary—to become involved in repressing those who are seen to be unacceptable on the basis of their religious beliefs.[94] This is precisely the practice employed in the Inquisition. The inquisitors could go only so far in their actions before it became necessary to "relax" the victim over to the secular state apparatus for final disposition, that is, death by burning at the stake. Notably, the Lateran Council at this time, out of concern for the souls of priests, forbid them to serve as surgeons, so they would avoid shedding blood.[95]

Bévenot is fully aware of the reputation and implications of the Inquisition's past actions. Echoing Maycock's "We cannot indict a whole civilization, a whole continent, a whole era of human activity" sentiment, Bévenot addresses the matter of the Inquisition's death penalty for heretics: "To call into question the rightness of these actions would seem to be denying the inherent holiness of the Church .... [W]e cannot admit that it was all a horrible mistake." Indeed, it is the Church's duty to request that the secular state should use its "powers of restraint and capital punishment" when heresy threatens the lives of Catholics.[96]

He seems aware that the twentieth century would not be hospitable to this violent way of punishing private beliefs, but he looks forward hopefully to that
happy day "when better times return, [when the Church] will be enabled to exercise its right again, and it will be the duty of all to lend their aid in fulfilling
this holy task."[97] It is highly significant that Bévenot sees the Church as *having a right* to ask the state to exercise the death penalty for the sin of heresy and
that people have a *duty* to assist in achieving this goal. His rhetoric clearly man-
ifests significant vestiges of the theology of sacred violence. Note that Bévenot,
a Jesuit priest writing in the mid-twentieth century, sees a heretic as not having a right to life. Although heresy is not an evident issue for the general
public today, we must wonder if heresy is an issue of concern for secular governments. Would Bévenot simply seek out those who practiced heresies in the
Church's past? Or would he extend sacred violence in the form of capital punishment to today's contemporary beliefs that defy Church doctrines? Would he
support the sixteenth-century Spanish crown's death sentences for all people
living in Holland? Indeed, what would Bévenot propose be done with that group
of people whose existence defined heresy at its most basic level for the medieval
church—the Jews? If they were an affront to the Christian *weltanschauung* in
the thirteenth century, surely they pose as much threat today to the theological sensibilities of the modern inquisitor. Given the Church's inherent right to
request state involvement, what would stop him? Bévenot's value system seems
to be locked into a period from before the American and French revolutions, before separation of church and state became a fact of modern political life in the
Anglo-European West. He is, however, consistent as he assumes universal truth
resides only within a specific religious institution, good for all time, for all people. In fact, there would be no Other if we were to see the return of the "better
times" Bévenot seeks. Other claims to truth, other views of human life, have no
standing here; they are simply in error, possibly a vile error, and represent a serious threat to the Church's hegemony, its proclamation of revealed truth, and
the souls of its faithful. Bévenot's better times, if implemented, would be yet another gardening operation. Perhaps modern gardening procedures would make
the operation far more successful than in the original better times of the Inquisition, before modern technology could make sacred violence as all-encompassing
and efficient as humanly possible. In a stunning passage in his discussion,
Bévenot cites with approval the suggestion of Alexis Comnenus, a twelfth-
century Byzantine emperor, for a chilling way of detecting heretics from the
truly faithful with certitude: build two funeral pyres, one with a crucifix, one
without. Give the condemned person the choice between the two: "thus the true
Christians could at least die as such, and achieve martyrdom."[98] The heretic obviously meets perdition. As in the case of Bishop du Fauga, those who would
build such a funeral pyre would be operating with the sacred higher purpose of
serving God, humanity, and the world they actively seek to build and promote.
This is difficult and unpleasant work, no doubt, but necessary if one is to reside
in a world where one's religious truth properly prevails over all other claims and

peoples, where any kind of difference is a threat to cultural and religious unity, and where Other religious perspectives are an affront of the worst kind to one's God. There is, perhaps, no higher calling than eliminating such error. Bévenot's value system is firmly based on an "imperial ecumenism" in which there is "no room for dissent, minorities, heterodoxy, or discrepant positions in a state designed for a religious goal."[99]

As discussed in this chapter, Jews and heretics were almost identical in the eyes of the Inquisition. Both groups exist as Disconfirming Others. Both groups do not assent to the various truth claims proffered by Christianity. They could be seen by some within certain wings of Christianity as hostile to the dominant religion, even if they are not. For Bévenot, simply stated, and consistent with the ideology of the Inquisition, members of these groups do not have the right to life. In Nazi terminology, these groups are life unworthy of life. It is important to remember that Bévenot, a Catholic priest and a member of the Society of Jesus (who is supposedly the Prince of Peace), is writing less than a quarter century after the demise of the Nazi German death camps, and is arguing eloquently in a public venue for, in essence, mass murder. Might this not be another example of a unified self in its doubling capacity? A priest, a man of God, a member of the Society of Jesus, calling for the deaths of those offending Others who have no right to life. Simon Wiesenthal had not completed his work as a Nazi hunter at the time Bévenot's essays were published. President Lyndon Johnson, although entangled in a wretched war in Vietnam, was arguing for the just merits of "The Great Society" and furthering human rights legislatively as the civil rights movement in the United States spread its influence to people of conscience. Bévenot seems not to have thought of the implications of his proposals in light of major advancements in the field of human rights in U.S. history. Furthermore, apparently the lessons of the Holocaust had not penetrated Bévenot's consciousness, or, if they had, they were ignored or discounted, or, more likely, counter-argued in the course of his strict Jesuit education. As a Catholic priest, at virtually every Mass he had celebrated or attended up to this point in his career, he would have been asking for the prayers of the congregation to help Jews convert to Christianity. It is likely that he would have been actively engaged in seeking conversions at some point in his priesthood. We must question whether Bévenot would recommend reinstituting past Inquisition practices, such as public executions in the form of the *auto de fé*, or torture to break down the heretic's reluctance to confess and convert? His stance is clear and internally consistent. Damage to the soul is worse than harm to the physical body. Heresy harms the soul. The Catholic version of Christianity is the one truth; anything else is false. Falsehood is harmful; falsehood must be eliminated. Christianity has the right to ask the state to come to its aid in eliminating falsehood, using violent means if necessary. The private citizen has a duty to help the state assist the Church in meeting its sacred obligation. As Ervin Staub dryly observes, people will kill for a higher cause.[100]

Bévenot asserts, "[W]e cannot admit that it was all a horrible mistake." He does not have available to him, or has not chosen to make use of an ideological critique that would allow him to find a way to come to a perspective that would see the problematical nature of the terror-producing practices of the Inquisition. If the state accepted his assertion and cooperated with his directive, could we then suppose that it would not be a horrible mistake if the Inquisition's practices were reinstituted? Would it not be a mistake for the state to use capital punishment to remove, for instance, Jews, as an affront to the majesty of the truth claims and, thereby, the souls of the members of the dominant religion? Strictly speaking, such state-sponsored genocide would be religious anti-Semitism, not the racial anti-Semitism of the Nazis. One must ask, however, if a dead Jew killed by the Nazis and a dead Jew killed by state apparatus at the behest of Christianity, as argued by Bévenot, are significantly, qualitatively different? Both Jews would have been killed in the process of the attempt to achieve the kind of world sought by those with the ideology and the means to enforce their sense of the one truth, a racist vision in the one case and a "sacred" vision of world uniformity in the other. We must also ask the question that is central to this study: Is there not a link between the ideology and supporting beliefs, the culture, that empowered the Inquisition when it acted violently against Jews and heretics many centuries ago and the empowering ideology, the sustaining and informing culture, that brought the immense power of the totalitarian Nazi state to bear directly against the lives of Jews trapped within that state's control? Is there not a very direct cultural and ideological link between the Inquisition as operated by the Dominicans and the proposals offered by the Jesuit, Father Maurice Bévenot? Is it not true that a Jewish life in the thirteenth century had no value in the eyes of the Inquisition? And that a Jewish life in the mid-twentieth century, under Nazi German control, likewise had no value? One would die as a result of religious anti-Semitism, the other from racist anti-Semitism. The clerical functionaries of the Inquisition would not be committing a sin. Nazis likewise did not see themselves at fault; the victims deserved what they suffered in the German cleansing actions. We cannot help but wonder if the charges of crimes against humanity brought forth in the Nuremberg proceedings have any relevance conceptually with regard to earlier atrocities, beliefs, and practices. The bystanders in both eras functioned as expected. Perhaps they were disturbed by the implications for themselves of what they were witnessing, but they were forearmed with a cultural configuration for their circle of moral obligation that did not cause them to behave at a humane level of empathy and concern. Bévenot and scholars such as Maycock cannot bring themselves to indict an entire civilization, its culture, its perpetrators, and the instruments of mass death. For them, that is unthinkable. Operating from within a certain cultural context, the mind of the devout believer cannot grasp the concept that wrong was done on a massive scale. The cultural mandate is too strong. Nothing evil happened. They believe the people responsible for mass death did nothing wrong. As stated by historian of religion William Clebsch, the dominant culture demands that its

sacrality dominates over its morality. It is important to note that there are scholars who see the criminality of the Inquisition. Benzion Netanyahu finds that it
was a crime against humanity; Cecil Roth calls it a crime against the human
race.[101] Bévenot, to the contrary, cannot bring himself to this position. Needless
to say, there are powerful cultural forces at work that do not allow him to "admit
that it was all a horrible mistake." I suspect that he is not alone, that the implications of this study's findings will be equally difficult for many to assimilate.

One charitably supposes that Maurice Bévenot was not a madman, although
if he was indeed sane then there are further, disturbing concerns to be considered. An exquisitely educated person, Bévenot makes a cogent argument for
mass murder. As Moore notes in his seminally important *Formation of a Persecuting Society*, the "tremendous extension of the power and influence of the
literate" is a component of "the development of persecution in all its forms."[102]
There appears to be no restraining factor. Bévenot had to be intelligent enough
to persist through the rigorous educational regimen of the Jesuit order. He had
to be remarkably self-disciplined to follow the strict behavioral guidelines the
Jesuits impose on their neophytes. Obedience is a characteristic with a supremely
high value placed on it by the Jesuits, as evidenced by being one of several Jesuit traits that impressed Reichsführer Heinrich Himmler as he set about organizing the Nazi SS in the image of the Jesuits. Bévenot surely had to excel in
obedience. It is most likely that his superiors were aware of his scholarship and
provided the permission he needed to devote himself to his ideological task.
The editors of the *Heythrop Journal* may also be assumed to have been socially
functional human beings, who shared the usual concerns about the larger human
condition. They also were literate people, supposedly capable of exercising independent judgment and reaching humane decisions. Given the times in which
they lived, they had to be somewhat familiar with the major issues facing humans in the mid-twentieth century. They read his scholarly submission, all four
parts, accepted it, and published it—then led the rest of their lives as usual. To
be editors of a journal in the 1960s indicates that they were probably young
adults during World War II, or perhaps they received their educations in the immediate post-war years. What were their thoughts about the Nazi death camps?
Did they have any concerns about Nazi state-sponsored genocide practiced
against the same people, the Jews, that Bévenot's beloved Inquisition burned to
death in sacred orgies of mass death? Did they see Jews as within their circle of
moral obligation, or not? What did they know of the depredations and terror of
the Inquisition? Did the thought ever cross their minds that the repression and
violence practiced against Jews and Others for centuries of European history
were in any way possibly related to the horrors of the Nazis' ideology and genocidal practices? Given those concerns, we must wonder if there were editorial
discussions or serious concerns or reservations about the meaning and intent of
Bévenot's work? Or did the editors simply agree with the thrust of his work?

Obviously, to my way of thinking, what is lacking here on several levels of
discourse, is the application of an ideological critique. I cannot speak for the

editors, but Bévenot's publicly printed words are clear enough. Perhaps it would be fair to say that the moral, philosophical, cultural, theological, and ideological ramifications of the Shoah had not fully penetrated the Western consciousness. It is more likely, however, that there was simply no perceived connection on the part of these people between the various elements of the culture in Bévenot's study and the many complex elements of the concentrationary universe of Nazi genocide practiced against Jews. I do not think that this is at all unusual; my hope, however, is that this chapter's discussion will heighten awareness in this regard. Bévenot's position demonstrates Ervin Staub's points, made in his study of evil: In the process of harming people, "it becomes increasingly difficult to stop and break the continuity." And, as people move along a continuum of destruction, "moral equilibration becomes more automatic."[103] For Staub, torturers often operate in and perceive an Us versus Them world dichotomy, believe deeply in a Just World (that is, people deserve what they get), and devalue the victims.[104] Bévenot's work once again shows features of Staub's theories at work. The Inquisition obviously divides people into the faithful and The Others—Jews, heretics—and then sets out to inflict a variety of punishments on those who are not among the faithful. Their fate is already decided by virtue of their error, unless, one supposes, they convert to the one religion with the only truth. Finally, we should not be surprised in Bévenot's essays to find a total lack of concern for those who suffer at the hands of the repressive measures sponsored by the agents of the Inquisition. Instead, his primary value is for the truth as claimed by the Church, and the souls of those exposed to that truth. M. Scott Peck, a psychiatrist who studies the relationship between religion and science, makes an acutely insightful and helpful observation: those who hold themselves to be faultless and blameless are themselves evil.[105] This perception is not a position that can be gained from within the cultural perspective of those who claim sole access to the universal truth. Such people define those discursive elements, conditions, and characteristics regarding which people can be charged with blame and fault, project these matters on The Other, then act against them, sometimes achieving the level of mass death, or even genocide. The consequences of such ideological practices in the culture, as we now know all too well, can be utterly disastrous for The Other.

5

Contact with
Indigenous Peoples

"The earth is the Lord's and the fullness thereof. The Lord may give the earth or any part of it to his chosen people. We are his chosen people."
—New England assembly, 1640s

"Colonialism cannot be understood without the possibility of torturing, raping and killing."
—Frantz Fanon

"It begins to look as if, through shame or fear of being racist, the West will not admit to having been so at any time."
—Léon Poliakov

"The Anglo-Europeans who came here had one goal: the destruction of life ... one of the best ways I know to discover purpose is to examine outcome."
—Paula Gunn Allen

Before the ships carrying Christopher Columbus and his crews were first seen by the indigenous peoples of the Americas, the destinies of the natives had already been declared in a variety of texts. The words, written in a dead language the targeted people could not possibly have known, inscribed theological concepts of dominion that were entirely alien to them. Boniface VIII's 1302 papal bull, *Unam Sanctum*, asserted the pontiff's absolute right to dominion: "that to be submitted to the Roman pontiff is for any creature a necessity for salvation."[1] In stark contrast to this, the Wintu people of California reportedly had no words with which to express "personal dominion and coercion .... so foreign were those concepts to their way of life."[2] Pope Nicolas V issued a papal bull, *Romanus Pontifex*, in 1454 that seemed to reach the logical extension of the 1302 position. It denies non-Christians the right to their own possessions, and gives to the Portuguese the right to invade and conquer the lands of non-Christians, force their expulsion, vanquish them, enslave them, and "expropriate their possessions" (actions to be taken against "pagans and all other enemies of Christ wheresoever placed").[3]

Nicolas's bull bears certain attitudinal similarities to the subsequent Spanish *Requierimento.* Loyola's Jesuits could read in his *Exercises* of the order's desire to "conquer the whole world," especially "all the lands of the infidels."[4] In the case of failed attempts to convert non-Christians on *terra nullis,* colonizers could kill the natives as "an act of faith and a religious duty."[5] The grounds for this treatment derived from the medieval interpretation that there was no legitimate secular power aside from the Church and that after Christ, "all legitimate secular power was transferred to the Christian faithful."[6] This theological and cultural orientation to The Other had its initial major outreach during the crusades, when war fought on behalf of the interests of the Church was automatically considered to be just,[7] and was "grounded in transcendent goals."[8] It is not surprising that the first European-built structure in the New World was a fort, or that Columbus would plant a cross in the soil of the new lands he was claiming on behalf of Christianity,[9] although he claimed that "nobody objected" to his taking possession of their lands.[10] The sum total of these attitudes and beliefs permeated the culture and the lives of all who lived within it and believed its messages. "A religion becomes much more than a set of doctrines and rituals; it was immanent in the total behavior of its adherents."[11] This "total behavior" would lend itself readily to genocide in the Western hemisphere as Christianity continued its development away from its early days as an institution serving the needs of the oppressed to becoming "a church of the oppressors."[12]

A portentous confluence of several historical streams exists. Each is propelled by the Western European culture of Christianity. Even as Columbus was leaving on his first voyage and eventual contact with a new Other, the Jews of Spain were being expelled under the pressures of the Inquisition, the continent's crusading efforts were not yet finished, and the slavery trade involving Africans for European needs had long been under way. Columbus himself was the first to unite the western thrust of European colonization with the notion that the indigenous people would make good slaves for their masters.[13] Djelal Kadir, in his study of Columbus, notes that the Christian West's expansion represents the "conjunction of two concomitant ideologies: the conquering or 'missionary' imperative of the Church Militant and the imperial dreams of the Universal Church, both ultimately invested with a prophetic narrative of the *ecclesia triumphans,* the Church Triumphant and its messianic eschatology."[14] In *The Invasion of America,* Francis Jennings notes, "[I]t was hard to proclaim a righteously defensive war against an enemy who had never ventured within a thousand miles of one's domain. Happily there was a saving precedent: the Crusades had well established that war conducted in the interests of the Holy Church was automatically just."[15] How appropriate, then, that Columbus reported that the natives he encountered in the New World were ignorant of warfare and weapons and had no words for it.[16] Here is yet another example of the collision between a potent, militarized Western culture sustained by centuries of a theology of sacred violence with a relatively nonviolent culture lacking a symmetrical theology, as well as the will to destroy. As Leonardo Boff notes of Spanish thoughts on sacred violence: the natives only heard the Gospel when it was accompanied by the cannon's roar. Gonzalo Fernández de Oviedo thus called for "Gunpowder against the infidel, and incense for the Lord!"[17] Furthermore, Columbus could rely upon papal assurances that all humans were obliged to recognize absolute papal authority over their souls, which in practice also translated into authority over their bodies and possessions. The observation that we "are all fellow travelers in the Colombian wake"[18] should give us pause as we consider the cumulative effects from the cultural past. The past definitively contributed to the formidable base for prevailing attitudes that helped facilitate the atrocities perpetrated against Other innocent, helpless people.

Given the enormity of what he would find, Columbus was not very well prepared for whatever it was he hoped to encounter. He did, however, see to it that he had a translator on his first expedition. This person was qualified to translate Hebrew and Aramaic.[19] What motivated the great admiral of the seas to include someone in his venture, supposedly to India, with these qualifications? To what cultural mandate was he responding? Did he expect to encounter people from the Holy Land? Were there expectations lingering from Europe's various crusading expeditions to the Holy Land? What sense of Judaism did Columbus and his supporters possess? Had he actually come face to face with someone speaking Hebrew, after a voyage of several thousands of miles, what cultural expectations would Columbus have brought to the moment? Would he have seen a Christ killer, and behaved accordingly? In light of the expulsion of Jews from Spain, would he have seen a person unworthy of living under the crown he served? Would he have initiated Christianity's usual conversion efforts? There were no priests on his first voyage, but there were thirteen priests accompanying the second.[20] Roy Harvey Pearce captures a salient point about conversion for the indigenous people, one that would hold true for the next five centuries: "Save him, and you save one of Satan's victims. Destroy him, and you have destroyed one of Satan's partisans."[21] Echoing many other scholars' thoughts, Kadir, who sees Columbus as "a cultural phenomenon,"[22] notes that Columbus undertook his voyage by sailing in God's name, "an unquestionable form of enablement that justifies all acts and sanctifies all means."[23] The royal charter that sustained Columbus, the Capitulaciones de Santa Fe, signed on 30 April 1492, authorized him—no less than *seven* times—"to discover and conquer."[24] Later, Englishman John Cabot's letter patents was somewhat more circumspect in this regard at first; he was authorized to "seek out, discover, and find." However, Cabot's document then immediately adds that he is also to "subdue, occupy, and possess." Kadir makes a crucial point: nowhere do we find the objects of these verbs, The Other humans in those distant lands, mentioned in these texts. "They are 'metonymically' displaced into annihilation,"[25] much like Jews were often absent in German documents dealing with their annihilation. The English felt they had a right to "just invasion and conquest,"[26] which is a clear echo of the role of sacred violence in the service of dominion.

In 1513, Palacios Rubios devised a written text Pedrarias Davila's used during his colonizing expedition to the mainland of the New World.[27] A key example of Western European Christian discourse that targeted The Other, the *Requierimento* required the indigenous people to agree to be in the Spanish crown's service. It did not mandate conversion,[28] although the missionaries would see to that in short order. Within a century of its initial colonizing efforts, Spain sponsored six ecclesiastical provinces, thirty-two dioceses, sixty thousand churches, and four hundred monasteries.[29] From the *Requierimento*, the Spanish colonizers read the following:

I certify to you that, with the help of God, we shall powerfully enter into your country and shall make war against you in all ways and manners that we can, and shall subject you to the yoke and obedience of the Church and of their Highnesses. We shall take you and your wives and your children, and shall make slaves of them, and as such shall sell and dispose of them as their highnesses command. And we shall take your goods, and shall do you all the mischief and damage that we can, as to vassals who do not obey and refuse to receive their lord and resist and contradict them.[30]

It is a fairly easily seen how the *Requierimento* represents disturbing vestiges of cultural and theological attitudes toward The Other that had been forming and evolving within Western European Christianity over a span of several centuries. Luis Rivera, for example, in his *Violent Evangelism,* traces the willingness to use capital punishment as a device against heresy to Aquinas's *Summa,*[31] thereby implicating one of the leading minds of the Church in later events that would culminate in genocide. Accordingly, in the *Requierimento* is seen a solemn promise, or threat, regarding the use of the sacred violence that had previously afflicted The Other countless times; the expectation for obedience; the dominion of the Church over the property, bodies, and souls of people for whom nothing could be more alien; an acceptance of and threat to use slavery; and complete disregard for the sanctity of the central family unit. First used by Oviedo in 1514,[32] the Spanish were required to read this statement to all new groups of natives they encountered. It was immaterial that those for whom this was intended could not understand the strange language and its even stranger ideology, much less the attitudes behind it.

In 1502, Bartolomé de Las Casas, who would become a famous Dominican friar, is recorded as having arrived in Spain's new possession in the Western hemisphere, Hispaniola. His father had been involved in the earliest Spanish contact with the indigenous people a few years earlier. The younger Las Casas recalled seeing some of the Native Americans taken to Spain by Columbus after the initial contact.[33] Las Casas's life was changed permanently in 1511 when he heard an impassioned sermon preached by Father Antonio de Montesinos, a Dominican priest. Montesinos insisted on the need to recognize the basic humanity of the native people.[34] His sermon was quite direct:

You are living in deadly sin for the atrocities you tyrannically impose on these innocent people. Tell me, what right have you to enslave them? What authority did you use to make war against them who lived at peace on their territories, killing them cruelly with methods never before heard of? How can you oppress them and not care to cure or feed them, and work them to death to satisfy your greed? And why don't you look after their spiritual health, so that they should come to know God, that they should be baptized, and that they should hear Mass and keep the holy days? Aren't they human beings? Have they no rational soul? Aren't you obliged to love them as you love yourselves? ... You may rest assured that you are in no better state of salvation than the Moors or the Turks who reject the Christian Faith.[35]

Montesinos's concerns reveal both a genuine, loving, humane concern for the suffering people, as well as vestiges of the dominant culture's belief system of theological superiority and supersessionism. The cathedral in which he preached his sermon was filled with Spanish officials of the colonial government, who reported his words to the crown, enraging King Fernando.[36] Although he challenges the conquerors' brutal methods, he doesn't go so far as to challenge the underlying assumptions, but that would perhaps be to ask too much. His voice and moral concerns, crying in the moral wilderness in deep anguish over the suffering wrought upon innocents by his co-religionists and countrymen, had not been heard often enough over the centuries. The lack of such concerns articulated in his passionate manner surely contributed much to abetting the murderous sacred violence inflicted upon Other innocents across many centuries.

After witnessing Montesinos's impressive performance, Las Casas devoted much of his long remaining life to bringing to the Spanish crown's attention his view that violent Spanish practices against the natives in the New World were unworthy of his sense of the most basic Christian principles. The first priest ordained in the New World, he appeared to have an enlightened, humane view of how to bring the Christian Gospel to nonbelievers. He reached a decision to reject what this study identifies as sacred violence; in other words, Las Casas proved that it is possible to conduct an ideological critique while also being an active participant in unfolding events. The two men, Montesinos and Las Casas, thus revealed their ability to take the crucial steps necessary to assume a position of "disruptive empathy"[37] which refuses to indulge in the self-delusion that the world of atrocity and genocide is normal. The sheer persistence of Las Casas in this matter resulted in a "debate" in 1550 with Father Juan Ginés de Sepulveda, the Crown's chaplain and chronicler,[38] who argued in support of the violent, inhumane Spanish policies and practices as the best means of bringing the natives to the supposedly loving bosom of the Church. Sepulveda found in Deuteronomy his support for armed conquest,[39] the sacred violence that led to as many as four to five million natives being killed in a fifteen-year period by Pedro de Alvarado, according to Las Casas.[40] Sepulveda sought for the natives "to be placed under the authority of civilized and virtuous princes or nations, so that they may learn, from the might, wisdom, and law of their conquerors, to practice better morals, worthier customs, and a more civilized way of life."[41] In a stunning insight, he argued that Native Americans were like Jews, whom God wanted destroyed.[42] His argument is central to the culture and rhetoric of dominion that had developed over the centuries: the natives have no right to self-determination; they lack civilization and virtue. Sepulveda trusts those Christian Europeans with power to be moral, wise, and civilized. His assertions are completely in line with the attitudes inculcated by a series of papal decrees originating with the crusades, views that have had terrible repercussions for The Other. In the debate with Sepulveda, Las Casas, however, prevailed and eventually the crown mandated changes in Spanish methods, although Native Americans never enjoyed any complete respite from European-inspired depredations.

Note, however, that Las Casas had his limitations. Despite enlightened, humane attitudes toward the indigenous people of the New World, he supported both the Inquisition and the sending of Africans to the New World to be enslaved.[43] Indeed, he owned black slaves as late as 1544.[44] George Tinker observes that Las Casas was committed to the conquest, but was reacting to the violence he saw.[45] In this, Las Casas's life recalls the tortured existence of Kurt Gerstein, a German nationalist, SS man, potential war crimes witness, man of conscience, and self-confessed mass murderer. Gerstein was trapped nevertheless by the unperceived limitations of his commitment to a certain culture and worldview, and a failure to grasp the depths of the evil he was vainly attempting to destroy almost single-handedly. Taken together, Las Casas and Gerstein perhaps reveal the extreme difficulties encountered when people must attempt to reinterpret events of atrocity going on around them in order "to be able to integrate it into [their] own vision."[46] Both men seem to have known very well that there were terrifying larger events taking place in their lives that had to be stopped. Both men took action against the evil forces surrounding them; both men were devout, faithful Christians. However, what inherent limitations in their views failed to lead them to see the precise nature of their own involvement in the evil they opposed? They clearly had the capacity to go just so far in their actions and beliefs. What restrained them from going further? What flaws, if any, existed in their respective moral structures? How do the flaws relate to discussion of sacred violence? Djelal Kadir makes a point that requires repeated emphasis: "Clearly, ideological and rhetorical determinants suffuse a culture's world view and practices so thoroughly that those conditions are operative and determinant in corroborative as well as dissenting actions of a society's members."[47]

In his report to the crown, *The Devastation of the Indies: A Brief Account*, Las Casas recorded an unbelievable litany of atrocities inflicted by the Spanish conquerors upon the nearly helpless natives. After detailing numerous accounts of mass slaughters, one particular atrocity stands out:

Now, in God's name, you who read this, consider ... whether it is accurate to call such Christians devils .... I am going to tell of another action the Spanish engage in ... and it still goes on at the present time ... the Spaniards train their fierce dogs to attack, kill and tear into pieces the Indians. It is doubtful whether anyone, whether Christian or not, has ever heard of such a thing as this. The Spaniards keep alive their dogs' appetite for human beings in this way .... And the Spaniards have butcher shops where the corpses of Indians are hung up, and someone will come in and say, more or less, "Give me a quarter of that rascal hanging there, to feed my dogs until I can kill another one for them." As if buying a quarter of a hog or other meat.[48]

A butcher shop selling body parts of human beings for dog food is only one vivid example of many such instances, attitudes, and behaviors. The chronicle of Las Casas is filled with many similar examples: dismembering natives like animals in a slaughterhouse, killing infants in front of their mothers, cutting off hands, roasting natives on fire grids, feeding burned humans to dogs, practicing 100:1 reprisals, burning people in their straw huts,[49] torturing people to death, burning people at the stake, disfiguring children's faces with swords.[50] Gonzalo Fernández de Oviedo, the crown secretary, had the assigned task of being the "official keeper of the branding iron for captured slaves." With each branding of a slave, de Oviedo received a royalty,[51] signifying yet another example of a government official standing to benefit from inhumane practices. Some Spanish, however, did not see much value at all in the natives, as exemplified on those occasions when they would decapitate a native rather than go to the bother of unlocking a chain.[52] Hernando Cortés achieved unbelievable heights of mass murder in the splendid Aztec city of Tenotchtlitán, killing twelve thousand people in one day's work; the murder of forty thousand basically helpless men, women, and children occurred the next day.[53] Sacred violence was conducted in close quarters within the city, in virtually face to face conditions. Not entirely satisfied, the Spanish burned holy books and fed the native priests to their dogs. They also fed native babies to their dogs, and killed other babies for the purpose of using them as roadside markers.[54] As Jalal Ahmad observes, all was done in the name of Christian peace and love.[55]

These atrocities were perpetrated by Spanish soldiers who felt, according to Las Casas, that they had the God-given right to do so; they were following the orders of their superiors.[56] The practice of invoking the Christian God as the ultimate warrant for such violent acts enjoyed a plethora of scriptural and theological sources. Just as a complex support services system was needed to keep the Nazi death camps fully operational, a butcher shop featuring choice human selections for dogs would also require a considerable degree of complexity among supporting personnel. The existence of such a shop requires that the conquerors see the natives as non-human or sub-human. Being mere objects to exploit,[57] as reflected in the debates within the Church as to whether or not the natives possessed souls, no one of a different conscience was on the scene to contest the matter. There is ample evidence of prevailing attitudes. Juan de Matienza, for example, in 1567 in Peru, said that Native Americans are "animals who do not even feel reason, but are ruled by their passions."[58] Despite such beliefs, could not an argument be made with some justification that such a shop would be unknown on the European mainland at that time? It was located, after all, thousands of miles from the mother country, with a vast ocean separating it from the homeland. Such a location also presupposes a crown charter. Support services needed for a significant maritime venture in colonialism would include church involvement, military personnel, various adventurers, individuals with capital interests, a variety of general laborers, supervisors, accountants, government representatives, the judiciary, and so forth. All these people would have seen the butcher shop. Upon their return to the homeland, would they have discussed the butcher shop with their families, friends, former co-workers, their confessors, and neighbors? Were they the same kind of people who might have received the boxes of body parts sent from the Holy Land back to Europe during the crusades?[59] We may justifiably ask, however, if those who had witnessed the butcher shop's horror, or any of the other atrocities detailed by Las Casas, were so hardened that they never felt the need to make comment to those close to them? Or, if they did, in what terms and attitudes were the descriptions couched? How would the information have been received? To what extent did the outrage of Las Casas find a counterpart among his contemporaries, both the supporting personnel behind the effort and people in the homeland? As asked previously, how many people cared? Did they perceive a problem? Did they feel anguish over the plight of the innocents? Did they feel any dissonance between the "difficult words" of Matthew's account of the Sermon on the Mount and their experiences of atrocities, or the accounts of such? Other than Las Casas and Montesinos, were the clergy assigned to the colony so immured within the cultural mandates regarding The Other that the atrocious scenes did not cause them to shudder in revulsion or reconsider theological underpinnings? Would the clergy or the laymen have noticed or even been concerned about the Spanish conquerors' habit of executing Native Americans in groups of thirteen "in honor and reverence for our Redeemer and the twelve Apostles"?[60] That they did not feel the need to make comment or protest speaks volumes about the strength of the dominant culture's assumptions and beliefs about The Other as well as the lingering influence of Inquisitorial thinking.

Indeed, the revelations of Las Casas led eventually to the controversy known as the Black Legend, based essentially on an unwillingness to believe the particulars of his allegations, downplaying their significance, or banning his books. The argument may be indicative of the Western culture's difficulty in fully coming to terms with the facts and the implications of atrocities like those practiced in the Americas, and genocides such as the Holocaust (not to mention what Holocaust denial and revisionism reveals). The cultural core values that did much to contribute to these events may be especially difficult in this regard. The ubiquitous, incessant claims of universality, transcendence, and triumphalism—allied with the obvious historical significance that vast resources and material prosperity represent—make it difficult for those who are fully invested in those claims to see anything else, to see fully and clearly the brutal impact Western culture has had on hundreds of millions of innocent people constituting The Other. Indeed, Christianity provided a "triadic formal model," composed of (1) Christians, (2) infidels (Jews, Muslims), and (3) idolators (pagans), that provided believers with a reliable schema for making decisions about moral commitments and obligations. The triadic model could also help a believer determine The Other's status as a human being, or something less than human. In yet another example that such culturally mandated attitudes about The Other persist in the contemporary world is found in the action of the Southern Baptist International Mission Board in publishing a "prayer guide" that was distributed in 1999 to forty thousand U.S. churches. The prayer guide was released to coincide with Rosh Hashanah in order to convince Jews to convert to Christianity.[61] Just as Europeans sought new lands and peoples to find new candidates for conversion, many large-scale Christian missionary efforts continue today "to invade the most sacred inner precincts of another man's being."[62] Such efforts were and are impelled by the basic claims to universal truth made by Christianity and the imperative to disseminate that truth worldwide, thus contributing to the perceptions of The Other as lacking an essential component of full humanity, or of existing in danger of eternal damnation. There is a direct cultural and discursive connection between this current Baptist document and a 1650 book by Thomas Thorogood. Titled *Jews in America*, it sought conversions through missionary activity.[63] In *The Inconstant Savage*, Harry Culverwell Porter notes that Native Americans were seen as "degenerate Jews."[64] In light of the litany of devastating cultural results, there would be considerable merit in assessing conversion attempts as an aspect of cultural genocide. Luis Rivera estimates that each Franciscan converted 300,000 people in Mexico,[65] a statistic that offers a sense of the dimensions.

Encountering the indigenous people of the New World proved to be an experience that "didn't fit within Christianity's explanation of the moral universe."[66] Given this, we should not be surprised to see Christianity using what was familiar—the template it had created many centuries earlier as it set about dehumanizing and persecuting Jews. Luis Rivera makes a crucial point by noting that Native Americans were perceived by the Church as suffering from "invincible ignorance"[67] of the truth as seen by Christianity; the exact same charge had been leveled against the Jews centuries earlier. Europeans had considerable experience in uniting military efforts with overt religious actions. For example, Spanish statutes required natives to attend religious instruction and Mass. George Tinker sees this kind of Christian evangelism serving as an integral part of a conquering army's strategy of conquest.[68] It may also be said to be an example of scholar Edward Said's concept of the "moral epistemology of imperialism"— blotting out knowledge of natives.[69] Having done all in its power to negate and nullify the knowledge of existence as recorded by Jews, it was not difficult to practice similar negations with The Others in the New World.

Sylvia Wynter contends that the truths people live by "once put into place, must necessarily be not only 'impervious to philosophical attack' but impervious also to empirical counterevidence."[70] Luis Villoro strikes a crucial note:

If the meaning of history is the final triumph of Christianity, if its development is governed by the design of Providence, that which is irreducible to Christianity can only be that which contradicts that design. And the one who contradicts it has, in our cultural tradition, a name: Satan. The [O]ther's culture, insofar as it cannot be translated into ours, cannot be but devilish. This is the most common interpretation amongst the missionaries and chroniclers. Their basic belief of the world holds that there can be only one truth and one destiny for man .... If some other culture intends to have another truth or destiny, it denies our picture of the world .... The other is the obscure and the occult, that which says "no" to the world, [it is] the Satanic. Then, by definition, it is what cannot be integrated into our world, that which is open to destruction.[71]

The cultural expectations and truth claims that empowered and sustained Europeans in their treatment of the indigenous peoples of the New World five centuries ago are still operating today. Sylvia Wynter identifies "the deep-seated belief in the genetic nonhomogeneity of the human species" as the "belief system ... responsible not only for innumerable atrocities that were to climax in Auschwitz, but also for a sociosystematically produced series of savage inequalities."[72] Francis Jennings argues that such beliefs constitute the "myths created by the cant of conquest [that] endure in many forms to mask the terrible tragedy that was Europe's glory."[73] Savagery has been a chief feature of the belief system that has, over many centuries, created definitional categories that led to perceiving the saved apart from the damned, those with souls and those without, the white good and the dark evil, the Aryan and the non-Aryan, and the Christian and the non-Christian. Few people over the centuries have summoned the courage or strength to challenge the evil and inhumanity of this belief structure. After all, it seemed normal, right, scriptural based, correct, and verifiable.

The disturbing example of the butcher shop that Las Casas witnessed and recorded has a horrifying but revealing counterpart from the Holocaust. As recounted by Regina Landau, the Gestapo used Jewish children to discover adult Jews being sought in a follow-up sweep after a massacre of Jews in the town of Lanzut, Poland. The children were tortured by the Gestapo, but the children did not reveal what they knew of the adults' whereabouts. According to Landau, the Gestapo ended the affair this way: "As the children were led to the cemetery they were urged not to cry, for they would 'go to heaven, and meet their mother, father and aunts.' After the children had been shot the Gestapo took their bodies to the circus performing in Lanzut, to be eaten by the beasts."[74]

This enormity engenders concerns similar to those articulated in the case of the Spanish butcher shop for canines. Revealed, obviously, is the Gestapo's ability to dehumanize The Other totally, to see Jewish children as unworthy of life, thus following the cultural blueprint created by Christianity as it defined and acted against the Disconfirming Other, the nemesis Jews. But we should note in particular the willingness to use a reference to a heaven and an afterlife as a means of "consoling" the children about to be murdered. The usual values associated with a heaven are here completely perverted; the Gestapo perpetrators were making their atrocity work easier for themselves, attempting to create fully compliant victims, rather than primarily offering "comfort" to the doomed children. The utter emptiness of their gesture is underscored by the subsequent use of the children's bodies to feed circus animals. As in the Spanish case, the implications of the stark facts of humans consciously being used by their tormentors as food for animals is not isolated to the perpetrators. The horror in this case extends to the larger surrounding social context. A circus is a place for family enjoyment, entertainment, and frivolity. Indeed, it is a place for children to indulge themselves and live out their innocent fantasies. The circus became a site of ultimate degradation, but also a site where the dominant culture expresses itself and its values, revealing once again individuals acting out yet another mandate and permutation of the sacred violence so highly valued in their culture.

The depredations practiced by the Spanish and Portuguese did not go unnoticed by the victims. Don Carlos, *cacique* of Tetzcoco, states an awareness of central issues: "Who are these who have brought us low and who disturb and live among us and whom we have upon our backs and who subject us? Who comes here to lord it over us, to capture us and subjugate us, who is not our parent nor our blood and yet who makes himself equal to us?" He was burned, as were many of his peers, in a public square in 1539 for worshipping idols in the privacy of his home.[75] Don Carlos is just one example of a human being born at a moment in history when one dominant social and cultural reality would be imposed on another such reality. The defining elements of his cultural meanings would forever be changed when the dominant set emerged to challenge and subsequently destroy the meanings that had operated for his people for centuries. Pope Alexander VI, in a 1493 bull, had demanded that Native Americans must acknowledge the authority of the pope and accept the Christian faith,[76] a gesture that Don Carlos failed to honor as he practiced his independent, private spirituality, the culture of his ancestors. Nevertheless, with nearly four centuries of invasive spiritual tactics honed to perfection by the agents of the Inquisition, this man's death was nearly foreordained.

Much like Don Carlos, we also have the prophecy of Chilam Balam de Chumayel, from the Maya of Mesoamerica, in the *Libro de los Linajes*:

In the Eleventh Ahau there begins the counting of time ....
    It was only because of the mad time, the mad priests, that sadness came among us, that Christianity came among us; for the great Christians came here with the true God; but that was the beginning of our distress, the beginning of the tribute, the beginning of the alms, what made the hidden discord appear,

> the beginning of the fighting with firearms,
>
> the beginning of the outrages,
>
> the beginning of being stripped of everything,
>
> the beginning of slavery for debts,
>
> the beginning of the debts bound to the shoulders,
>
> the beginning of the constant quarrelling,
>
> the beginning of the suffering,
>
> It was the beginning of the work of the Spaniards and the priests,
>
> the beginning of the manipulation of chiefs, schoolmasters and officials ....
>
> The poor people did not protest against what they felt a slavery,
>
> the Antichrist on earth, tiger of the peoples,

wildcat of the peoples, sucking the Indian people dry.

But the day will come when the tears of their eyes

reach God and God's justice

comes down and strikes the world.[77]

We would do well to attend to the cry from the heart by this Mayan prophet. Echoes of the impact of the policies behind the blunt threats of the *Requierimento* abound in these sad Mayan lines: the true God, tributes, firearms, outrages, devastating losses, slavery, debts, suffering. Tens of millions, perhaps hundreds of millions of innocent people suffered these indignities for each of the centuries following contact between Christian Europeans and the indigenes, centuries in which mortality rates for natives in the Western hemisphere averaged 90 percent each century. One of the victims, Hatuey, was condemned to death but given an opportunity to repent in order to go to heaven. He asked the attending priest if Christians could be found there. Upon being told that this was indeed the case, Hatuey refused to repent, preferring to have an afterlife devoid of his zealous oppressors.[78] Hatuey thus successfully resisted the cultural mandate to accept "the superiority of Europe [and come] as close as possible to the ideal model as possible."[79] We have almost no way of fully realizing what might have eventuated from these Other cultures for the good of humanity, although their contribution to the world's food supply today is perhaps an indication of what was lost. Their historical trajectories were altered forever by contact with Christian Europeans and all that went with it. Not only did the dominant culture bring with it its claims to all spiritual truth for all time and all people, it brought with it the will to impose those truth claims in such a way that competing cultural truth claims, even though they had been operative for many centuries, were all but destroyed. The supporting technology and weaponry, of course, had much to do with the victorious outcome for the Christian West, but the empowering beliefs and attitudes also contributed, including the perceptions engendered by various papal decrees and bulls. The Native Americans had no idea of what they were facing. They could not know of the experiences of the Jews of Europe with this dominating, aggressive culture that was armed for sacred violence with a theology that had, for many centuries, motivated perpetrators to murder The Other with impunity and bystanders to ignore or derealize the inhumanity of the situation.

In the Spanish conquest of much of the New World, we find a culmination of several important cultural streams involving sacred violence. Edward Hyams and George Ordish offer useful insights contrasting the native religion of Peru with the Spanish church:

despite men like Las Casas who was far ahead of his time, Spanish Catholicism was, by Peruvian standards, atrocious. [The Inca religion] consisted in the propitiation of the lesser gods, iconolatry, and a profound and prayerful humility in their attitude to the Almighty. In this respect ... it closely resembled the religion of the Spaniards, who propitiated the saints, worshiped relics and other idols, and abased themselves before their triune Almighty. But, whereas the Inca Church was relatively humane in its practices, forcing no conversions, absorbing rather than suppressing alien cults, and practicing human sacrifice, if at all, then with such moderation that it certainly sacrificed fewer victims in a year than did the Church of England under the first Elizabeth, the Spanish church was horrifyingly different. It forced conversions by torture and fear and death, it suppressed alien cults with ruthlessness and, in its numerous autos-da-fé, it practiced human sacrifice by means of burning, the most painful of deaths, on a vast scale. It is necessary to stress this fact because a religious excuse is frequently offered for the destruction of native Peru by the Spaniards. It is true that the Spaniards sincerely believed that they were serving their god by such practices.[80]

Quite appropriately aware of the nature of the atrocity facing the indigenous people, the authors' language brings forth the ideological point that "natives" offer human sacrifices, but not Europeans. This is an excellent example of the limitations created by cultural perceptions. Limitations permeate the ways in which the culture permits itself to be passed on from one generation to the next in the form of one's education, indeed, limitations in the very way that people can think. Mass murder committed by the agents of Christianity in serving the higher purposes and the exclusive truth claims of that religion cannot possibly be equated in the minds of the devout faithful with similar acts perpetrated by non-Christians. Acts of atrocity have often been perpetrated within a sanctified context, as we should expect because this is sacred violence. For example, just prior to the planned slaughter of the Incans escorting Atahualpa, Pizarro and his men attended a Mass celebrated by Father Valverde. David E. Stannard notes that the "destruction of a few hundred or thousand Inca bodies, as a means of bringing a few million Inca souls to Christ, was a good act, a religious deed .... It was with a sense of righteousness, of holiness, that the Spaniards in Caxamarca barracks square that morning called in song upon their God to arise—*Exsurge domine!*—and judge His own cause."[81] Shortly after celebrating Mass, the slaughter commenced against The Other, largely unarmed people.

The situation still exists. Djelal Kadir finds that "Christian cosmology and its prophetic narrative" constituted the empowering agents that permitted the Christian West to claim "proprietary rights to the land, culture, history, and bodies" of Other people. These "authorizing mechanisms, rhetorical and ideological, remain intact and continue to be operative."[82] The constituent elements of the dominant religion also empowered human agents who were charged, cynically or otherwise, with spreading religion among The Others in their path. In light of Kadir's points, George Tinker, in *Missionary Conquest*, poses highly pertinent questions: "How are our thoughts and actions today controlled by this same systemic whole? And how can we begin to stand apart from it with some intentionality?"[83] Tinker's study interrogates the possibility of resistance, a behavior considered on several occasions, but more to the point he is cognizant of the controlling features of the "systemic whole"—the culture.

The culture and its oppressive acts in history are not isolated to the Iberian peninsula. The English brought with them to the New World attitudes very similar to those that sustained the genocidal activities under Spanish and Portuguese control. New England colonial leader John Winthrop and Columbus both saw themselves with a "conviction of divine election"—a "fundamental premise"[84] in their personal makeup. The Virginia colonists marked Jamestown with a cross,[85] as Columbus had in his initial contacts. Robert Johnson, in 1609, said the colonists' first concern should be to "advance and spread the kingdom of God, and the knowledge of his truth, among so many millions of men and women, savage and blind, that never yet saw the true light." Johnson, like Sepulveda a half century earlier, also believed that conquest by the sword can be honorable,[86] keeping alive a current of thought within Christianity that had persisted for more than a thousand years. Robert Gray, also in 1609, articulated that a Christian king "may lawfully make war upon a barbarous and savage people."[87] Augustine had argued a similar point, when the young religion was in its formative period, even as Other cultures developing elsewhere in the world were in a state of ignorance about the fervent partisans of a sacred violence half a world away that would eventually destroy them and their cultures.

A consciousness of divine calling characterized the exploits of Europeans as they sailed westward and encountered a pagan world unknown to them. Extending power was not without its cultural antecedents, however. Europe's Christian *gladium spirituale* dominated over many centuries. Europeans had responded to papal calls with sacred violence many times; colonial expansion involved the same kind of motivations. Although not operating under a papal mandate, the 1606 Virginia charter is replete with references to Christian scripture and garden images,[88] with the New Eden awaiting their devout cultivation, including the native souls living there. The colonists of Virginia felt themselves "marked and chosen by the finger of God to possess it."[89] Using the template of Christian interpretation of Hebrew scripture, William Symonds preached a sermon in 1609 calling for the propagation of the Gospel in Virginia, citing God's command to Abraham in Genesis 12:1–3. Robert Gray called for the casting out of the Canaanites living in Virginia.[90] The Reverend Samuel Worcester found the indigenous people to be without "hope, salvation, or eternal light."[91] Father Paul LeJeune, a Jesuit priest, believed that "because the Indians were pagan their conduct could not be called in any strict sense moral."[92] Allied with these views is Robert Gray's notion that God gave the world to people like him, but it is unlawfully possessed by wild beasts, unreasonable creatures, and brutish savages.[93] Increase Mather, six decades later, repeated Gray's point: New England is the New Israel, occupied by "Heathen People ... whose land the Lord God of our Fathers hath given to us for rightfull Possession."[94] Mather saw the natives as "rubbish,"[95] the kind of attitude that enabled Christian Europeans to become actively engaged in decimating native populations with impunity and a total absence of moral qualms. Showing virtually no concern over the welfare of the natives, William Berkeley, governor of the Virginia colony, proposed killing all adult males in order to sell women and children into slavery.[96]

Such attitudes, combined with the widespread perception on the part of the colonists that the indigenous people were "culturally and religiously inferior,"[97] would prove to be a deadly ideological mix that would contribute directly to genocidal acts throughout the period of contact between Europeans and Native Americans. For example, in the massacres of the Pequot War, Captain John Mason deliberately burned to death seven hundred men, women, and children in 1637.[98] Bringing his soldiers with him to a native village, Mason had surveyed the scene and quickly concluded, "We must burn them."[99] Following the slaughter, colonist John Underhill wrote, "Sometimes the Scripture declareth women and children must perish with their parents.... We had sufficient light from the word of God for our proceedings."[100] Underhill's *Newes from America* also referred to the Pequot deaths as a "sweet slaughter."[101] Of course, for the devout faithful, such a claim is "true" if it is scriptural, because then it is indelibly related to Christianity's truth claims and could now be applied as a model for the new garden of Eden being so assiduously cultivated by the Europeans. Four decades after the Pequot slaughter, during King Philip's War, English soldiers under Josiah Winthrop murdered a group of Narragansett tribal people within one of their forts, burning "to death all the women, children, and wounded men in the wigwams." Increase Mather's history of the war comments on such incidents: "A Sword, a Sword is sharpened, and also fourbished ... to make a sore slaughter, *should we then make mirth.*"[102] William Bradford, when told of a similar slaughter, expressed his interest in seeing that some of the victims had converted before their demise.[103] English accounts of such atrocities often reflected the rhetoric such as "thus doth the Lord Jesus make them bow before him, and to lick the Dust."[104] A century and a half later, and to the contrary of Bradford's position, American troops slaughtered a village of Delaware Moravian Christians in Gnadenhütten, Ohio. The unarmed Delawares were cut down without mercy, even though they were begging and pleading for their lives.[105] Conversion to Christianity meant nothing in the scale of value used by the Americans facing these Others. Stockam, an English minister, articulated the prevailing attitude that had operated at Gnadenhütten: conversion is useless, just cut their throats.[106]

That same divine light often revealed to the colonists that Indians, motivated by Satan, "are ordained for destruction."[107] The year 1622 proved to be disastrous for the natives in Virginia. They had rebelled against the colonists, then suffered a "war of extermination" that began, ironically enough, on Good Friday.[108] Apparently not satisfied with relatively crude methods, two years later, Dr. John Pott, a physician serving the English crown as the interim appointee as governor of the colony of Virginia, "conceived a project ... of exterminating the Indians by poison."[109] A century later, in 1763, Lord Jeffrey Amherst employed smallpox against the Ottowas in Pennsylvania; this tactic was used again in 1717 and 1783.[110] Ward Churchill claims more than 200,000 Native Americans died from smallpox-infested blankets from hospitals in later decimations.[111] Roger Williams, often associated with the individual and institutional quest for religious freedom, in 1645 said, regarding "these Heathen Dogges, better kill a thousand of them than that we Christians should be endangered or troubled with them."[112] The faithful of the Plymouth colony, upon seeing neighboring natives dying in droves in 1617, spoke of "God's Visitation of a Wonderful Plague" on the hapless innocents.[113] With some singular exceptions, the attitude of these cultural forefathers persisted for several more centuries, certainly to the time of the American Declaration of Independence and its reference to "merciless Indian savages." In 1818 U.S. Representative Henry Southard called for either moralizing or exterminating Indians.[114] The sacred violence attitude may have even perhaps extended beyond the Seventh Cavalry's slaughter of unarmed native Others at Wounded Knee in 1890.

To further understand the American experience we must analyze the famous and frequently encountered "Manifest Destiny." James Treat offers a succinct version of this doctrine: Manifest Destiny "states that God has destined the Christian world to conquer the rest of creation in His name."[115] Coined by New York journalist John L. O'Sullivan in 1845,[116] it came to be used widely in the press in subsequent decades, reaching its apotheosis in John Fiske's 1885 article appearing in *Harper's New Monthly Magazine*. Fiske's rhetoric, typical for much of American nineteenth-century discourse, unites or reflects many of the cultural threads being traced in this study. He assumes that men who are self-governing must be allowed to work together "on a grand scale." Small groups, in his view, with only primitive governance, are "perpetually at war" among themselves; we should read here Fiske's code for the nineteenth-century stereotype of "Indians." Smugly, he goes on to add that the "industrial phase" of civilization causes men to be "less inclined to destroy life or to inflict pain,"[117] which is an amazing claim in light of the devastation brought to the lives of countless Native Americans through the advanced technologies of America's industrial capacity. He is consistent, however, as he next proposes that world peace will only be ensured by gradually concentrating the "preponderant military strength into the hands of the most pacific communities." Fiske sees these communities as seldom showing awareness of the danger of "outside attacks, whether from surrounding barbarism or from neighboring civilizations of lower types." He uses Imperial Rome as an example of the proper kind of response "against menacing barbarism" and reveals the awareness that theirs was "murderous work, but it had to be done by some one [sic] before you could expect to have great and peaceful civilizations like our own." Speaking of "frontier disturbances," Fiske asks that his fellow Americans should sympathize with Roman military history.[118] Using rhetoric that echoes Heinrich Himmler's Posen speech to his SS comrades, Fiske admires this difficult task of the Romans as they faced the "giant barbaric force" of the Gauls. "This great work was as thoroughly done as anything that was ever done in human history, and that we ought to be thankful to Caesar for it every day that we live." He rhapsodizes about the Teutonic

Knights, and notes with admiration that the "Aryan people, after attaining a high stage of civilization in Europe, are at last beginning to recover their ancient homestead."[119] Is it pointless to ask if he would have admired the murderous work of Aryans and its results that began less than sixty years after he wrote this article? He reveals concern over Muslim threats and the "*asiaticization* of European life."[120] He is not without hope, however, because Americans are the inheritors of "the indomitable spirit of English liberty" that has prevailed wherever "men of English race have set their feet as masters." In language containing echoes of his praise for Rome, Fiske argues that the "conquest of the North American continent by men of the English race was unquestionably the most prodigious event in the political annals of mankind."[121] In a final paroxysm of praise, Fiske sees "the United States as stretching from pole to pole.... Indeed, only when such a state of things has begun to be realized can civilization, as sharply demarcated from barbarism, ... [o]nly then can the world be said to have become truly Christian."[122] In 1889, Fiske maintained a consistent viewpoint when he argued, "The world is so made that it is only in that way [violence] that the higher races have been able to preserve themselves and carry on their progressive work."[123]

Fiske's work is a prime example of the discourse of the larger culture at work, one based on dominion, might, racism, and, apparently, what amounts to sacred violence—the "murderous work" that leads to a "truly Christian" world. Those who subscribed to the tenets of Manifest Destiny, such as the members of the Big Horn Association, mirror key elements of Fiske's thoughts, although Rome serves a different rhetorical purpose. "The same inscrutable Arbiter that decreed the downfall of Rome has pronounced the doom of extinction upon the red men of America."[124] A pernicious form of cultural imperialism is at work: a smug acceptance of superior and inferior status, an inability to see any worth in The Other, life unworthy of life for those who must execute the murderous work. All are matters that can be traced in other places and at different times. Fiske is writing about, and his audience is reading about, genocide, even though the harsh reality of it is covered up with patriotic, chauvinistic rhetoric. American political and journalistic rhetoric had for more than a century been filled with references to the extermination and annihilation of Native Americans.[125] Thomas Farnham, a Vermont lawyer, demanded that the "Indians' bones must enrich the soil, before the plough of the civilized man can open it.... [They] must fatten the corn hills of a more civilized race!"[126] Farnham's rhetoric about human bones serving as fertilizer becomes Nazi fact in the twentieth century. Native Americans had faced government-mandated relocation programs, loss of homelands, and various forms of direct and institutional violence very early in the young republic's history. The pressures mounted and the violence increased. Little more than twenty years before Fiske's article Colonel John M. Chivington, an ordained minister, led his Colorado Volunteer troops in the massacre at Sand Creek. Black Kettle's villagers, including the elderly, women, and children, were decimated even though they flew an American flag and waved white flags during the vicious attack. Furthering the work of cultural genocide, in the decade before the publication of Fiske's article government policy ensured that the seemingly endless herds of buffalo in the Great Plains were wiped out. Thus the basic food supply for many tribes was destroyed, as well as one of the central cultural images for many tribal religions. Other inhuman practices faced by the indigenous peoples abounded. The Republic of Texas offered a bounty for *any* Native American scalp. Californians burned whole villages of natives at night. Such practices lead to 80 to 85 percent of the remaining U.S. native population being destroyed in the first century of the nation's existence.[127] The governor of Colorado, John Evans, revealed the prevailing attitude when speaking of one of his state's military units: "But what shall I do with the Third Colorado Regiment if I make peace? They have been raised to kill Indians, and they must kill Indians."[128] Chivington showed his warrior's mentality, as well as his racism, when he cried out to those who wished to avert bloodshed just prior to his attack on Black Kettle, "Damn any man who sympathizes with Indians! I have come to kill Indians, and believe it is right and honorable to use any means under God's heaven to kill Indians."[129] In his cry we hear echoes of the papal doctrine of dominion over non-Christians, as well as yet another instance of the end result of more than a thousand years of Christianity's Just War (and Just World) theorizing and practice of sacred violence. To be sure, there were simultaneous efforts designed to help the suffering indigenous peoples, but these often had the string of religious conversion or racism attached and were seldom done out of a spirit of disinterested humane concern. U.S. Senator John Logan, speaking to Sitting Bull, discloses this point: "The government feeds and clothes and educates your children now, and desires to teach you to become farmers, and to civilize you, and make you as white men."[130] In short, the natives in the United States found precious few people who accepted them as they were; to the contrary, they faced ubiquitous demands that they change their religion, their culture, their preferred lifestyle, their clothing, their family structure, their language, and their sustaining mythologies. As The Other, their lives and the meaning structures embedded within were not valued whatsoever by the dominant culture. Sacred violence succeeded almost entirely in destroying them. For the few not destroyed, they faced a cultural process in which they would become "essentially self-colonizing, eternally subjugated in psychic and intellectual terms" for the purpose of becoming functional units within the new Eurocentric dominion.[131] All was done within "a religious culture that was as theologically as arrogant and violence-justifying as any the world had seen."[132] The Reverend John Thompson, a missionary of the American Board, observes, "It may be part of God's plan in promoting the interests of His church to destroy the majority of the Cherokees. ... The Redeemer's cause may, for aught I know, be promoted in the end by such an event."[133] William Gilmore Simms offered rhetoric that prefigured violent twentieth-century Nazi notions: Americans should obey "our destiny and our blood" and "our destiny is conquest."[134]

The dominant culture's sacred violence was not isolated to the acts of military and paramilitary units operating in isolated areas. Natives in California believed that mission priests allowed Spanish soldiers to commit rapes, even as the priests practiced floggings and used shackles and stocks to punish recalcitrant natives chafing under the mission's strict regimes.[135] One priest, stricken with pangs of conscience over the abuses, much like Las Casas centuries earlier, complained to higher authorities. He was declared insane and forced to leave California.[136] An echo of the Black Legend that haunted the work of Las Casas, it is also an excellent example of the culture's inherent difficulties in coming to moral and intellectual terms with its own evils and hypocrisy.

Ward Churchill writes eloquently about the Nazis' need for "psychological preparations for an entire population to accept a genocide" that was *about to occur* while Americans faced a process of "rationalizing and redeeming a process of conquest and genocide *which has already transpired.*"[137] Such psychological preparations have been a necessary aspect of Western cultural existence for a long time, especially with regard to debasing and dehumanizing The Other. Simultaneously a powerful set of transcendent motivations and palliations is offered to those tasked with killing and for those who stood by passively. Furthermore, the process for such preparations necessarily transposes into rationalizations and post hoc justifications, as is often seen in current U.S. educational literature that attempts to deal with this country's own genocidal past as well as that of many of its neighbors. With regard to cultural genocide, it is likely that "the good intent of some may be so mired in unrecognized systemic structures that they even remain unaware of the destruction that results from those good intentions." Cultural genocide almost always attacks "the spiritual foundations of a people's unity by denying the existing ceremonial and mythological sense of a community in relationship to the Sacred Other."[138] Countless acts amounting to cultural genocide have undoubtedly constituted a policy of the Christian West since the fourth century C.E., and have been allied with the military projection of social, political, cultural, and ideological power. In their study of genocide in California, Rupert Costo and Jeannette Henry Costo observe that genocidal "manifestations were so numerous and so rationalized by institutional opinion and academic equivocation that any implication of conspiracy or complicity in the crime is vehemently denied or rejected out of hand."[139] George Tinker, in his study of missions and their impact on cultural genocide in North America, finds that "the problem is so systemic and so deeply ingrained that it has become part of the unarticulated foundations of all Western thought and behavior and goes unrecognized even by those whom one would expect to be most acutely sensitive." He concludes that we "must come to an understanding of the pervasiveness of culture in determining structures of intellectual development as well as other, more physical patterns of behavior."[140] I would argue that the very rationalizations and equivocations that concern the Costos and Tinker in their respective studies have been operative within the Christian West for a considerable span of time, certainly longer than the existence of what passes for the modern educational system. Djelal Kadir speaks of the "empirical contexts of a certain system of beliefs that actually governs the experience of a particular culture."[141] This observation is insightful enough, to be sure, but I would alter the relationship to speak of culture's impact on one's belief system. Harry Culverwell Porter notes that empirical observation was "more often than not conditioned by pre-conception . . . Biblical preconception."[142]

An overview of the atrocities detailed against The Other in this chapter supports the Costos' views that the "Western paradigm whereby rationalization leads quickly to dehumanization of objectified others [and] an ideology of exclusiveness and discriminating datum" provides "the seeds of a dominion for greater and more efficient deaths."[143] A good example of this point is found in the late nineteenth century, when Charles Kingsley gave a lecture at Cambridge University. He argued that God made the Teutonic race such that it alone was qualified to rule the world. For Kingsley, the well being of this chosen race is the well being of the whole world. He concluded with the opinion that other races are better off dead.[144] Kingsley's lecture, given at one of Europe's leading educational institutions for the better part of seven hundred years, is obviously a representative sample of Christian Europe's "discourse about other cultures and their right to flourish."[145] The dominant culture's position on this matter is that The Other does not have the right to flourish on its own terms; it will face incessant, ubiquitous demands to change, to convert to the one, true model, often accompanied by either explicit or tacit threats of destruction. When given the opportunity, the dominant culture opts for destruction via sacred violence. After all, as Luis Rivera notes, the first commandment in the Decalogue requires the believer "to destroy idolatry."[146] This fervor is based on the inability of the Christian culture "to find a trace of God in the 'otherness of others.'"[147] Once again, it is important to recognize that the paradigm has functioned for at least seventeen centuries, and has been executed against many Others. The willingness on the part of the perpetrators to commit sacred violence against The Other in the service of a higher cause has been central to this pattern, and the bystanders must also be held accountable. In essence, Christianity successfully inculcated an ideology and a culture that involved hundreds of millions of its faithful believers in the most heinous acts committed against The Other over seventeen centuries. It created conditions that led to indifference on the part of believers to the massive suffering they caused or witnessed. Edward Hyams and George Ordish make the sobering point that the indigenous peoples of the New World "found themselves opposed to a new kind of human being who waged war à outrance, inspired by a terrifying religion which enabled them to use treachery, hypocrisy, cruelty, torture and massacre in the name of the God of Love; who were indifferent to the suffering they inflicted."[148] These unfortunate characteristics were not isolated to the Spanish or the English. Lamentably, Others had also encountered these very matters when Christians were in a position to exercise the power of theological dominion and sacred violence over them. David Stannard observes that the conquerors in the New World were not unique; other Europeans were "of equally genocidal temperament."[149] Gradually, over the centuries, Christian perpetrators and bystanders came to be extremely proficient in their respective functions. Christians came to reach impressive proportions both for their sheer destructiveness and for their ability to find ways not to show concern over the fate of The Other, even as they decimated them in the most abhorrent ways. In conclusion, Leonardo Boff and Virgil Elizondo strike a crucial note when they observe that "the genocide and massacre which began in 1492 would not have been possible without an appropriate theology. The historical violence was accompanied by theological violence."[150]

6
Slavery

"There never was a civilized nation of any other complexion than white."
—David Hume

"In order to persuade a good moral man to do evil, then, it is not necessary first to persuade him to become evil. It is only necessary to teach him that he is doing good."
—Leonard W. Doob

"The White American could not, even when he wished to, transcend his own values."
—Gary B. Nash and Richard Weiss

"Forgetting one's participation in mass murder is not something passive; it is an active deed."
—Adam Hochschild

Slavery has been a fact of human life in all corners of the globe for virtually all its recorded history. As such, it is decidedly not a specifically Christian phenomenon. Once Christianity emerged as a dominant cultural force in history, however, its relationship to slavery took on a certain reality that can only be found within a Christian cultural context. In Western annals, slavery has been one of the most recognizable forms of human organization. While all legal, political, social, religious, philosophical, educational, cultural, and psychological forces were mustered by the educated elite to justify slavery over many centuries, untold millions of human beings led lives of misery and terribly diminished circumstances and hopes. This is not to say that some slaves did not have a measure of comfort, status, and security in their lives. But the absence of what could be recognized as modern freedoms, as well as simple dignity and human respect, meant that most slaves basically could not achieve full personal fulfillment or the realization of their true human potential.

As with other aspects of the maltreatment of The Other seen throughout this study, slavery in the Christian West eventually developed a large discursive presence and a massive institutional reality that impacted virtually all components of culture and society. At its height in North America, slavery found itself supported by arguments that could appear in virtually any form available to the public: in letters, legal briefs, catechisms intended for the use of slaves, and seminary lectures supporting Bible study,[1] as well as in the many forms of the popular press such as newspapers, magazines, literature, and songs. All is evidence of the view that Christianity came to be a "keystone in the ideological justification of slavery."[2] Christian social ethics emphasizing hierarchical models of social organization were likewise easily accessed by the faithful from scripture, classic writings by Christian leaders, Lutheran and Calvinist catechisms, and modern clerical attacks on the "infidelity" of natural rights theories.[3] The latter is worthy of consideration because it associates anti-slavery views with infidels. Unlike most other areas under investigation in this study, over time there developed a competing set of claims on behalf of the enslaved victims. We know which view eventually triumphed, but this did not occur without a vigorous fight. Disturbing vestiges of original attitudes still exist. One instructive example serves to demonstrate the difficulties faced when counterclaims displeased authorities. A 1573 book by University of Mexico law professor Bartolomé de Albornoz offered a "radical attack" on Negro slavery. The book, *De la Eclavitud*, is now difficult to locate, and not merely because of its age. Eventually, the Holy Office placed it on its Index; that is, the Inquisition censored the book.[4]

Furthermore, as discussed, cognitive dissonance emerged from Christianity's message of love and peace versus the reality of brutal Christian practices in the service of sacred violence. A similar level of dissonance exists between this religion's views of the brotherhood of man and human dignity versus its claims and practices involving humans not deemed to have legitimate access to the highest ideals claimed. Without that access, other roles and places were assigned to these people in the Christian scheme of things. Late in the history of slavery, for instance, the Church of England came to the position that there was no inconsistency between Christianity and slavery,[5] a view certainly ratified by many centuries of practicing the theology of slavery. John Locke believed that slavery could be justified because it lay outside the social contract; in this regard, slavery was akin to war.[6] Furthermore, we must not forget that a victim-centered description of the problem tends to diminish the focus on the perpetrators and the bystanders, which, in the case of slavery, was perhaps the most massive phenomenon and grouping of those under scrutiny. It is important to remember that slavery, as it developed to its greatest extent, touched on all elements of human life. It involved large numbers of people directly, and virtually everyone indirectly. The products of slavery included the food people ate, the jewelry with which they adorned themselves, and the very clothes they wore.

The full genius of Western Christianity applied itself to the subject of slavery. St. Augustine believed that slavery was both a punishment for and a remedy of sin.[7] St. Thomas Aquinas, for instance, bridges my concerns in his magisterial *Summa Theologica* when he noted that Jews were destined for "perpetual slavery" as a penalty that legally entitled "sovereigns of states" to "treat their [i.e., the Jews'] goods as their own property."[8] Herein, we see the convergence of several important streams, including Christianity's self-declared principle of dominion, and its concerns with Jews as the Disconfirming Other, their status as free or enslaved, the legal status of their personal property, and the rights of state sovereigns to dispose of that property. We can wonder if Hitler's Nazi legal theoreticians were aware of this document's historical precedents for their own projects and designs involving the Jews under their control. Jewish women and children in fifteenth-century Spain accordingly found themselves being sold into slavery; Jews leaving Spain became the crown's slaves.[9] Ultimately, the widespread trade in human slaves presupposes "a general accord ... between the church, the state, the nobility and public opinion."[10] In 1436, Pope Eugene IV offered his papal blessings in support of Portuguese slavery.[11] Pope Nicholas V added considerable impetus to events that would emerge shortly after his death in 1455 when he "legitimized slaving expeditions anywhere."[12]

Orlando Patterson, in his magnificent *Slavery and Social Death*, makes a connection to this matter of dominion. Keeping in mind the cultural importance of Christian claims of dominion, Patterson notes that in the third-century B.C.E. *dominus* meant slavemaster. Later, *dominium* came to mean absolute ownership.[13] We find echoes of these lexical concerns in later papal pronouncements and attitudes toward The Other. Patterson points out that in the project of exercising authority, those who seek to use power "must first control ... appropriate symbolic instruments."[14] In the Christian world, there is no greater appropriate symbolic instrument than the Bible. Those who control its interpretation are strategically placed to use it as a weapon of sacred violence against The Other, who may not even know of the Bible, or who may have different interpretations of it entirely. In the case of slavery after the emergence of Christianity as an integral part of the Roman Empire, Christian interpretation of scripture became "the most important source for establishing the morality of slavery."[15] It is equally important to realize the synergistic relationship of slavery to the symbolic instruments: "the slave experience was a major source of the metaphors that informed the symbolic structure of Christianity."[16] With this observation, we are better able to understand the degree to which slavery interpenetrated the culture of Christianity, thereby contributing to the theology of slavery. Furthermore, as William A. Clebsch observes, in slavery we find the "attitudinal cousin of genocide ... and the earliest intuition of blood—or gene—superiority is the parent of both." From Clebsch's perspective, the transition from the world of slavery to genocide is not difficult to traverse.[17]

It would seem that the rise of the new religion might have provided a paradigm shift for Roman slaves, who were, from the Roman legal viewpoint, not deemed to be fully human.[18] Although Christianity claimed to be inclusive in its eagerness to embrace new souls to be won for the glory of its God, it basically left Roman practices unaltered. Thus the religion left for itself a haunting problem, the matter of humans suffering the immiseration of enslavement and social death on this earth as the devotees of the religion all the while were honoring and worshipping a God who allegedly saw no distinctions between and among his human creations. In the mid-fifth century, Pope Leo the Great refused to have former slaves serve the Christian God as priests.[19] The irony includes a medieval church council mandating that a parish had to have one hundred slaves in residence before a parish priest could be assigned. Despite the Church claims about the equality of souls before the eyes of God, former slaves found it a difficult matter to become priests, monks, and nuns.[20] Eventually, this would manifest in the American dilemma of the treatment of Christianized Negro slaves. By then, according to George Kelsey, modern Christianity and Christian civilization both had "domesticated racism so thoroughly that most Christians [stood] too close to assess it properly."[21] Thus Christianity and its major interpreters, from "St. Paul through Martin Luther to Cotton Mather and Bishop Asbury ... had to grapple with the profound revolutionary implications of [the religion's] doctrines. Social stability always depended upon maintenance of rigid distinction between two spheres, a distinction which rationalized the equality of souls with the inequality of persons."[22] To alleviate the dissonance, Christians could always avoid the distinction simply by declaring some element of The Other not to be human, that is, lacking a soul, and thus not subject to the circle of moral obligation usually honored by believers. Many plantation owners, for instance, saw slaves as lacking souls.[23] Richard H. Popkin notes that the prevailing "true idea of humanity" was only to be gained by those who lived in the geographical locations between the Caucasus Mountains and Paris.[24] In the 1550s, Richard Eden considered Negroes and Moors "a people of beastly lyvynge, without a god, religion, or common wealth."[25] Edward Long thought Negroes were "a brutish, ignorant, idle, crafty, treacherous, bloody, thievish, mistrustful, and superstitious people," a separate species vastly inferior to humans.[26] In a 1693 case in England, Negroes were defined as "merchandise and compared with musk cats and monkeys."[27] Thomas Jefferson, even though sexually involved over a period of some years with one of his domestic slaves, found that "blacks, whether originally a distinct race, or made distinct by time and circumstances, are inferior to whites in the endowment of body and mind."[28] This particular pattern of dehumanization emerges time and time again.

Christianity's cultural template, originally set for use against Jews, was alive, well, and active. Winthrop Jordan observes that Christians were "sufficiently acquainted with the concept of heathenism that they confronted its living representatives without puzzlement."[29] As James Walvin points out, the racist images of blacks and the theology of slavery rested upon preexisting cultural attitudes.[30] Betty Wood, in her study of slavery, notes, "By the sixteenth century the link between the lack of Christianity and eligibility for enslavement had long been in place."[31] She finds that slavery was a state established for occupation by strangers and outsiders, based essentially on the victims' religious identity rather than other considerations.[32] Accordingly, both Africans and the indigenous people of the New World were quickly identified by Christian Europeans as "heathen brutes."[33] Christian Europeans were predisposed, according to

Walvin, to see Africans as culturally different.[34] For the dominant Christians, "Biblicism, fundamentalism, and social piety were learned traits that cropped up in the same process that gave rise to proslavery ideology."[35] Spiritual status in a lawsuit led a Negro youngster in 1694 to be returned to his owner "because he was a heathen."[36] Once Christian perceptions based on these factors lodged in the cultural matrix, as the Jews knew all too well, the process of making victims was well under way. The end result was a new iteration of a "hierarchical, organic, social ideology" that produced a more or less predictable "comprehensive outlook ... a coherent ideology"[37] that would prove to be lethal for millions of slaves.

The nexus point between Christianity's belief structure and issues involving slavery is the Christian concept of sin.[38] Proslavery Christian thinkers traced the establishment of slavery to the Garden of Eden, when mankind fell from grace through the sin of Adam and Eve. Subsequently a male-dominated hierarchy, man over woman, was created.[39] Living in a fallen world, humans can expect to live within imperfect social arrangements. A powerful rationale within the theology of slavery is that God nowhere proscribes the practice in the scriptures. Indeed, there are numerous biblical references to masters and slaves with no opprobrium attached. Over time, the Church itself came to hold slaves. It is especially significant that its theological and pastoral representatives, Spanish and Portuguese priests in the New World and, later, Congregationalists in New England and Jesuits in Maryland, held large number of slaves. Institutional slave grants were awarded to monasteries and convents.[40] Mission boards and the missionaries used slaves to help build missions.[41] Although the practice of direct involvement in slavery appears to fly in the face of papal proclamations and a later declaration by the Church that slaveholding was a sin, the history of the Church's moral compromises perhaps obviated its own influence upon its agents. Believing hierarchy to be a "natural" human and social phenomenon for the organization of society, slavery is deemed an unavoidable feature of human life. Thinking this way, slavery replicates such recognizable, "natural" patterns as the hierarchy found within the family, with the male at the head, as well as the natural leaders taking charge on behalf of the natural followers as is seen in the military or within government, with kings ruling over the masses. Of course, doubting any of these arrangements is an act of infidelity, a sin, because it defies the very structure of the world as created by God and thus could lead to disaster and anarchy. The proslavery writers went further, however. Stith Mead, writing in the 1790s, argued that "familiar, and unequal, domestic relations" such as slavery and wives submitting to husbands fulfill "the law of Christ."[42]

Another important scriptural consideration for the proslavery position is found in Genesis 9:18–27. Eventually known as the Hamitic argument, Noah's curse upon Ham allegedly explains the existence of races on earth. Negroes supposedly descended as Ham's accursed progeny, and the Other races from Noah's other sons, creating the situation in which claims of polygenesis furthered the cause and support of slavery.[43] This form of racialism proved to be "the foundation of Christianity's universalism."[44] Furthermore, Ham's enslavement "accorded with God's will for the advancement of civilization."[45] Apparently, an important cultural part of that plan for the advancement of civilization was the existence of chattel slavery.[46] It is somewhat difficult, however, to see precisely how an impressive cultural edifice could ever sustain itself based, as it was, on slavery and all that this institution entailed. The proslavery argument would, nevertheless, find that the hierarchical arrangement of master and slave replicated God's design and that the underling's unquestioning obedience is the model behavior. A proslavery advocate, physician Samuel Cartwright, argued that it is against God's decree to raise Negroes above their state in life to equal that of whites, an act that abuses God-given power over inferiors.[47] Racist restatements of the Christian doctrine of dominion abound. Solace and comfort are found in the admonition in I Timothy 6:1–2, for slaves to obey their masters: "Let slaves who are under the yoke account their masters deserving of all honor .... Teach and exhort these things." Reverend Fred A. Ross, citing this passage from Timothy, claimed that arguments on behalf of the abolition of slavery are "destitute of the truth."[48] Reverend Thomas Bacon developed this message to the point where he echoes Luther's demands to obey authority: slaves must obey their owners because their "Masters and Mistresses are God's overseers."[49]

Proslavery advocates almost always cited the fact that the patriarch Abraham owned slaves, using Genesis 14:14, 17:27, 20:14, and 24:34–35. Ross, who had completed his Divinity studies before becoming deeply embroiled in articulating the proslavery argument in the 1850s, discussed Abraham's slaves and then added that one of God's angels sent back to the rightful owner the fugitive slave, Hagar.[50] He also argued that "God's command *made it right* for Moses to destroy the Midianites and make slaves of their daughters.... [for] a thing is right ... because God makes it right."[51] Proslavery writers also cited Leviticus 25:44 and 46 to support their cause.

In sum, God created all these differences between people; efforts toward achieving equality will only serve to "invert the Order that God had set."[52] In other words: Know thy place. As the vice president of the Confederate States of America, Alexander Stephens, proclaimed, "until Christianity is overthrown ... the relation between master and slave can never be regarded as an offense against the Divine Laws."[53] Educated as a lawyer, and elected eight times to serve Georgia in Congress, Stephens may be presumed to have known something about laws.

Reverend Fred A. Ross offers a religious perspective. "*Sin is the transgression of the law, and where there is no law there is no sin.* As a mental state, it is self-will, not submitting to God's will."[54] His viewpoint is based on a hierarchical set of values. Ross continues, "*Shall man submit to the revealed will of God, or to his own will?*"[55] Note the reliance upon powerful others, in this case God, and a total reliance upon scripture as revealed. Being a stance based on a Christian truth claim, there is precious little room for any reassessment of the position.

Ross continues, virtually removing human agency as a factor. "*[C]onformity* to that law [is] *right*, and *non-conformity* [is] *wrong*. Why? Simply because [God] saw it to be *good*, and *made it to be RIGHT*." He also states, "Man, then, having this revelation, is under obligation ever to believe every jot and tittle of that WORD" and "REVELATION ... does fix forever the foundation of man's moral obligation in the benevolence of God."[56] Reginald Horsman's *Race and Manifest Destiny* adds a nineteenth-century view that it is God who directs the extermination of races, which is "all right because it is necessary."[57]

The theology of slavery, while not unrelated to the theology of violence and sacred violence, matured into the experience of America. Castilian slave laws harkened to the past, eleven centuries earlier, their authors basing the laws on Justinian's Roman laws regarding slavery.[58] Later, Reverend Devereaux Jarratt argued that "inhuman conduct does not condemn an institution or a social relation as unchristian." For Jarratt, "As fallen and corrupt beings, humans could not avoid sin." Jarratt sees that "slavery had always received divine approval and thus could not be inherently evil."[59]

St. Paul had perhaps anticipated the "inhuman conduct" that tugged at Jarratt's conscience. The good saint had advice for slaves facing the expected brutality: acquiesce.[60] A Jesuit priest, Antonio Vieira, echoed St. Paul's position. He held that "slaves, while free in soul and equal before God, should acquiesce in their external fate." Vieira actually told slaves to bear their sufferings with patience as a form of martyrdom, and to not shirk their duty.[61] The Elizabethan William Gouge—educated at Eton and Cambridge, the minister of Blackfriars Church in London for nearly half a century, and an outspoken advocate for Just War—argues that slaves must even "acquiesce in unjust beatings."[62] Such stated positions reflect the view that Christianity promoted social control and prevented rebellion, especially in the forms of obedience and docility.[63] The supreme law of religion, according to one source, is obedience to the master.[64] Such attitudes clearly reflect the emphasis placed by Christianity on the "principles of order and duty."[65] Although seeming to run counter to the notion that this religion blazed a revolutionary trail, it is more likely that the same kind of compromises seen earlier with regard to war and military service also came to function again in regard to issues of social organization.

St. Paul and others advised acquiescence. An Irish Jesuit, visiting twelve thousand acres owned by the Maryland Jesuits that was worked by slaves from 1711 until 1838,[66] was appalled to see pregnant female slaves being whipped.[67] One of the Jesuit brothers, Joseph Mobberly, believed that the slaves were granted too many freedoms. He called for even more whippings.[68] Visitors found the dwellings for the Jesuit slaves "almost universally unfit for human beings to live in."[69] The slaves under Jesuit oversight (God's overseers, perhaps?) were provided $1\frac{1}{4}$ pounds of meat per week[70] despite the whippings and extremely hard work. After considerable discussion, it was decided in 1838 that it would be best for the Jesuits to sell the slaves and divest themselves of the operation. European-born Jesuits on the site unanimously opposed the recommended sale because they "imagine the master-slave relationship as an idealized master-serf relationship."[71] Nevertheless, the sale proceeded and the largest single institutional slaveowning operation in the Western hemisphere passed into history.[72]

Is there something unseemly about the highly educated Jesuits whipping defenseless pregnant slaves? Did any moral qualms cross their minds as the terrified women writhed in agony beneath their flails? We may argue with some certainty that these highly devout Christians, like their fellow Christian slaveholders, had massive supporting evidence, both cultural and theological, to assist them in their slaveholding activities. We today may be shocked by the brutal events conducted on this Jesuit property 170 years ago by the elite of the Catholic Church, as perhaps we are similarly shocked to learn of the Jesuit Father Maurice Bévenot's appeal for the assistance of governments in executing infidels in 1967. Is there not cultural significance to the fact that these same Jesuits were the organizational model upon which Heinrich Himmler built his SS empire, complete with its ambitious plans for massive feudal slave labor operations in the Nazi-occupied Slavic east? It is important to remember that these instances directly involved Jesuits, even separated as they are by more than a century. In the former case, slaves bore the curse of the religion's interpretation of the scriptural past and may actually have originally come from a "heathen" background. In the latter case Bévenot had demarcated moral lines of responsibility between the pious faithful charged with seeing that no sin be committed and those modern infidels who would deny the truth claims of the Church. With these startling examples in mind, we can better appreciate Forrest G. Wood's notion that "English North Americans embraced slavery *because* they were Christians, not in spite of it."[73]

Jesuits in Maryland were not alone in their use of violence against hapless slaves they owned. As is likely in the case of the Jesuits, we sadly learn that terribly "evil acts are sometimes committed by individuals who take themselves to have a morally decent character."[74] Devout, faithful involvement in the truth claims, transcendent value system, and system of eternal rewards proffered by Christianity is enough to serve as confirming evidence for most people of the inherent rightness of their acts and beliefs. Furthermore, as Laurence Mordekhai Thomas notes, most people simply assume that legitimate authority is right,[75] a thought that echoes Luther's demands as well as a mild version of typical Nuremberg defense claims. Thomas is thus not surprised to find that one member of the Stanley Milgram experimental group was an Ivy League Divinity school faculty member, who had no qualms about the appropriateness of what Milgram had the group doing.[76] Fred Ross and Devereaux Jarratt, vocal supporters of slavery, along with German theologians such as Gerhard Kittell and Paul Althaus, supporters of the Nazi regime, found themselves mired far more deeply in morally compromising positions in their respective eras than the Ivy League theologian in Milgram's experiment. As ministers and theologians, advocates of slavery and the Nazi regime alike were often removed from the horrible physical acts (unlike the Jesuits in Maryland) of violence perpetrated against Other victims. Distance, however, does not serve to reduce their culpability. Their support helped provide the necessary layers of cultural insulation for those entrusted with the actual physical violence.

As previously discussed, the Spanish butcher shop that sold human body parts for canine consumption is one example of sacred violence. The Spanish also intimidated their slaves by cutting off noses, branding foreheads, and cutting off ears or limbs. Such typical brutal acts served to nurture and sustain slavery.[77] Arguments used by Sepulveda to counter those of Las Casas in 1551, for example, that it is permissible to use violence to bring the indigenous to the bosom of the Church, were later used to help justify the enslavement of Africans.[78] Of course, the Spanish had no monopoly on the use of violence with those unfortunates who fell under their control. In London nearly two hundred years after the Las Casas and Sepulveda debate, the Society for the Propagation of the Gospel in 1732 was advised to try to help stop the practice of branding the word "society" on slaves' chests.[79] The litany of violence, both physical and structural, committed against African slaves is endless: floggings, confinement in chains, shootings, hangings, legal restrictions, rapes, mutilations, the destruction of families, psychological terror, and amputations.

The violence that beset Negroes throughout the period of slavery in the New World had its own counterparts in Africa itself, even after slavery had formally ended as a legal practice in the Americas. While not formally using slavery as a system, forced labor was used instead. Although a fine distinction, it was nevertheless supported through the usual cultural explanations and incentives. Belgians in the Congo in the late nineteenth century cut off hands, noses, ears, and feet to "motivate" the Congolese to meet periodic rubber quotas.[80] Adam Hochschild's account of the brutality in the Congo contains the account and photograph of a destitute Congolese father, Nsala of the Wala district. He disturbed the completion of a breakfast for Europeans when he appeared in tears on their veranda holding the foot and hand of his five-year-old daughter, Boali.[81] She had been mutilated as punishment for failing to meet her quota. Hochschild describes the piles of hands and feet, as well as decapitations and various mutilations, that observers noted on their travels through Leopold's African kingdom.[82] The Black American historian, George Washington Williams, after seeing these conditions, claimed all this was a crime against humanity.[83]

The brutality witnessed by Williams was not confined to the nineteenth century. In 1920, 26,579 lashes were administered to Congolese workers and recorded by their overseers, eight lashes per full-time worker.[84] Someone had to handle these whips; someone had to write down for posterity the results. The twentieth century is not unfamiliar with the exquisite accounting of mass suffering and inhumanity inflicted against The Other in the service of some higher European cause. Written by the conquerors, a 1959 textbook for Congolese soldiers paid high compliments to the Belgians who had "brilliantly completed the most humanitarian campaign of the century."[85] One overseer, Léon Fiévez, who had decapitated one hundred natives as a motivational tactic, claimed that he had done it as a humane gesture, saving five hundred lives in the process.[86] As atrocities mounted and the natives sought relief from any source available, one British missionary was approached by a Congolese. He asked, "Has the Savior you tell us of any power to save us from the rubber trouble?"[87] No salvation from rubber is on the official record, but Hochschild does note that 80 percent of the uranium needed for the atomic bombs deployed against Japan in 1945 came from a single mine in the Congo; the mine's workers had their annual days of forced work increased to 120.[88]

Africans displaced into the New World were faced with incredible institutional prejudices. Perhaps we should not be surprised to learn that the first edition of the *Encyclopedia Britannica* published in North America, in 1798, contained the following entry for Negroes: "flat nose, thick lips ... ugliness.... Vices the most notorious seem to be the portion of this unhappy race; idleness, treachery, revenge, cruelty, impudence, stealing, lying, profanity, debauchery, nastiness, and intemperance ... strangers to the very sentiment of compassion ... an awful example of man when left to himself." A century later, the invective had not changed measurably.[89] Once again, we see the educated elite contributing to the dominant culture's discourse about The Other. The editors and writers most likely had attended colleges available to Americans of the time; these educational institutions had tightly woven ties to the various wings and sects of Christianity. Situated at the center of the culture's discourse, they well represented its attitudes and dominant values. One wonders if the thought ever crossed their minds, individually or collectively, that the charges being leveled against the Negroes derived largely from the actual practices of the white European Christians who had devastated the lives and hopes of the people they enslaved as well as those they left behind. Did these editors and writers encounter any of theological and moral dissonance? Or, were they simply confirmed in their views by the massive weight of the culture's perceptions and dictates?

The dissonance between social ideals and proslavery claims had its counterpart outside the realm of theological matters, notably with regards to the basic revolutionary documents of America's break from Britain. Discussing the American Declaration of Independence, Fred A. Ross states, "God gives no sanction to the affirmation that he has *created all men equal;* that this is *self-evident,* and that he has given them *unalienable rights;* that he has made government to *derive its power solely from their consent,* and that he has given them *the right to change that government in their mere pleasure.* All this—every word of it, every jot and tittle—is the liberty and equality claimed by infidelity."[90] Ross reiterates his basic point: "*This is the affirmation of liberty claimed by infidelity.*" He next calls this passage in the Declaration of Independence "an *execrescence* on the tree of our liberty."[91] In such rhetoric we see once again that a claim of freedom entails allegations of infidelity, a clear outgrowth of the Christian demand for obedience and hierarchy. We can also see here how difficult it must have been for proslavery advocates to have seen such arguments rendered null and void when the Union triumphed over the Confederacy in 1865. An entire worldview, an ideology of human dominion that had stood for nearly twenty centuries, was subverted in the North's victory. It once again raises the difficulty of sorting out the sane from the insane, the moral from the immoral, the humane from the inhumane, and also the significance of theological contributions to inhumane social practices.

These considerations suggest the serious implications associated with eisegetics (reading into) as opposed to exegetics (reading from). In some ways, this has been at issue throughout this study. Given the idea that scriptural interpretations constitute the symbolic center of the dominant religion and the complex power dynamics of who gets to control that symbolic center, the controversies surrounding the problem of slavery make eisegetics a concern of tremendous importance, perhaps a paradigm of the larger issues involving the religion, the culture, and those who live within that culture acting as bystanders or perpetrators. Were proslavery partisans such as Ross executing an "incorrect" reading of the Declaration of Independence? If so, what had to change in the basic theology and culture to render interpretations incorrect? A very strong case could be made that Ross was reading the declaration and rejecting it from within the context of a discursive social history and a culture that had helped inform the shape of Christian ideology for centuries. Slavery had not been illegal in the Christian West over the period of the religion's dominance, in North America in 1776, nor at the time during which Ross was writing, and, indeed, some of the framers and signers of the Declaration of Independence owned slaves. Highly charged and very public battles had been fought through the American political and legal systems, and elsewhere, over decades. The controversy was not unrepresented in the deliberations of the various sects and wings of Christianity. Only the Quakers expelled members who held slaves.[92] On the contrary, we have seen the Catholic Church as deeply involved in slaveowning and popes taking positions on both sides of the issue. Orlando Patterson finds that the Catholic Church declared slavery to be a sin even though it was one of the largest slaveholders.[93] The Catholic Church in the South offered biblical support for slavery. Catholic bishops were quick to give their blessings to Confederate regiments as they departed for the war, and gave general aid to secessionist fortunes, including a southern bishop working toward papal diplomatic intercession.[94] Methodists in 1784 demanded that believers free their slaves, but this position became the target of widespread disagreement and it was withdrawn. In 1785, Baptists found "hereditary slavery to be contrary to the word of God" but popular discontent once again overturned this position.[95] Marcus Jernegan records an instance of a Presbyterian congregation being given a slave as an endowment,[96] apparently widely practiced. John Hughes, whose prominence within the Catholic Church led to his becoming the archbishop of New York, was "an unblinking enemy of abolition."[97] In sum, one could be a good Christian while being fully supportive of slavery for the entire history of slavery as it was practiced in the New World.

All these instances demonstrate James Walvin's assertion that so few criticized slavery because so many benefited from it.[98] Such had been the case throughout the history of Western Christianity, a fact that helps explain the theological dissonance within Christianity as well as the involvement of both the religion and its adherents in both roles of perpetrating and bystanding. With regard to this latter point, it must be kept in mind that the perpetrators and bystanders represented a huge number of people in Western European Christianity and in the New World. As in Nazi Germany, virtually all levels of society and the economy were involved in supporting the prevailing inhumane practices. Government officials; those in the legal profession, the military, and the churches; educators; people in commercial and agrarian enterprises; and consumers all performed functions that helped support the institution of slavery.

7

The Holocaust

"It never occurred to us to doubt the order of things."
—Albert Speer

Christianity provided the "model for the plan of exterminating the Jews."
—Hyam Maccoby

"The equal toleration of all religions ... is the same thing as atheism."
—Pope Leo XIII

It remains to be seen whether this long litany of sacred violence conceptualized and implemented by Christianity against The Other was instrumental during the Shoah. I believe that a very strong case may be made that there is a definite line of intent running from the late fourth century until the twentieth century in which there are very clear indications that institutional Christianity was quite willing to exercise all the considerable power at its command to change ("convert") or destroy The Other whenever and wherever encountered. Indeed, in *The Jew in Christian Theology*, Gerhard Falk argues that Christianity very early developed the notion that Jews did not have the right to exist.[1] This was simultaneously accompanied by the notion that Jews and their suffering were necessary as proof of their sins against God as well as of the triumph of Christianity. The instances of Christianity's various encounters with a wide variety of Others are too many to enumerate, but suffice it to say that the representatives of Christianity quickly developed a general approach to the experience that was somewhat uniformly implemented in each case. The ideology for this was created in theological terms. The agents of the Church—popes, cardinals, bishops, priests, inquisitors, teachers, and Protestant clerics and other leaders later in history—often carried out the actions. But the ideology was delivered to the masses of the faithful in countless documents and declarations of the Christian churches, helping to create a discursive universe and contribute to the larger culture with enormous implications for The Others through the centuries. Frederic Cople Jaher notes the widespread transmission of anti-Jewish images in the Middle Ages through a complex discursive interplay, including "religious propaganda by sermons, treatises, canons, dogma, and liturgy; in folklore by ballads, tales, legends, incantations, charms, jokes, passion and miracle plays, and carnival sketches; for the more intellectual audience in chronicles and pamphlets; through such literary devices as satire, scatology, and ridicule, ... in sacred and secular art and sculpture ... church sculpture, iconography, painting, stained glass windows, illuminated manuscripts, prayer books, hymnals, Bibles, woodcuts, and monuments on bridges, city halls, and public squares."[2] Egon Schwartz also offers a perspective that provides substantial support for the culture studies approach:

In its claim to both secular power and a monopoly on salvation, the Catholic Church manipulated the ignorant masses, instigating plundering and mass murder. It staged burnings at the stake, forced baptism, and mass expulsions, passed special laws and humiliating dress codes, and ordered the exclusion of Jews from respectable occupations and their incarceration in ghettos .... Papal bulls, anti-Jewish sermons, polemic treatises, inflammatory pamphlets, literary and pictorial caricatures poured out the poison and hatred and derision into the masses, laying the foundations for a bias that made possible the pogroms of the nineteenth century and the mass exterminations of the twentieth century.[3]

Based on an all-encompassing cultural presence, it would have been difficult to find any believing Christian adult during these sixteen centuries who was not quite aware of "the difference" between a Christian and a Jew, whether or not that Christian had ever met a Jew in person and developed enough of a relationship to share in a dialogic manner. Such awareness could rather easily be translated into a wide variety of actions against the Jews. Those not in a position to exercise a hatred of Jews directly against them in violent ways had very few incentives to come to their aid when violence and repression struck Jews. That is to say, Christian bystanders constitute a very large majority of the human behaviors during those sixteen centuries, an excellent example of moral indifference being enabled by the dominant culture. Gerhard Falk states that hatred of Jews became state policy throughout Europe.[4] A study of the Holocaust argues, "genocide [was] conceived, supported and technologically perfected by Christians."[5] Victoria Barnett argues that the "moral permission" to murder Jews "had been given at another level of society."[6] Norbert Elias, in *The Germans*, reviews the historical record and concludes that the Nazi decision to exterminate the Jews "may appear to have been predictable."[7] It is not surprising to learn that the largest massacres of Jews during the Middle Ages took place in Germany, including the slaughter of converts during the Black Death.[8] Even without the plague to motivate them, when there were no Jews readily available to slaughter, Léon Poliakov points out, Germans in the Middle Ages would hunt down and kill Jewish converts to Christianity. In addition, Poliakov also notes that the first charges of ritual murder and profanation of the Host appeared in Germany in 1146.[9]

In her study of bystanders, Barnett asks a highly pertinent question of great importance: "Why do disrespect and indifference contribute to something far more malignant?"[10] There is no doubt that modern sensibilities are shocked by the events and supporting behaviors during the Holocaust. The malignancy of the perpetrators has been recounted in endless, horrifying detail and is easily perceived. In a certain way, Barnett's question is one that would not have been asked with such urgency in earlier centuries. It would seem that conditions have changed. What would make humans more aware of disrespect, indifference, and the resulting inhumanity? Slavery and dueling were both legal and widely accepted in 1800 in the Western world; both were largely relics one century later. Many social, theological, and legal factors contributed to the changes in thinking. Yet we see that anti-Semitism persisted and flourished in the twentieth century. Barnett's question recalls earlier discussions: How are small acts of racism and hatred conducive to mass atrocities, how do the small yet vicious flames lead to the all-consuming conflagration? Small, individual acts are empowered to a large extent by larger surrounding forces, such as the prevailing culture, social attitudes, ideology, and discursive realities. They are symptomatic of deeper concerns; they do not exist in isolation. They require fertile ground in which to germinate. Disrespect and indifference indicate the presence of a larger malignancy. In the cases studied, malignancy emanates from one of the central, most significant institutions in the shared human experience of Western Europeans. If the dominant religion, supported by its truth claims, makes a declaration about the spiritual worthlessness of an entire group of humans, recapitulates that message countless times, rewards those who support its claims, and acts accordingly against the interests of the anathematized group, it would be unusual for most of the religion's devout believers to create a private, personal meaning construct for their human relationships that deviates significantly from the religion's fundamental pronouncements.

A truism in Holocaust studies is that the Nazis did not "invent" anything, that they built upon the practices of the past. There were countless prefigurings for them to draw from. For instance, Moshe Herr notes that the Romans thought Jews sought to conquer the world.[11] Rosemary Reuther identifies early Christianity as the original architect of the ghettos[12] that came to mark much of Jewish existence from an early Christian period. Popes Pius IV and V, in the middle of the sixteenth century, ordered ghettos extended across all of Europe; this condition existed until Napoleon's reign.[13] The Council of Narbonne in 1235 forced Jews to wear an identifying yellow patch on their clothing.[14] Judenrate existed as early as the Middle Ages in Germany.[15] Endless accounts exist of popular uprisings and state-sponsored pogroms against Jews, not to mention the more highly organized forms of violence such as the crusades and the Inquisition. We have recounted the myriad legal devices, wrought by Christianity and leading Christians, used against Jews from the Roman period until most recent times. The most advanced forms of technology and weaponry within each period under consideration have been unleashed against Jews as sacred violence and devastated their lives. A Christian-inspired discourse of extermination developed from the religion's foundational documents and the works of the most sophisticated theologians to enable and sustain the ongoing sacred violence. The basest means of dehumanization targeted Jews in the vilest ways. The dominant religion, in both its Protestant and Catholic forms, allied with state power to bring immense pressure to bear against Jews in the most private aspects of their lives. Large numbers of the faithful were involved as the institutional arms of church, state, and municipal authorities moved inexorably to ravage the lives, possessions, hopes, and the futures of the Disconfirming Other.

Robert Jay Lifton argues that the Nazis thus built upon a "universal phenomenon."[16] If so, then we are justified in seeking to examine the genesis of this universal phenomenon. It may be said to have started with the possibility, articulated by Irvin J. Borowsky, who heads the American Interfaith Institute, that the "New Testament has led to the murder of one out of two Jews in history, all based on the idea that Jews killed Jesus."[17] We cannot operate under the illusion that contemporary Christians and the religion they serve will readily agree to these assertions. Norbert Elias makes the point that religious "creeds or principles" that are "absolute, unyielding, unalterable" cannot easily be challenged "in the light of new experiences or reasoned argument."[18] That insight strikes me as valid for the humans and their beliefs over the centuries as well as for people today. Personally experiencing the disbelief and conceptual rejections of the views contained in this study, I am not insensitive to what is at stake here. Victoria Barnett discusses the role of group psychology in the Holocaust. She finds that the boundaries of the individual self become weakened under the onslaught of group pressures. The "I" becomes embedded, enveloped, and defined by the "We."[19] Under these circumstances, ordinary humans can become deeply involved in atrocity, "simply doing their jobs, and without any particular hostility."[20] I add that they may just as easily become apologists for the cultural situation in which they find themselves, even if that means they must somehow account for the culture's involvement in atrocities such as genocide. Not unusual, Barnett's insight has been articulated in many ways over the years. It is a phenomenon not isolated to the Shoah, although it seems to have achieved an apotheosis of sorts there. It was also exquisitely recorded in ways not available to humans in other eras. We must wonder, then, whether this erosion of self was qualitatively different for those living under the Third Reich than for those who heeded the hate-filled words of Chrysostom in the fifth century C.E., or those who devoted themselves wholly and faithfully to crusading, or those who served the interests, directly or indirectly, of the Inquisition. Obviously, people living in the past did not live under the kind of a propaganda regime that the Nazis created. Nevertheless, there were terribly powerful forces operating within the culture that contributed to the formation of both group and personal identities. Because the dominant religion is able to call forth a complex set of incentives involving the condition of one's soul for all eternity, there existed potent inducements for believers that are difficult for a state to match for sheer efficacy. In Barnett's view, humans face the pressure to conform that already exists within the social system. Coercion is not typically needed because there is an evolution within the group of its beliefs, values, and aims.[21] Indeed, Allan Fenigstein, following the work of Holocaust survivor Henri Tajfel, finds that people will manifest a group mentality without the need for the usual inducements; "simply imposing a shared membership category" can create the conditions needed for the formation of a group mentality,[22] which can then operate violently, if need be, against The Other. When the "I" becomes a "We," there is a loss, to be sure, but the loss is compensated for by the addition or creation of a new identity, one largely informed by the dominant group. The new "I" then behaves according to the accepted patterns of behavior or thought favored by the dominant group.[23]

James C. Russell, in *The Germanization of Early Medieval Christianity*, touches on matters that have a certain bearing on this study's subject. He notes that Christian vernacular, following the religion's contact with German pagans, subsequently made "considerable use of the terms of pagan warfare" and that the papacy eagerly supported "warfare to spread Christianity and convert the heathen."[24] We can see an intriguing interplay between the religion and a certain spirit of violence, but it is perhaps more important that Christianity was already a fertile locus for martial matters and influence, and thus it is not shocking to find a papal benediction for spiritual warfare. The implications extend to the crusades; Russell notes that for the crusaders "war was ... a form of moral action, a higher type of life than was peace. All of this stood at the opposite pole from Christian morality."[25] I tend to disagree with Russell's latter point: Christian morality is most certainly not isolated to a pacific morality, much of its rhetoric notwithstanding. As discussed, there is a long history of strong military influence following the fourth century.

Gerhard Falk finds Martin Luther to be a precursor of Nazi bloodshed and "the supporter of religious hate such as the Christian world had not seen before." The Shoah was the "direct outcome of Luther's teaching" with it being possible to "trace a linear connection" from Luther to Adolf Hitler. Goethe, for instance, declared that Germans were initially shaped into a Volk through Luther.[26] Falk supports his contention by noting that Julius Streicher used Luther as a key part of his Nuremberg defense.[27] Léon Poliakov's earlier work on anti-Semitism supports Falk's point: with his status as a national prophet, and his notion of unconditional obedience to the authority of the state, Luther helped lead directly to Hitler and the Holocaust.[28] Jaime Contreras, a scholar of the Inquisition, notes that one of the results of Luther's ideas and influence was the "necessity of the repression of intellectual and religious dissent."[29] Herein we find a specific argument with important implications for the matter of the ideological critique that typically has not been activated in many of the instances examined in this study. How ironic that Martin Luther, one of the chief leaders in the Protestant Reformation's challenge of Rome, would serve as a key figure in Germany's failure to develop a meaningful religious and ideological challenge to the genocidal "sacred violence" practiced by the Nazis and their helpers.

Luther's relationship to the Jews serves as a central point of concern for later developments. Certainly, his eventual rejection of Jews, with all of its incredible ugliness, did not spring from nowhere. His position had origins from more than one thousand years earlier. He seems to have brought much of the earlier menacing rhetoric into an even sharper focus. His rise to prominence in German and world affairs makes his contributions to later historical events extremely problematic and sobering. For instance, Luther's "The Jews and Their Lies" discloses several important cultural streams of thought:

What then shall we Christians do with this damned, rejected race of Jews? Since they live among us and we know about their lying and blasphemy and cursing, we cannot tolerate them if we do not wish to share in their lies, curses, and blasphemy. In this way we cannot quench the inextinguishable fire of divine rage (as the prophets say) nor convert the Jews. We must prayerfully and reverentially practice a merciful severity. Perhaps we may save a few from the fire and the flames. We must not seek vengeance. They are surely being punished a thousand times more than we might wish them. Let me give you my honest advice.

First, their synagogues or churches should be set on fire, and whatever does not burn should be covered or spread over with dirt so that no one may ever be able to see a cinder or stone of it. And this ought to be done for the honor of God and of Christianity, in order that God may see that we are Christians, and that we have not wittingly tolerated or approved of such public lying, cursing, and blaspheming of His Son and His Christians ....

Secondly, their homes should likewise be broken down and destroyed. For they perpetrate the same things there that they do in their synagogues ....

Thirdly, they should be deprived of their prayer-books and Talmuds, in which idolatry, lies, cursing, and blasphemy are taught.

Fourthly, their rabbis must be forbidden under threat of death to teach any more ....

Fifthly, passport and traveling privileges should be absolutely forbidden to the Jews. For they have no business in the rural districts .... Let them stay at home .... You ought not, you cannot protect them, unless in the eyes of God you want to share all their abomination ....

Sixthly, they ought to be stopped from usury. All their cash and valuables of silver and gold ought to be taken from them and put aside for safe keeping .... [E]verything that they possess they stole and robbed from us through their usury ....

Seventhly, let the young and strong Jews and Jewesses be given the flail, the ax, the hoe, the spade, the distaff, and spindle; and let them earn their bread by the sweat of their noses .... [L]et us drive them out of the country for all time. For, as has been said, God's rage is so great against them that they only become worse and worse through mild mercy, and not much better through severe mercy. Therefore, away with them .... [I]f this advice of mine does not suit you, then find a better one so that you and we may all be free of this insufferable devilish burden—the Jews.[30]

Obviously, Luther's invective in "The Jews and Their Lies" reflects and brings together several items of concern. The clear nexus point is that Luther sees the "race" of Jews as damned, utterly beyond the grace of the God of Christians. Jews had been seen as a race by Christians long before Luther, and race is a concept that has taken on somewhat different meanings over the centuries. But having one of the chief religious leaders in German history and culture using a term that would have such murderous developments in the twentieth century is one of those

seemingly small, insignificant points that we might think would be of little consequence. Indeed, we may never know about any possible consequence, at least
not in any empirically or statistically verifiable way. But we do know that Luther's
words have much theological and cultural history behind them. They betray attitudes long held by believing Christians. They are the kind of words that had led
to unbelievable cruelties targeted against Jews for hundreds of years. Given his
prominence in German history, given his demands for obedience to authority, we
may justifiably suppose that Luther's words carried great weight into the Nazi era.

Luther seeing the Jews as damned is to be expected; the Church had promulgated this viewpoint for more than one thousand years before his lifetime and
countless Jews had suffered incredibly for it. To believe anything else would have
been a difficult matter for a Christian. It is an essential belief, one around which
exist several highly significant clusters of Christian beliefs and truth claims. That
the claim of damnation dehumanizes and makes diabolical the subjects of the
claim is not to be considered. They are God's outcasts; the circle of Christian
moral obligation has no place for them. Jewish beliefs are unworthy of respect,
devoid of merit. Their beliefs have been replaced by a new dispensation, a new
truth good for all humans for all times and conditions. The closed hermeneutic
circle of Christian beliefs about Jews leaves virtually no room for a different perspective. Luther, having been bitterly disappointed in his hopes for Jews to convert to Christianity, is responding to what amounts to a cultural mandate.

For Martin Luther, physical proximity to Jews—for "they live among us"—
runs the risk for Christians of becoming infected with pernicious Jewish influ-
ences, specifically their lies, curses, and blasphemy. Christians must remain un-
defiled, pure, and unharmed by the evil designs and machinations of this fallen
race. Jews are a constant threat to Christian beliefs and the desired religious uniformity sought by Christianity. Luther's anti-Semitic rhetoric is nothing new,
but his prominence in German history means that his views persist, filtering
down to and involving all subsequent generations of Germans, thereby providing a crucial discursive base to the Nazis.

Echoing earlier Christian sentiments, Luther associates Christians with the
anger of God against Jews, and reiterates Augustine's notion of using "merciful
severity" in the absence of the hope for conversion. Merciful severity would
prove to be the essence of Sepulveda's argument against Las Casas with regard
to the treatment of yet another group of people, Native Americans, whose lives
and beliefs are similarly unworthy of respect in the Christian moral universe.
Knowing that Jews constantly face divine wrath, Luther smugly asserts that
human punishment can never hope to match God's retribution. He nevertheless offers a plan of action, based partially on earlier precedents, that bears unmistakable similarities to subsequent events. He calls up images that preview
Kristallnacht—burn the synagogues of Jews, destroy their contents, then cover
them with dirt "for the honor of God and Christianity" so that "God may see
that we are Christians." God may not have noticed, but this certainly would be
recognizable to Jews, and Others, who have come to be viewed as God's enemies

by Christians. Luther calls for the invasion and destruction of private residences, where Jews perversely continue to commit the crimes they perform in their houses of worship. Luther continues the invasion against the private lives of the Disconfirming Other by denying Jews access to their holy books and stripping the rabbinate of the right to teach religion. Indeed, he had them killed if they violated this provision. With his recommendation to limit the right to movement across borders by Jews, Luther continues the papacy's historical trend to control all facets of Jewish life and presages the severe restrictions Jews would face under Hitler. After the usual call for an end to Jewish usury, Luther once again heralds Nazi rhetoric by demanding that Jews be put to work, and relies upon a racist stereotype with his demand that Jews "earn their bread by the sweat of their noses." In sum, "away with them ... this insufferable devilish burden," thus echoing the brutal Christian cry that had carried across the centuries, one that would continue to resonate across the remaining centuries to mid-twentieth century Germany and the Europe it controlled.

"Away with them": the sum total of the moral universe inhabited by untold millions of Christians when Jews are involved, vicious racist invective in honor of the Christian God, language that could just as easily have been used in the White Aryan Nation compound of Hayden Lake, Idaho, in 1995, or by the Ku Klux Klan at any point in that group's lamentable history of violence. If Luther's words do not capture the evil essence of the Christian theology of sacred violence, of how far the religion has departed from its original message of universal love, then nothing can. Having said that, however, it is important to recognize that such awareness is certainly not guaranteed from within the Christian hermeneutic, given the central, almost tortuous place reserved exclusively for Jews within Christian eschatology.

In "The Jews and Their Lies," however, Luther had not exercised his full capacity for vitriolic hatred. His 1543 pamphlet, which not surprisingly has all but disappeared from the printed record as a cultural reflex to efface its lamentable religious, racist past from the record, is titled "On Shem Hamphoras [the Ineffable Name] and the Descent of Christ." Following the standard Christian view that Christian scripture had been foretold in Hebrew scripture, and that Jews were perversely incapable of understanding their own sacred writings, Luther erupts with an astonishing rhetorical stream:

I, a damned *goy*, cannot understand where they have their great skill in interpreting, except, perhaps, that when Judas Iscariot hung himself, his bladder burst and his gut split. Perhaps the Jews had their servants there with golden pots and silver bowls to catch Judas's piss and other reliques (as they are called). Then they ate and drank the shit mixed with piss to become so sharp-eyed in interpreting the Scripture. They see things in Scripture that neither Isaiah nor Matthew, nor all the angels saw, and that we damned *goys* can never hope to see. Or did they look into their god's ass and found it written there? It is after all not in the text, that is certain. Nothing can be removed from there.... Therefore we damned *goys* have to leave the holy Jews their celestial wisdom which they have found outside the text in their Judas piss and their Jewish sweat, that they alone are the wise and we are the fools. [31]

We may ask with justification about the effect these words had upon Luther's audience. His vicious views of Jews remained a part of his clerical duties until the end of his life. He reportedly devoted his entire final sermon, four days before his death, to the subject of the Jews and their alleged perfidy.[32] Would he have persisted in his obsession had he not enjoyed a receptive audience? Did his listeners and readers comment among themselves about his remarks, or about their own personal knowledge of Jews? Did children have Jewish friends or acquaintances and feel any need to ask questions of right and wrong of their parents? If so, what would have been the adults' likely answer? Were there any signs whatsoever of disgust over or resistance to Luther's diatribes? Did anyone care? Léon Poliakov offers insight into these questions when he notes that Germany has been the most notable country over time for its expression of anti-Semitism.[33]

Gerrit Jan Heering, in his study of Christianity, the state, and war, finds Luther to be in a direct causal line to "the phenomenon of the armed Christian bully."[34] For Luther, the soldier can function "as a servant of justice and peace." His can be "a godly office." Furthermore, for Luther, "The hand which bears the sword [i.e., the sword of government] is as such no longer man's hand, but God's, and not man it is, but God who hangs, breaks on the wheel, strangles and wages war."[35] Given his violent attitudes toward Jews, and his expectations for obedience to the state, we can see from this passage that Luther makes a significant contribution to the sense of the individual's helplessness vis-à-vis the state's operations. But more to the point is the concept that it is God behind the armed might and actions of the state. The longstanding anti-Semitic views of Christianity align perfectly with these views; God punishes the Jews for their perfidy. The believing Christian is thus the action arm of God's justice and plan for His diabolical enemies. As if aware that such armed Christians might have twinges of doubt and conscience, Luther advises, "When in doubt, obey."[36] This chilling directive rings down through the ensuing centuries to calm later doubts among those people also charged with executing God's will through the sacred violence of the state enacted against The Other.

Germans had more opportunities than those provided by Luther in the sixteenth century to encounter Christianity's views of Jews and Judaism. Jacob Katz studied anti-Semitism in Germany from 1700 to 1933. He details the 1819 "Hep! Hep!" riots of Wurzburg, Bamberg, Bayreuth, and Munich, in Bavaria, as well as violence against Jews in other German cities such as Breslau and Hamburg. Homes were ransacked and destroyed, synagogues were attacked. Jews were forced into hiding, pamphlets and papers attacking them were widely available, and security forces often failed to protect the victims.[37] Such attacks, in Katz's view, resembled the pogroms Jews suffered in Russia, and clearly indicate that the basic hatreds that had been festering just below the surface of public life could be easily inflamed.

Katz notes that the first references to the term, "the Christian state," took place in the years 1842–1844, in pamphlets and books that purported to deal with the proper place of Jews living in a Gentile society. He identifies a pamphlet by Wolfgang Bernhard Fränkel, titled "Die Unmöglichkeit der Emancipation der Judem im christlichen Staat" (The Impossibility of the Emancipation of Jews in the Christian State), and cites other works along these lines by H. E. Marcard, Constantin Frantz, and Philip Ludwig Wolfart. All reflect the anti-Jewish influence of Friedrich Rühs and Friedrich Julius Stahl, a Jewish apostate. In essence, once a state has been identified as a Christian state, the horizons of Jews become severely prescribed.[38] In 1892, the Conservative Party of Breslau stated that a Christian state depends on Christian authority "and the teachers of our people can only be Christians." Furthermore, this group feared that alien forces in the population would "infect" their legislative process and the life of the citizens.[39] Once again, there is nothing new here; this had been the practical social practice and experience for centuries. It is significant because it is a specific and popular response to the gradual process of assimilation happening in certain European countries, most notably France after the Napoleonic reforms. Jews are perceived as a threat, an encrustation on the Christian body politic. In 1888, the academicians at the University of Giessen conferred an honorary degree upon Bismarck. While doing so they noted that "only the Christian religion can redeem the social reality."[40] German universities, it should be noted, were seen as byproducts of the Christian spirit; outsiders such as Jews had nothing to contribute to their advancement.[41] Half a century later, Theodor Fritsch published his *Anti-Semite Catechism*. Later re-issued as the *Handbook of Anti-Semitism*, it went through no less than thirty-six editions between 1896 and 1914. His works reflect the typical Christian approaches to Jews: the Jew is a member of "a pernicious and destructive species .... [and is] a deceitful, parasitic creature, an enemy of mankind, incapable of reforming himself, either by baptism or otherwise." Katz estimates that this kind of rhetoric reached millions of German readers.[42] In what seems to be an evolutionary development to such publications, Houston Stewart Chamberlain's *Foundations of the Nineteenth Century*, published in 1899, and Alfred Rosenberg's *Myth of the Twentieth Century*, published in 1930, both reached at least hundreds of thousands of readers.[43] As in so many other instances mentioned, such materials necessarily require the existence of a supportive cultural matrix, one that certainly runs deep within the countries in question, in their religious realities, and in the social myths to which people subscribe.

Walter Zwi Bacharach, a Holocaust survivor personally familiar with the ravages of anti-Semitism, has traced the vilifications against the Jews found in German Catholic sermons. He asks the pertinent question: "whether historical and ideological continuity is discernible between Christian anti-semitism and the atrocities committed by the Nazis."[44] His study focuses primarily on the delivery of such views to a wide, popular audience, including the rural areas. He finds that much of the Catholic discourse involving Jews took a personal angle in its attack on Jews. For example, L. Hammerstein's 1900 publication, *Begruendung des Glaubens*, a publication that spoke of the Jews' stubborn rejection of the messiah, Judaism is described as being merely the empty "husk which remains after the butterfly has emerged from the larva."[45] In one instance, a Catholic priest led his congregation in a call for "the annihilation of these impudent desecrators of Divine law." A religious instruction manual used in many schools spoke of the "eradication" of Jews.[46] In rhetoric recalling the inflammatory words of Chrysostom, or Father Ferrán Martínez, other German sermons for the edification of Catholics included other charges against Jews: they are "murderers, criminals, evil ones, sinners, enraged, inhuman, despicable, corrupt, desecrators, impudent, cunning serpents, poisonous, enemies of God ... garbage." Sermons designed for the moral improvement of Catholic children were little different.[47] In a collection of 120 sermons for children, one sermon in particular stands out for Bacharach; in this sermon, he finds two primary concerns: "the Pharisees as the foes of Jesus and the symbol of evil .... base heretics [who sought] to vilify the deeds and words of the divine savior."[48] The same concerns from Chrysostom and Martínez obtain here; it seems that not much changed in the intervening sixteen centuries from ancient Antioch to medieval Castile to modern Munich and Berlin. We must wonder how these calls for annihilation and eradication and other sordid accusations were received by those who heard the various priests' words spoken from the pulpits across the country or who read the instruction manuals in schools or churches. Did these men of God leave the same kind of impression John Chivington, a pastor and colonel, left with those who knew him and his views of Native Americans? Did the priests' words reduce the listeners' unwillingness to behave in cruel and violent ways against their fellow human beings? Did these words contribute to dehumanizing Jews in the minds of Catholic parishioners? What of those who wrote, edited, and disseminated the instruction manual? Did they give any thought whatsoever to the evil they were perpetrating, or, more likely, did they simply assent to these views, finding them to be morally accurate in terms of the culture in which they lived? What did the teachers using this manual tell the children who were studying its message? Did any children reading this manual or hearing these sermons ask about the Christian message of love and how that did or did not accord with the eradication of the Jews? What might the teachers have answered? Did all involved in these overt manifestations of the Christian culture fail to grasp any of these considerations? Did the culture's truth claims override basic humane behavior? Robert Wistrich argues that a long period of "ideological indoctrination" was necessary to create the Nazi bureaucrats and SS killers. The willingness of Germans to become involved in genocide was conditioned by Nazi propaganda that had emphasized the eradication of Jews from German life.[49] Obviously, the Nazi ideological indoctrination seeking eradication of Jews was not isolated to the twelve years of the Third Reich. Germans who found Nazi rhetoric agreeable were definitely not taking a sharp turn away from previously established cultural norms in European Christendom.

Bacharach notes that 43.1 percent of Germans under Hitler were Catholics. Of those who served in Himmler's SS, 22.7 percent maintained their loyalty to the Catholic church.[50] His study raises haunting speculations for those who are concerned about the lingering effects on the population of the virulent anti-Semitism that emanated from Catholic pulpits, catechisms, pamphlets, magazines, newspapers, and educational materials. The Catholics in Hitler's Germany, including Catholics in the SS, had been raised within their religious tradition and experienced a constant stream of vilifications against Jews, wrapped in the usual discursive pieties. They had been hearing or reading these words from respected, educated authority figures in an intellectual context that adamantly discouraged doubts or challenges. The insults against Jews were not isolated to Sunday school catechisms. An 1876 German textbook for medical school claimed that Jews were idiots and insane. Thomas Frey published the *Anti-Semites' Catechism* in 1887.[51] A racist novel first published in 1917, Artur Dinter's *Die Sünde wider das Blut* (*The Sin Against One's Blood*), reached over two million readers in the following turbulent decade.[52] In all these cases, including similar examples from other countries, the usual discursive complexities are factors to be considered. Such books do not just appear from nowhere. They represent the merest tip of an intricate complex of economic, social, intellectual, and cultural realities. The charges and the claims made become the perceived cultural norm, the familiar social reality. Bacharach's investigation leads him to determine, "Anti-Jewish prejudices stemmed from the Christian heritage and remained imprinted on the public consciousness." He probably would arrive at similar results looking anywhere in Christian Europe. Bacharach is to be commended for his perceptive conclusion: "one cannot ignore the link between theological anti-semitism and Nazi anti-semitism, and Christianity cannot evade its responsibility for the existence of the interrelation between them."[53] He does not focus specifically on culture, as is being done in this study, but he is essentially dealing with key elements of the culture and discourse experienced by Catholic Christians in Germany. His work is crucial, because it stands as a model of the kind of work that needs to be done in the many areas suggested in this study.

Robert Wistrich's work takes Bacharach's study into the twentieth century, noting the beliefs of Adolf Lanz von Liebenfels, a "renegade Cistercian monk" who published a racist journal, *Ostara Bände,* and flew a swastika flag at his castle on the Danube, "as a symbol of the Aryan movement for race purity." Both von Liebenfels and Hitler came to believe in the "God-given right of the Aryan-Germanic people to dominate the world."[54] Robert Ericksen makes an acutely disturbing observation regarding the difficulty "of distinguishing the insane from the believers,"[55] a problem that takes on awesome dimensions from the perspective of The Other. Looking back over the litany of the Christian atrocities against and doctrinal statements about The Other surveyed here, Ericksen makes a staggering point. Remembering the difficulty encountered when trying to distinguish between sane and insane believers, we can see that a repulsive view such as this has components and precedents deriving from the Christian past, not the least being its racist elements and transcendent expectations of uniformity based on a self-proclaimed doctrine of dominion over others. Basically, racist nonsense had to come from somewhere. Perhaps the initial thrust of these ideas, many centuries prior to the twentieth century, was not particularly malignant in terms of mass murder or genocide at its inception. But the seed had been planted and carefully nurtured, sustained, and impelled by subsequent developments, such as colonialism and imperialism, as well as the encounters with other races and non-Christian belief systems.

Hitler used other elements of the Christian past as well. In 1926, he proclaimed "Jesus as the first National Socialist."[56] We must wonder if anyone from a religious background in his entourage, or average Germans in their private lives, would have found this objectionable. Hitler announced that the Jew's "spirit is as alien to true Christianity" as it was to Christ himself two thousand years ago.[57] He could rely to a certain extent upon his adoring public being previously influenced somewhat by the work of Max Bewer, who had published a work containing his lectures in 1892. It was Bewer's view that Jesus could not possibly have been of Jewish extraction, because Jewish blood had long been defiled by various lusts. Instead, Bewer theorizes, Galilee had long been populated by blond, blue-eyed Germans. In Jesus, German blood had thus triumphed over Jewish blood.[58] With this kind of remythologizing influencing readers, Hitler's public speeches as well as the widely read *Mein Kampf* often reminded the German public that Jesus used a whip to drive out of the "temple of the Lord this adversary of all humanity."[59] Wistrich's study of Hitler points out that Hitler saw himself as the chosen Redeemer of his people and of the entire non-Jewish world. Hitler deemed himself a leader designated to foil a Satanic plan.[60] He exhorted followers, "We want to prevent our Germany from suffering, as Another did, the death upon the cross."[61] The nature of this appeal is obvious. Did anyone object, or was public and private agreement more likely and more common? What might someone such as Pope Pius XII have thought of such a claim, for instance? Did Hitler's rhetoric help link Nazi policies successfully in the minds of Germans with pre-existing cultural attitudes and discursive realities? Hitler viewed politics in distinctly Salvationist terms, to be experienced as a sequence of "either-or choices which would lead to deliverance or catastrophe."[62] Perhaps it was this kind of an appeal that led Father Stempfle to serve as a proofreader for Hitler's *Mein Kampf*.[63] We may justifiably inquire as to the motives, thoughts, and reactions of this priest as he read Hitler's prose, with its deep anti-Semitism searing many of its pages. Did this priest find anything in its pages that struck him as sinful? Did he feel concerned for the psyche of its author, or the moral condition of his soul? Was he at all concerned on behalf of the human targets of Hitler's prose? If not, then it is likely that the moral vision of the book complemented the views of the priest, who most likely had an upbringing that involved the vicious religious education detailed by Walter Zwi Bacharach's study. Following his return to public life after his incarceration, and declaring that in his provocative words and deeds aimed at Jews, "I am acting for the Lord," Hitler used a "perverted religiosity" to project himself into German consciousness, fostering the Holocaust as "the logical culmination of [his] messianic self-conception."[64]

Paul Althaus, a leading German theologian during the Nazi years, brings together some of the concerns of this study from the Roman past, when Christianity moved inexorably away from its pacifist roots. For Althaus, the soldier kills out of love and faith,[65] a stunning assertion linking sacred violence as theorized and practiced in the Christian past with the German soldiers operating on behalf of Hitler and the Nazis. Theologians in the conservative group known as the *Christlich-Deutsche Bewegung* (CDB), working at the time of the rise of the Nazi party, echoed a decision reached early in the Christian church when they rejected pacifism. They also resolved an important conflict that afflicted Augustine when they argued that the Gospel cannot rule the world.[66] Other principles would have to operate, rather than the Gospel, in the world of *realpolitik*. They also declared that war could be a moral duty, and that world brotherhood was not to be given a higher priority than the Volk.[67] Such statements by church leaders surely helped provide some impetus to the militaristic designs of Hitler and the Nazis serving his aims and helped guide young German males into roles that would prove to be murderous. Finally, in an echo of the proslavery dogma of Reverends Fred A. Ross or a Devereaux Jarratt, CDB leaders stated that the Gospel does not support human equality, but only equality before God.[68] In these various positions, we see a curious, almost tortured rendering of scripture as both efficacious and useless. It is permissible to kill, and the Gospel must defer to *realpolitik*. Yet the Gospel is used to endorse human inequality in the social realm, presenting a clear case of selective theology. So, just as Hitler made use of religious symbols and values, trained theologians also made contributions to the cultural realities in which people lived.

Another important leader who also ostensibly acted on behalf of the Lord was Eugenio Pacelli, Pope Pius XII. He may never be fully understood by Holocaust scholars, but he is likely to remain a controversial subject for study. The published record involving Church records and Pius XII is not complete and is likely to remain so for a considerable time. Yet he is a compelling, intriguing individual—austere, aloof, intellectual, supremely gifted in many personal dimensions—who commanded a central position in the moral and historical landscape of mid-century Europe. John Cornwell, in *Hitler's Pope*, argues that Pius XII was not an evil person, but that his is a portrait of a "fatal moral dislocation ... a separation of authority from Christian love."[69] Nothing new in this observation, the moral dislocation Cornwell describes has afflicted Christianity virtually from the time of Constantine. Reasons of state have consistently nullified any dynamic of Christian love, but especially when the target is The Other. Furthermore, "Christian love" can be defined and acted out as primarily a love for the God Christianity serves, which prioritizes into a hierarchical set the motives, attitudes, and acts of those subscribing to and involved in a wide variety of endeavors. To be low in this set of priorities, or to be absent from the list, is another way of describing the marginalization of The Other, another way of denoting the shape of the moral universe in which people live and operate.

The Vatican that Pius XII led when he ascended to his papal duties was the site of an 1858 incident and scandal. Involving the kidnapping of a Jewish child, Edgardo Mortara, from his parents by the papal police under Pius IX, Edgardo was not allowed to return to his family. Instead, Pius oversaw his formal instruction in the Catholic faith, a process that led eventually to Edgardo's ordination as a Catholic priest.[70] Here, once again, is nothing new. Christianity had many precedents for forced conversions, refusals to return "converts" to their former religious status, and incentives for acts of conversion. Simply stated, from within this interpretive position what is at stake is a soul, a soul to be "saved" from involvement in a fatal error. Involvement in a false religion, one that serves Satan's evil designs according to the claims of the dominant religion in European culture, presents no conflict to be negotiated by the Christian believer. Instead, one must celebrate the victory, the saving of the soul that could have been forfeit for all eternity. Little of this would have seemed alien to Pius XII.

Cornwell uses the letters of Pacelli in 1917 to reveal a certain attitude in his personal dealing with Jews. It was a simple matter, a polite request from a German Rabbi under wartime conditions for assistance in releasing palm fronds purchased earlier in Italy for their celebration of the Feast of Tabernacles. Pacelli more or less deflected the issue so that it became impossible to meet the request in a timely fashion. His explanatory letter to a colleague refers to "their Jewish cult." The colleague, Pietro Gasparri, made a point of noting Pacelli's "well-noted shrewdness" as the rabbi's request came to naught. By using delaying tactics and the excuse that the Vatican had no diplomatic relations with the Italian government, Pacelli had effectively guaranteed that the German rabbi's request would not be met. The incident reveals a basic personal attitude toward this "cult," even though it had preceded Christianity by some 3,600 years. Pacelli's personal views of Jews are repeated in another letter describing his experience with a group of German revolutionaries following the end of the war. He finds them to be "a gang of young women, of dubious appearance ... Jews ... with lecherous demeanor and suggestive smiles." Of a young Jewish man, Pacelli notes "drugged eyes ... vulgar, repulsive ... sly." He takes care to observe "an armed hunchback."[71] Pacelli, an extremely fastidious person by nature, seems to have found this encounter to be almost too much to stomach. He appears unable to avoid relying on stereotypical, negative descriptions and observations. These perceptions were, after all, handed down to him as culturally appropriate and accurate; these were the interpersonal tools and interpretive devices of the dominant Christianity with which he had to work whenever he encountered the Disconfirming Other, the Jews. The Christian message of love does not appear to have been activated. After all, Pacelli is in these small incidents dealing with people outside his Catholic circle of moral obligation. Cornwell supports this observation when he notes, "Pacelli was not concerned about the fate of parallel faiths, religious communities, or institutions, or about human rights and social ethics."[72]

At the thirty-fourth International Eucharistic Congress in 1938, according to Cornwell, Pacelli represented the pope and delivered remarks that once again reveal certain attitudes and beliefs. Discussing "the message of love in action," he contrasted Christian love to those "foes of Jesus who cried out to his face, 'Crucify him!' [whereas] we sing him hymns of our loyalty and our love. We act in this fashion, not out of bitterness, not out of a sense of superiority, not out of arrogance toward those whose lips curse him and whose hearts reject him even today." Moshe Y. Herczl quotes these words in his study of the Holocaust and Hungarian Jews, and concludes that Pacelli's "comprehensive love" did not extend to Jews.[73]

We will perhaps never know the full extent of whatever Pacelli did or did not do on behalf of the Jews who lived in Christian Europe during the Holocaust while he was pope. Cornwell, however, does note that Pius XII did have a priestly concern for a certain Catholic individual—Adolf Hitler. The pope apparently performed exorcisms in the quiet of his papal apartments, deep in the night, hoping to rid *Der Fuehrer* of whatever demons afflicted him.[74] In the midst of one of the largest wars ever to engulf humanity, with civilization itself on the brink, and with tens of thousands of Jews dying horrific deaths daily across the European map, the pope chose exorcism of one man as a response to his reading of the horrific events swirling around him. Rolf Hochhuth's play, *The Deputy*, raised the issue of where the good Christian should stand during the Holocaust. Why not at the gates of Auschwitz? His play presents a Pius XII beset with economic worries about the Church's various manifestations of wealth, brooding over the threat posed by atheistic Bolshevism if Nazi Germany is unable to make the center hold in Christian Europe. It is an interesting dramatic dilemma, and Hochhuth succeeds in at least raising the philosophical issue of what it means to be one's brother's keeper. Hochhuth's pope takes an extremely narrow view of the definition of "brother," an interpretation that appears to accord with historical reality. Yet it strikes me that his pope is perhaps too much a Machiavellian, using one power source to thwart a dreaded one, never really thinking in terms of the potentially wide array of spiritual weapons that could be brought to bear in the crisis. The difference can be appreciated by replacing Pacelli with Gandhi in this crucial position. Cornwell thus at least shows the pope *doing something* on a personal level about the wartime situation in Europe, but his anecdote also reveals a stunning limitation of perspective on the part of the pope. The pope appears to have concluded that *something* was amiss with the German chancellor. News reports from across the globe, as we know well today, had been detailing accurately the sufferings and deaths of those European Jews over the years they were under Nazi control. Representatives of the Vatican had been approached by individuals such as Kurt Gerstein with accurate accounts of the genocide. Europeans had witnessed publicly Nazi party intentions and acts against Jews over the years. The data and evidence available were massive and irrefutable, even if difficult to fully assimilate. No intelligent, aware, conscious person could have missed what was happening on such an enormous scale over so many years. And we also know that many people—though far, far from a majority, indeed only a tiny fraction—did actively or surreptitiously attempt to do something to help the victims of the Nazis, either on behalf of individuals being threatened or groups. We also know that such assistance took many forms. The human imagination is capable of creating a wide array of helping behaviors in the face of extreme danger and threats. We must wonder, then, just how many well-informed and well-intended people seeking to make a difference in the presence of genocide eventually settled on exorcism as the appropriate response? The focus of the attention in this case, once again, betrays a certain set of values and attitudes as well as the foreclosing of other options through the limited set of potential cultural responses. The primary goal of the pope seems to have been to try to make Hitler into a functional international diplomat, a goal that would have helped support the papacy's hopes for a stable Europe led by a strong Germany to keep godless communism at bay. One might also then hope that an exorcised Hitler, his personal demons cast somewhere else, could then have issued the order to stop the machinery of death at the camps. But, no, that is an unrealistic, dreadfully naive expectation and interpretation. Two thousand years of Christianity had associated the Jews with demonic forces, and there is absolutely no evidence that Pius XII was unfamiliar with this characterization of Jews. Indeed, as Cornwell demonstrates, Pius XII seems to have imbibed on a personal level the vicious stereotypes that had afflicted Jews for many centuries. Pius epitomizes the nature of the individual's expression of cultural expectations and norms, as well as the way in which those norms can contribute to the narrowing of choices and options. The Christian culture of Europe, simply stated, had a different set of values, one that had developed over a vast expanse of time, one that ultimately placed very little value on the lives of Jews. This being the case, is it reasonable to see in the pope's exorcisms of Hitler an effort to help the Jews, an act of faith that would stop the genocide in the death camps? No, that was not the concern at issue. The pope had looked within Hitler and from his priestly, pastoral perspective found evidence of spiritual pathology. What he seems to have failed to perceive—perhaps could not have perceived—was the moral state of the religion and the culture he served and led. He performed exorcism rituals for Hitler, entirely missing the larger point, that is, the task of rooting out the pathologies that have marked the culture of Christian Europe in its countless dealings with The Other throughout its history since its ascension to a position of dominance and power. The way in which the pope acted in this instance is a crucial piece of evidence regarding the worldview and culture he both served and led, one that had done much, in its turn, to create the pope's attitudes and prejudices. While Pius XII was exorcising Hitler's demons, Catholic priests were assisting in the destruction and elimination of Croatian Jews and Gypsies, often helping the Ustasha as they executed their slaughters,[75] even as some of their colleagues attempted to help the victims. Even when the pope managed to bring himself to speak in protest on behalf of Hitler's victims, he could not find a way to be specific about Jews. In yet another telling vignette of his views of Other people, Pope Pius XII had communicated to Allied leaders in London in January 1944 his hope that the Allied occupation forces garrisoned in Rome following the German withdrawal would *not* contain what he called "coloured troops."[76] Surely this man, imperious and aloof, was nevertheless deeply beset by the prejudices of the day, and was either unwilling or incapable of taking the necessary measures to recognize the signs of these personal and cultural malignancies and then act upon this acquired self-knowledge.

While Pius XII was in Rome exorcising Hitler's demons, hundreds of thousands of German Jews were grievously suffering from the incessant attacks perpetrated against them by Hitler's Nazi henchmen. We have before us today an incredible testament to the daily experiences of Jews in Germany in Victor Klemperer's two-volume set of books based on his diaries covering the entire Third Reich era. Klemperer's diary entry for June 7, 1942, contains a passage that reverberates throughout my concerns in this study: "Every idea is present in almost every age as a tiny individual flame."[77] When speaking of the Shoah, the all-consuming firestorm that annihilated millions of Jewish lives, we must heed Klemperer's insight. If we accept his insight, then we are better able to see the connection between the attacks against Jews in the fourth century by men later designated as Christian saints, Jews being slaughtered in the crusades and in the Inquisition, and the manifold depredations inflicted on indigenous peoples and African slaves. All are functions of a rejection of The Other and a turn to the use of a theology of sacred violence to justify and execute to the fullest extent possible the implications of that rejection. Over time, the "tiny individual flames" of hate-filled ideas were carefully protected, nurtured, fed, and then whipped into the frenzy that obliterated all in the Shoah. Yet it is absolutely crucial to recognize that there are countless tiny flames in the world of ideas, including those of unconditional love, acceptance, and tolerance. These flames can burn just as intensely as flames of hatred, rejection, and prejudice, and they can save lives as surely as the flames of hate destroy lives. A valid concern is whether one set of flames is more or less likely than the other set to become activated in a way that brings about mass good or mass evil. What are the cultural dynamics that go into the creation of mass good or mass evil expressed and activated over long periods of time? Why did the early pacifistic leanings of incipient Christianity not become the cultural, social, and theological norm for believing Christians, and thus create a world in which The Other could be left free of militant conversion tactics, their Otherness honored and respected rather than despised and rejected? Better yet, perhaps the simple act of defining and then perceiving The Other would never have developed as it did. Is there something about the unification of church and imperial state, with the transcendent claims of an aggressive religion armed with a complex, powerful military apparatus, that guarantees that the combined structure will become a zealous, hostile force in history? When the new structure came into existence, were there preexisting elements that compelled sacred violence to dominate the thoughts, beliefs, and actions of the religion's believers? Were Victor Klemperer and his fellow

Jews in mid-twentieth-century Europe basically foredoomed by decisions reached in the first four centuries of Christianity's existence? Was there no turning back? Could Christianity change the elements within it that ran counter to its highest ideals? What countervailing cultural forces and ideas could have turned back the tide of victory for a forceful, proselytizing religion newly armed with imperial military strength and attitudes to help it promulgate its message of dominion and a single truth?

Klemperer's diary depicts in minute detail the all-pervasive fear, acts and words of barbarism, oppression, lack of freedom, cowardice by Germans, diminished prospects, legal violence and restrictions, corruption of language, shattered social bonds, ruined careers, alienation of parents and children, brave private acts, mob violence, pettiness, terror, hunger, and suicides that Germany's Jews faced on a daily basis from the world around them throughout the Nazi era. Readers become intimately familiar with the haunting fears and devastating personal anguish registered by this sensitive consciousness. Klemperer's observations lend tremendous weight to the claim that the neighbors of Jews in Germany often turned on them almost immediately following Hitler's coming to power as chancellor.[78] It is not an altogether unrelieved reading experience; there are definite signs of humane values and behavior to be found in the non-Jewish contacts in his life. Ultimately, Klemperer finds no evidence that *all Germans* are anti-Semitic. A compilation of episodes and events suggests a bi-modal set of experiences. Although the bulk of his perceptions are of the sheer, massive weight of Nazi terror, he also records many significant—usually fleeting and furtive—encounters and moments when a kind word or gesture took place, sometimes done in a potentially dangerous manner for the parties involved. Indeed, as the years go by, these moments appeared to happen more frequently, although the terror and near-paralyzing fear are simply always there. Often Klemperer records an instance of hate juxtaposed by a humane incident just moments later. What is less obvious are the innumerable acts of what Victoria Barnett terms "observant passivity"[79]—bystanders who actually see or hear a vile act, yet who ignore the plight of the human victims. The accumulation of both positive, life-affirming incidents and cruel, negative experiences seem to drive Klemperer into a quiet search for evidence to help him make up his minds about the true nature of the non-Jewish people who surround him.

To read Klemperer's diaries in light of the material discussed in the foregoing chapters of this book is a sobering, powerful experience. So many of the frightening experiences in his life, and the lives of his friends, recall similar traumatic events from prior eras. There is the constant sense that the inner turmoil for this man, the deprivations and indignities, and the sheer terror that grips him daily, all of these had their counterparts for Other people in other times. We may gain some insight into the likely state of mind for those who felt themselves to be hunted prey, who cannot possibly know where all the threats derive, who cannot fathom the hurtful motivations of the hunters. We are not privileged to enter within the minds of the perpetrators and bystanders in his diary but Klemperer provides numerous accounts of their words and actions, notably the complete immunity they seem to enjoy for their participation in evil.

Although not an exhaustive review of the diary's contents, the following items are worthwhile matters to consider. In March 1933, Klemperer finds a child's ball in a toy shop emblazoned with a swastika.[80] Such a sight indicates a significant chain of prior events, not the least being the eagerness of the Nazis to involve children in their political and social worldview. But this toy ball also brings into the child's life a direct element of socially sanctioned hate, all that the symbol had come to mean in Germany, the tip of a massive racist discourse. Toys do not just appear out of nowhere. Like anything else in a modern economy, they must be designed, produced, and marketed. They are the end product of a long line of decisions rendered by adults. When purchased by an adult for a child, what is the message that goes along with the Nazi toy ball to the child? Certainly, there is an indirect, perhaps direct, message of adult support for what the ball represents; it is no longer merely a toy. The child's innocent world of play now has taken on an additional level of significance, as most German children were to learn in the following years. Symbolic and actual irruption of vicious evil entered their play. We may also inquire about the experience of the Jewish child in Germany. In March 1933, the ubiquitous Nazi German restrictions on the public life of Jews had not yet been promulgated. Certainly, anti-Semitism was present in public life, thanks in part to Nazi broadcasts, publications, speeches, rallies, and parades. It is entirely likely that Jewish children would have encountered toy balls with swastikas in shops, or would have seen neighborhood children playing with them. If these balls bore ominous significance for Aryan children, what may be said on behalf of Jewish children? What thoughts and fears would Jewish children have experienced in the presence of a familiar object, but now one defaced with the official symbol of the political party seeking their destruction? How were their psychological horizons circumscribed or impaired? We know that Jewish children almost immediately encountered vicious rejections in their school classrooms, both from classmates and from teachers. Would the swastika on a toy ball have touched their lives in deeply personal ways difficult to perceive and measure? How much pain and distress might this have caused young children and their families? Finally, what might adults, Jews and non-Jews, have to say to any of these children about the significance of these toy balls? Would they explain it away, downplay it, exult over it, or ignore it altogether?

Klemperer records several instances where religious values and discourse from the past are allied with Nazi propaganda designs. He discusses the distressing experience of his "Aryan" friend and fellow teacher, Johannes Köhler, who had to collect signatures at school in February 1934 so he could buy a "Luther Rose" inscribed "With Luther and Hitler."[81] As with the Nazified child's ball, we see the markings of the Nazi party invading the conscience and work of a decent man, associating German religious history with the Nazi party leader and German chancellor. But Luther is no innocent child's toy. He is not without a significant degree of guilt because he contributed to the Nazi regime's ability to disarm any public expression of disagreement with the party's treatment of Jews. It is also likely that Hitler, a Catholic, was hoping to gain some additional support from Lutheran Germans by associating himself and his party with this supposed great leader from the past.

Similarly, Klemperer notes other Nazi items that seem to rely upon prior Christian rhetoric, attitudes, and prejudices. In May 1935, he records seeing a Nazi billboard proclaiming, "Whoever knows the Jew, knows the devil!"[82] A year and a half later, in September 1936, Klemperer reports the visit to Dresden of the Nazi propagandist Julius Streicher. He is accompanied by "all the features of an election campaign: posters, broad banners stretched across streets, processions, drummers and slogans chanted in chorus in the streets." In this year of the Berlin Olympics, when Nazi Germany tried to demonstrate to the world less of its official prejudice against Jews, Klemperer nevertheless notes that the newspaper records Streicher's words: "Who fights the Jew, wrestles with the Devil."[83] We must recognize in these reports the highly public nature of these venomous Nazi devices. They were not hiding their opinions, as the world well knew. In these particular instances, they simply reiterated the demonizing rhetoric that had marked Christian pronouncements and culture for nearly two thousand years, demonstrating Wistrich's view that the Nazis sought to rely upon "the centuries-old tradition of anti-Semitism for electoral purposes."[84] Hundreds of millions of Christians over years held similar opinions and acted out those beliefs, including those identified as among the holiest individuals in all Christendom, the saints of the Church. Such demonizing rhetoric had been articulated by its most educated and influential leaders in virtually all aspects of Christian discourse including sermons, scriptural commentary pamphlets, catechisms, tracts, conciliar proceedings, papal bulls, homilies, various art forms, disputations, speeches, articles, and books. Countless Jews over the centuries had been murdered by Christians holding these views. An entire bureaucracy within the Catholic Church in the institution of the Inquisition had been devised to bring its terror and power against Jews, with lay Christians fully involved in assisting the search for demonized Jews and Other victims. Untold millions of Christians had been bystanders while Jews died horrible deaths as a result of Christian beliefs. In light of what we know of prior Christian practices, the Nazis were not doing anything innovative or unusually disgusting with the rhetoric that riveted Klemperer's attention. Perhaps, in retrospect, people today have proved to be more sensitive to the human rights implications of Nazi practices, although this did not seem to be the case for many of those who were in the immediate vicinity of the practices and acts that Klemperer details. Indeed, Eric Johnson's study of the Gestapo in Krefeld identifies Franz von Vacano, a judge heading the Cologne Special Court, as a practicing Catholic with twelve children (with another on the way) who "had little trouble balancing his Catholic beliefs with his Nazi convictions."[85] The Nazis surely consciously relied upon what they knew of the German public; it is likely that the Nazis who promulgated such anti-Semitic rhetoric had encountered it at some earlier point in their lives, perhaps from some respected authority figure. As stated earlier, Hitler and his Nazi satraps invented very little. One scholar observes that the Nazi-inspired laws against Jews served to "create new standards of acceptable conduct [and] must have helped Germans to distance themselves from the Jews."[86] I would argue, however, that the standards of acceptable conduct involving Jews had been defined and made culturally operative by Christianity much earlier in the Common Era. There were clear periods covering considerable periods of time in which Christian-inspired atrocities against Jews were the norm. These surely had an impact on the cultural conditions for people living during the Shoah, thus helping to make the distance between Jews and non-Jews all the wider, all the more lethal. Hyam Maccoby, for instance, laments the extensive period of anathematizing the Jews, which eventually lodged in the "popular imagination" of the masses, assimilating the Christian rejection and fear of Jews into "the preconscious fear system of the people."[87]

Klemperer sees all this and comments on what he calls "religious madness."[88] He is aware that Hitler spoke to his followers of the Nazis who died in 1923 at the Feldherrnhalle: "My apostles .... 'You have risen again in the Third Reich.'" In July 1937, Klemperer notes a speech Hitler made in Wurzburg: "Providence guides us, we act according to the will of the Almighty. No one can make national or world history without the blessing of this Providence."[89] Such proclamations provide convincing evidence to scholars that Hitler was possessed of a certain Christ complex, as Christ Triumphant or the Christ of the Second Coming.[90] Norbert Elias notes that the Nazis "combined many of the traits of a religious movement with those of a political party."[91] We are abundantly aware of the pathologies in Hitler's psychology, although we may never fully understand them, but what of the public's reaction to the kinds of declarations preserved by observers like Klemperer? Surely there is a difference between hearing or reading a public pronouncement by a political leader, and fully understanding that leader's psychological profile. By all accounts, Hitler was socially functional, eccentric, and charismatic, all the while being a sociopath. His psychological state, however, was not a barrier to the acceptance of his views by a large segment of the German populace. This matter recalls Robert Ericksen's notion of the difficulty experienced in detecting a sane from an insane believer. In Hitler, we have a man who may have been clinically insane, but who espoused familiar slogans, viewpoints, and attitudes from the Christian past that resulted in genocide. We must wonder if the rhetoric in this instance served to obscure the insanity. What, then, of the millions of Christians who had held similar beliefs over the centuries?

Klemperer's acute observations offer ample, highly credible support for the view that the machinery undergirding the Holocaust involved virtually all segments of German society. The social revolution that stripped Jews of their civil rights necessarily required the assistance of the country's legal establishment and its judiciary, police, and various private and government bureaucracies. The legal changes devolved to impact life on the streets; transportation personnel, store clerks, and even librarians were involved in applying Nazi laws and regulations against Jews, often in fanatically rude and abrasive manners. Germans were bombarded with various forms of Nazi discourse: newspapers, books, films, pamphlets, posters, banners, postcards, stamps, graphics. All relied upon the preexisting cultural landscape. Aside from formal interactions with the state or social apparatus, Klemperer records numerous instances in which he was simply accosted with a crude remark or vile behavior in public, in full view of anyone who cared to hear or see the event. We also know that the education system was totally compromised and the churches represented a significant institutional disappointment with regard to taking a moral stand in defense of helpless, innocent victims. But this is to expect too much perhaps; we know that the churches, church officials, and their congregants would have had many internal cultural and theological obstacles to overcome to have behaved otherwise. Labor federations became part of the Nazi onslaught. Youth clubs, church groups, and social clubs all came under the direct influence of the Nazi party. Eventually, even the German military forces subscribed to a personal oath of loyalty to Hitler. Klemperer records the impact of Nazi propaganda on the German language, hoping to turn his careful observations into a book on the subject. One might also note that changes in language would, logically, have been accompanied by alterations in thought processes. The sum total of Klemperer's observations in this regard offer ample support for the view that "it took nearly the entire German population to carry out the Holocaust."[92]

The actual processes more directly involved with genocide also involved wide segments of German society and culture, or those areas adjacent to the death camps. Citizens would have seen their neighbors rounded up and moved to ghettos. Jewish properties were redistributed to Aryans; such property transfers necessarily involved considerable bureaucratic support services. Coworkers went to work only to find Jewish colleagues absent or removed while on the job. Other citizens or people under Nazi control lived nearby or adjacent to the ghettos and would have been able to see the countless scenes of terrified victims entering unknown territories with their pitiful belongings and meager hopes. Incredibly violent acts haunted the ghettos, both inside and outside the walls.

George Victor writes accurately and forcefully of the depths of involvement on the part of perpetrators and bystanders:

Hitler's regime was basically criminal, and a great many people were drawn into complicity. Officers of the justice system—police, prosecutors, and judges, aided by clerks and lawyers—became criminals by involvement in the system's operation. Many people participated by spying on others and denouncing them. Actions against Jews alone involved people who kept records, inventoried and audited businesses, and issued documents. From boycott to expropriation, professionals and business people participated passively or actively in the elimination of Jewish competitors, acquiring their clientele and assets. Ordinary citizens acquired homes, jobs, and property they often knew were taken from Jews.... Extermination involved medical and paramedical workers and about a million transportation workers over the years. And actions against Jews were only a fraction of the government's lawlessness. Industrialists and farmers used slave labor, paying little or no salaries.... In all, as accessories and beneficiaries of crimes, many millions of Germans became accomplices.[93]

Victor's points reflect the views of many scholars who see a widespread involvement on the part of many Germans in various phases of the Holocaust. Even though Victor is a practicing psychotherapist, his assertions may be said to share significant elements with the culture studies method of this study. We see that many people became involved in a widespread set of oppressive behaviors practiced against Jews, even if only in an indirect manner. But the machinery of massive oppression and genocide requires many assistants and a supporting cultural context that permits or encourages violence, sacred or otherwise. Starting with Christian-influenced laws and edicts during the late Roman era, and through each area of this study, we have seen a uniform pattern: identify The Other, anathematize them, then begin taking a variety of actions against them, including extreme violence based on a theology of violence. In most cases, with the possible exception of the crusades, a large bureaucracy is required to handle the many legal and social tasks involved. In addition, the active and passive support of the masses also comes into play. Especially in cases of coercive pacification, the threats of violence and actual violence are acted out in public; they are there for all to see—public humiliations, punishments, destruction of property, and mass executions. In many cases, the victims are known to participants or those watching the unfolding events. Often the perpetrators had to perform their functions face-to-face. The humanity of their victims might be thought to be manifest before them, but the empowering culture typically provided the necessary rewards and sanctions to overcome any reluctance one might have had about acting against The Other. Of course, anonymity was also a factor.

Scenarios described by Victor Klemperer were available to people from all walks of life, including children. Klemperer's account speaks often of the fears that characterized interpersonal relationships, and of how people had to articulate their doubts and concerns in private. He is writing, of course, of Germany. Surely, similar concerns afflicted the lives of people in the vicinities of the ghettos. Very few people mustered the courage to come directly to the aid of the ghettoized Jewish victims in their midst. We must wonder, in light of these matters, about the very question that haunted Klemperer: How many Germans and other Europeans were anti-Semitic?

This focus of this study changes Klemperer's question. Surely, there were many anti-Semitic people to be found throughout Europe, and Germany, by all accounts, was one of the central locations, along with Austria and Poland, for anti-Semitic values, attitudes, and behaviors. Rabid anti-Semites, such as the leadership of the Nazi Party, were by no means the majority. Klemperer encounters a few hardcore Gestapo types, for instance, but most of his interactions are with people far short of the evil, radicalized Gestapo personnel. Instead, his days and nights over the years under the Nazis are spent in a series of encounters with people across the entire political and moral spectrum. All these people, but most notably the non-Jews, would have had some contact with the culture's discourse, rhetoric, and theological instruction involving the Christian religion's rejection of Jews as well as that dominant religion's removal of Jews from the accepted circle of moral obligation. In his study of anti-Semitic stereotypes, Frank Felsenstein notes that Christians always provided a negative function for Jews in their religious "fantasy life."[94] Ervin Staub makes a crucial point: the deep structure of anti-Semitism was stronger in Germany than elsewhere, with an especially deep set of roots established in the medieval period.[95] Staub identifies ancient German attitudes toward Jews as a "cultural blueprint" for the later Nazi depredations.[96] In medieval Spain, the Church had relied upon the deicide charge to maximize the public rejection of Jews, leading to the implication that "the masses understood and embraced [this] as fitting their innermost desires."[97] It is highly likely that the Nazis consciously chose to rely upon the preexisting negative images of Jews, replicating the Spanish experience, thus exposing the "innermost desires" of large numbers of Christian Europeans in the middle of the twentieth century. With anti-Jewish propaganda having reached a new height of intensity for most Christian Europeans, we may also reasonably surmise that the underlying cultural attitudes and expected behaviors were thereby activated and also intensified. In their study of violence, Jennifer Turpin and Lester Kurtz observe that once a self is named or confirmed by an authority figure, that self is most likely to become more clear and definite in its various operations. They argue that "the Auschwitz self," for instance, takes on increasing prominence, achieving hegemonic proportions, on a daily basis.[98] Based on their analysis, I suspect that there was also a Nazi self, a Dachau self, an Einsatzgruppen self, a bystander self, and a rescuer self (although this was not defined by any state authority), among many others. A corresponding cultural template for each of these selves can be identified in the Christian past. Again, with the possible exception of the rescuer self, the basic Christian message of love apparently was not activated on behalf of Jews and Other victims in any significant manner until rather late in history. Although Jews had been able to live bearable lives prior to the rise to power of the Nazis, the increasing intensity of Nazi propaganda and an increased acting out of brutally racist attitudes forced them to deal with very real threats to their well-being.

What can we say of the Auschwitz self, the Western European Christian who operated as an agent of genocide on behalf of Nazi designs? The sun will grow into a red giant and obliterate the earth, along with the solar system, before anyone can fully understand the Auschwitz self. Perhaps it is better left not fully understood. Elie Wiesel has spoken eloquently for decades about the need for silence, the betrayal that accompanies words used to discuss the Shoah. We should listen carefully.

Elie Wiesel also has anger, deep from within, from his very soul, when he writes or speaks of the Shoah. He cannot see the world the way anyone who never spent one second in Auschwitz does. His anger is justified six million times over. What does this Auschwitz survivor, intimately knowledgeable about the Auschwitz self, think of Chrysostom's words about Jews? What does Wiesel think of a pope who wants the Jews burned? What does Wiesel think of Martin Luther's views of the proper treatment of the perfidious Jews? What does he think of the Inquisition's destruction of Jews? What are his thoughts about the Inquisition's torture instruments? Or forced conversions? Or public burnings of Jews over several centuries in Christian Europe? What has he to say about the many Christian saints who supported and implemented sacred violence? What are his thoughts of the Christian catechisms and their many defamations of Jews and Judaism? What does Wiesel think about the claims of papal dominion over *all* souls? Granted, these are not, most definitely not, gas chambers and crematoria, the Nazis' assembly line death, but they surely helped create the mind set for the Auschwitz self, the preconditions, the cultural base for genocide.

The Auschwitz self had to dehumanize the Jews radically in order to kill them. The cultural components of that process to dehumanize Jews started, perhaps, in the church services of Chrysostom's Antioch, or earlier perhaps, when the final Gospels were written as the alienation of Christianity from Judaism developed. The Auschwitz self saw Jews as a disease, a blot on creation, a threat, life unworthy of life. Prominent Christian saints also saw Jews this way, and, in many cases, applied all of their knowledge and expertise to the religiously sanctioned gardening project of killing them. The Auschwitz self was supported by a massive Nazi discursive effort that kept the nemesis Jews constantly before the German public as anathematized enemies, targets of opportunity with wide-open rules of engagement for attack. The Christian discourse was operative, obviously, far longer than the twelve years of the Nazi regime but lacked none of its rhetorical impact and hate-filled details. Moving believers to action succeeded. The Auschwitz self believed that it was serving a higher good, a transcendent project, and would thus return Germany to its self-declared position of prominence in Europe, leading a pure Aryan race to its appropriate position of racial dominion by eliminating the bacillus that plagued European life, the Jews. For Christianity, Jews served a dual purpose, both as living evidence of their perfidy against God and as proof of God's plan for the triumphant religion replacing them. The Auschwitz self was aided tremendously, as Wiesel has argued so eloquently, by the indifference of the millions of bystanders, people who lacked the "disruptive empathy"[99] to intervene directly on behalf of the innocent Jewish victims of Nazi evil. Such bystanding has been one of the chief characteristics discussed in this study. Very few human beings within Christendom were able to overcome all the cultural incentives offered by their religion in order to challenge the various elements of its dogma that served as weapons against The Other or to challenge those individuals who executed the aggressive, destructive elements of that dogma. Indeed, I doubt if there were many people the caliber of a Bartolomé de Las Casas at almost any point over the era of Christian domination who perceived anything of moral concern to themselves when it came to the sacred violence being practiced against The Other. Absent either the capacity or the motivation for an ideological critique of the claims of Christianity, the agents of the culture, indeed, the culture itself, performed the necessary gardening maneuvers against lives deemed unworthy of life. For at least seventeen centuries, lives were destroyed or diminished, and the Christian perpetrators and the Christian bystanders functioned as they had been directed, prodded, encouraged, and educated to do through the agents of the Christian culture. *No one saw very much wrong with all this.* As a crusader in Jerusalem in 1099 reported it, "Wonderful things were to be seen.... In the temple of Solomon, the horses waded in blood up to their knees, nay, up to the bridle. It was a just and marvelous judgment of God, that this place should be filled with the blood of unbelievers."[100] Similar thoughts may have been in the minds of inquisitors as they watched the fruits of their sacred violence with satisfaction. What would Pope Paul IV have recorded if his wish to see "the whole lot burned" was enacted? What thoughts would have passed through his mind if he were to have seen the Auschwitz burning pit filled with Jewish infants on the same terrible night that Elie Wiesel records seeing it? What might Martin Luther have recorded had he been able to see the murdered Jewish rabbis he demanded in his hate-filled writing? Assemble these individuals at the crematoria in Auschwitz, and what might their reactions be? There they would see what they had asked for all along, with firm scriptural, theological, and cultural support. Perhaps they would admire the efficiency with which the Nazis were exterminating this age-old plague. Perhaps, like the two young Polish priests celebrating a Catholic Mass after the war, they would thank their God for eliminating these Jews and see in the genocide further evidence of the triumph of Christianity. We may also ask, had such leaders been able to attend the Nuremberg war crime trials as witnesses, what would have been the nature of their testimony? Would they have offered exculpatory points of view on behalf of the defendants? Christianity has much invested in this, including the writing of an historical record that would minimize its contribution to the Nazis. Nevertheless, scholars such as Eric Johnson find that there was not "much real conflict between the Nazi state and the Catholic Church," for instance, and that Protestants were even more supportive of the Nazis.[101]

"Away with them." The Christian culture almost got its wish in the Shoah. Polish Catholic priests, among others, celebrated the event. Perhaps those who originally said things like this did not really believe what they were saying, but there is precious little evidence to support that. And now that the event will forever stand in Western history as an accusation of its fundamental belief structure, there will be massive denial behaviors. The implications are simply too much of a challenge. The authenticity of the culture, its very reason for being as it is, cannot for long withstand the harsh light of scrutiny that shines out from the death camps and mass burial grounds, from the Inquisition's racks, from the Spanish butcher shop, from Luther's prose, from millions of sermons, from the

Temple of Solomon with Jewish blood reaching the knees of the horses used by Christian crusaders. As for whether the Shoah is specifically a German event, as Daniel Goldhagen's work argues, the approach taken here helps to account for Germany's willing helpers—the Ukrainians, the Dutch, the Latvians, the French, the Lithuanians, the Romanians, the Estonians, to name a few. The Holocaust cannot have significance for the entire Western world if it is a German-specific event insofar as perpetration goes. As this study has argued, the underlying culture provided the fertile ground for the weeding operation to go forward, much as it had for centuries. During those centuries, all available means, including the most advanced technologies, had been applied as forms of sacred violence against The Other. As noted again and again, the Germans invented very little. They applied their keen organizational and bureaucratic skills to the matter of state-sponsored genocide, with staggering results.

Echoing the words of Elie Wiesel, it is time to begin again. It is time to turn aside from the single claims of truth, from all that goes with those claims, to turn away from the acts of perception that create the one and only truth and then The Others who cannot subscribe to that truth. It is now time to find the many truths within the worldviews of The Others, to let those truths thrive in a world that celebrates those Other views, those Other ways of seeing and caring for the world, those Other ways of celebrating the creator, creation, and the creatures within it. All human beings are gifts to all Other human beings, not threats, not satanic beings, not parasites. All human beings have lives worthy of life. May we all do what is necessary to bring about this new world that has been attempting to come into existence, but has been brutally thwarted throughout Western Christian history by the sacred, violent denial of its vision.

Conclusion

"Christians shed more blood than all other peoples taken together."
—Moses Ben Nachman

"To claim that Christianity has had 'an elevating moral influence' can only be maintained by wholesale ignoring or falsification of the historical evidence."
—Bertrand Russell

"[The] Holocaust was a window ... [through] which ... one can catch a rare glimpse of many things otherwise invisible."
—Zygmunt Bauman

I have not undertaken the writing of this book without trepidation, concern, and a self-imposed tortuous thought process. Well known to me as a fact is the matter that much of the contents of this book, both the details and the interpretation of those details, will most likely prove to be extremely painful to those thoughtful readers who are also devout, faithful Christians, people who have found peace, sustenance, consolation, guidance, and personal fulfillment in and through their religious beliefs and practices. The pain is not intended; it is a by-product of bringing to the attention of such readers historical and cultural facts and the implications of facts not previously encountered. The past rapidly recedes in our individual and collective memory. The conditions of human experience a century ago, or a thousand years ago, or two thousand years ago, seem remote, unavailable, perhaps utterly insignificant as components impacting and conditioning the lives of humans today. More important, one of the chief functions of a culture is to protect itself, and those humans who comprise it and live within it, from perceptions that challenge the legitimacy, authority, meaning, and significance of that culture. Among other things, this means that a culture's various aspects of an educational system will not readily emphasize matters that would not be conducive to creating enough support for the culture to keep it alive and intact. I have attempted to argue throughout this study that Christianity, as a major component of the dominant culture, does not foster an ideological critique of its various truth claims and their implications. Hyam Maccoby notes that a culture's myths are deeply intertwined with the instruments of moral evaluation. The myths help inform the culture; once those myths have become embedded in the lives and minds of the people in the culture, "the outlines of the culture are determined."[1] Part of the culture that today's Christians have inherited is a religion that long ago separated the human religious experience into two groups, the We and the They, believers and unbelievers. Humans comprising the latter groups were officially deemed appropriate for dominion and slavery.[2] This kind of dichotomy becomes part of the practical knowledge of those who participate in a dominant culture, a form of "'common sense' ... rarely made explicit... often in fact unconscious, but it too is built upon a comprehensive foundation of ideological premises."[3] While slavery is not as widespread as formerly, the claims of such concepts as an exclusive transcendent truth and dominion do not seem to have weakened appreciably. Ziauddin Sardar states it somewhat differently. "The universalizing principle of western civilization has always been to see its way as the only way and therefore the universal way. The West's use of the term universal is an intentional statement of the becoming of the Other.... It is always intended to be an act of will and force."[4] Frantz Fanon, annother intellectual writing critically of the Western European cultural norm, made an acutely insightful observation four decades ago: "The extensions of Otherness reach into the very recesses of our consciousness, so that we cannot perceive the world, and its inhabitants, outside of this filter."[5]

Part of the difficulty is that believing Christians must come to grips with the simple fact that over many centuries there are canonized saints of the church who spent considerable time and effort in their holy lives persecuting and even murdering Jews.[6] Such leaders, as well as the many generations of faithful Christians who revered them, took part in the long cultural process in which "certain of our hypotheses inevitably press us to conclusions and assurances which justify our way of life."[7] Nevertheless, Maycock refused to indict the entire civilization. This is to be expected; it is as difficult today as it was three-quarters of a century ago when Maycock was writing about the Inquisition. But we have considerably more disturbing information and evidence of atrocities in the center of contemporary Christian Europe to account for than he did. I suspect that we also have more readily available to us the tools needed to conduct the critique that will help us come to a particular appreciation of the culture in which we live, although this will continue to be a difficult matter, perhaps impossible, for many people. Many believers will look at these matters and basically fall into denial. And some will not care enough to bother to look at all. A measure of the difficulty in this area is offered by Forrest G. Wood when he observes that "recognizing Christianity itself as a source of immorality [is] unthinkable for the faithful because such recognition would have impugned their most profound beliefs."[8] Scholars studying the Native American experience find Anglo-European society and history to be guilty of a variety of crimes and they suggest that it is now the time to investigate the evidence supposedly supporting its claims to being a truly humane institution.[9] I believe that a similar charge can be brought in general against Western European Christianity. Indeed, as suggested elsewhere in this study, a strong case can be made that Western Christianity, its culture, and its agents have perpetrated countless crimes against humanity for considerably more than a millennium. We must wonder, then, about the implications for the individual believer today who has given his or her prayerful, deeply personal assent to a religion and worldview that has been criminally culpable in the deaths and immiseration of untold millions of human beings. How might those believers live their lives differently, how might they think, if they were not beset with destructive, violent, inhumane values? Perhaps now is the time for this portion of humanity, devoutly believing Christians, to review their presence in the lives of The Other over time to see if the culture can begin in earnest a different historical trajectory, so that those who are enculturated with its messages will be better able to achieve the kind of "disruptive empathy" that refuses to accept dehumanization and more victims of sacred violence.

It is possible to engage in an ideological critique but the effort may derive from a source outside the usual belief structure. An excellent example comes from the nineteenth century in the person of Robert Green Ingersoll, one of the century's leading orators, although he made his career on the basis of his radical atheism and his scathing commentary on the hypocrisy of institutional religion. One of his most popular lectures was "Some Reasons Why," first delivered to his public in 1881. In this lecture, Ingersoll told his listeners:

Religion makes enemies of friends. That one word, "religion," covers all the horizon of memory with visions of war, of outrage, of persecution, of tyranny, and death. That one word brings to the mind every instrument with which man has tortured man. In that one word are all the fagots and flames and dungeons of the past, and in that word is the infinite and eternal hell of the future.

In the name of universal benevolence Christians have hated their fellow-men. Although they have been preaching universal love, the Christian nations are the warlike nations of the world. The most destructive weapons of war have been invented by Christians. The musket, the revolver, the rifled canon [sic], the bombshell, the torpedo, the explosive bullet, have been invented by Christian brains. Above all other arts, the Christian world has placed the art of war.

A Christian nation has never had the slightest respect for the rights of barbarians; neither has any Christian sect any respect for the rights of other sects .... [E]ven now, something happens almost every day to show the old spirit that was in the Inquisition still slumbers in the Christian breast.

Whoever imagines himself a favorite with God, holds other people in contempt.

Whenever a man believes that he has the exact truth from God, there is in that man no spirit of compromise. He has not the modesty born of the imperfections of human nature; he has the arrogance of theological certainty and the tyranny born of ignorant assurance. Believing himself to be the slave of God, he imitates his master, and of all tyrants, the worst is a slave in power.

When a man really believes that it is necessary to do a certain thing to be happy forever, or that a certain belief is necessary to ensure eternal joy, there is in that man no spirit of concession. He divides the whole world into saints and sinners, into believers and unbelievers, into God's sheep and Devil's goats, into people who will be glorified and people who will be damned.

A Christian nation can make no compromise with one not Christian; it will either compel that nation to accept its doctrine, or it will wage war. If Christ, in fact, said, "I come not to bring peace but a sword," it is the only prophecy in the New Testament that has been literally fulfilled.[10]

Ingersoll's words are themselves prophetic. He died before the twentieth century dawned. Its atrocities even he could not have imagined. Now we have to add that Christian minds invented and deployed atomic weapons, holding the world hostage for four decades, a logical extension of the implications of Christian claims to truth for all, dominion over all, and sacred violence. The Marine officer's words about the Vietnamese village—"We had to destroy it to save it"—may be said to have been the operative rhetoric for this period, perhaps even for the entire time frame of this study, especially for the victims of the Inquisition and depredations against the indigenous people of the Americas. Indeed, Ingersoll possessed acutely perceptive insights into the cultural processes at work.

Along these same lines, Hermann Doerris notes that the Great Commission made the Christian responsible for the welfare of his neighbors, that the devout Christian was *obligated to take the measures to intervene* to save those in error from the torments of hell. Simply stated, a devout Christian had to do something about the faith of Others.[11] A fair assessment of the behavior of Christians since the promulgation of this Great Commission would seem to indicate that this obligation has not diminished appreciably over time. It has most likely taken on new dimensions. Using different instruments to achieve its ends, it might not be recognizable to those who originally conceived of the notion. Nevertheless, it continued to function at some elemental level over much of history and continues today in the lives of many different people across the globe. It is a function of Christianity's basic claim to universal dominion. It is important to note, however, that the Great Commission often struck against elements of human life that are some of the most basic components of an individual's sense and experience of a meaningful existence. José Oscar Beozzo states that people can come to face a form of deep personal humiliation that essentially nullifies reasons for living: "Language and religion are the basic structure of this dimension, and were to be used as a deliberate instrument of domination."[12] George Tinker makes a crucial observation in his study of cultural genocide: "We must come to an understanding of the pervasiveness of culture in determining structures of intellectual development as well as other, more physical patterns of behavior."[13] Equally important is Tinker's identification of our relationship to a "systemic *causal nexus*" in which the missionary perpetrators of cultural genocide were "entrapped, even as we are more or less entrapped in it today."[14] Ervin Staub finds that culture shapes human personality by providing an arena for common agreement over values, goals, and explanations for the various phenomena of the world.[15] We see evidence of this, for instance, in Benzion Netanyahu's argument that the hatred for Jews spearheaded by Spain's Father Ferrán Martínez's call for their annihilation was the "product of a long social evolution."[16] Its crucial early starting point may be Sophronius's view that Christians constitute a race unto themselves, formed by none other than Jesus Christ himself from all the Gentile nations.[17] As the initial components of the theological stance of dominion and sacred violence spread throughout Christendom and across time, Netanyahu notes that Christians came to hate and dislike "the whole being of the Jew, not merely his religion." Jews came to be seen not as merely alien entities in a population, but as enemy aliens.[18] As seen from the first, these claims were absolute, and demanded the undivided allegiance of its adherents and the total rejection of all the claims and beliefs of the Disconfirming Other.[19] Marcel Simon argues that anti-Jewish behaviors tended to become more widespread and frequent in their applications over time.[20] It is crucial to realize that Christianity and Western civilization, certainly since the Reformation, constitute an "unbroken continuum."[21] In the modern experience, conditions that foster atrocity are "so structured externally that the average person entering it will commit or become associated with atrocities."[22]

With these sobering points, however, comes the utterly crucial point that a culture studies approach does not absolve a person from individual responsibility for his or her actions in an atrocity. Nor, perhaps, in continued allegiance to a criminal institution. There is always an opportunity for the individual to take a position or behave in a way that runs counter to the cultural norm, even though this may be personally, socially, or psychologically difficult. "The culture made me do it" is simply an unacceptable substitution for the Nuremberg claim, "I was following orders." If we are "entrapped," to use Tinker's word, if we exist within a carceral social reality, as mentioned numerous times, it is so because we have, at a particular moment, as individuals, agreed in some way to do so. People make many choices, according to Staub, with little or no awareness, although they actually have available to them a wide variety of moral values and social rules from which to choose.[23] As actors in a social setting, we must never lose sight of this fact. To fail in this regard means that the individual has abandoned any claim to personal autonomy. Rather than forsake personal autonomy, we may take heart in the possibility Michel Foucault offers: for the individual to be able to create a self, to act upon oneself, "to monitor, test, improve and transform" oneself.[24] Likewise, the individual must always be on guard for the indications that one's personal autonomy is being misappropriated by some larger force or entity, such as a social institution or one's culture. In this regard, Zygmunt Bauman argued that individuals have a "moral responsibility for resisting socialization."[25] In sum, from the standpoint of culture studies, the matter of human agency is of paramount importance. We must also be cognizant of the insidious nature of the cultural process whereby the individual gives his or her assent to a belief system. "Guided by shared cultural dispositions ... people *join* rather than simply obey out of fear or respect."[26] The moment of choice for the individual may not be obvious or overt, but it can be more likely a quiet moment, perhaps one not even demanding reflection or forethought. The moment passes, the person's agreement is given, a bond is established, and a life is ineffably changed. It doesn't stop there, however, because that single life is part of a much larger social and cultural scene, one that brings various kinds of pressure and behaviors against Others, thereby altering their lives in turn. Countless such personal choices had to be reached over the centuries, rooted in the culture of sacred violence. Staub argues that the process that culminates in genocide involves a slow progression "over decades or even centuries and creates a readiness in the culture."[27]

I have tried to maintain a consistent position throughout this study that the culture operated—on its members and against The Other—as it had been designed to do, to create a certain desired state or condition of uniformity of beliefs. A gardening function was performed with exquisite precision. There is, perhaps, some comfort in failures during the Holocaust and in other lamentable episodes. Perhaps some higher calling exists, but human weaknesses did not allow its full realization. There is certainly scriptural support for this exalted possibility for human behavior, not the least being the "difficult words" recorded in Matthew 5, the Sermon on the Mount. However, Christianity does not offer its believers a univocal set of options for behavior. We have seen countless examples of sacred violence that seem to have become more readily operative when The Other is involved. Given this equivocal theological and cultural message, it is no wonder that a scholar sees the West as "ethically confused" and Christianity as virtually meaningless[28] in terms of its moral stances. The prejudices that people live with as part of the fabric of their lives in large part derive from social institutions such as the Church.[29] For example, in Christian Europe, France in particular, the Catholic faithful experienced over two centuries a certain catechism by Abbé M. Fleury that went into no less than 172 editions after its initial publication in 1766.[30] Seven or eight generations of Catholic children in France were raised and educated with the primary moral authority leaders in their impressionable young lives teaching from *Catechisme Historique*, filled with many vilifications of Jews and Judaism. We know of the depths of anti-Semitism in neighboring countries, fueled by similar discursive realities. As Sardar has pointed out, the stereotypes that afflicted Jews over the centuries served to separate "the Other from the existence of redeemed European Christian humanity."[31] Indeed, Mario Eidman, a Polish Jew raised as a Catholic in the years before the war, tells of hearing two young Polish Catholic priests offering a sermon at a Mass immediately *after* the end of the war, offering their devout thanks before the congregation to Hitler for having rid Poland of the Jews in their midst. Eidman and his father promptly left the church, never to return. They did begin practicing Judaism again.[32] George Kelsey finds that over time there has been a gradual shift from religious superiority to racial superiority,[33] although it appears that the two are often closely allied in social practice. The institution that has served as the dominant religion in Western Europe contributed in hideous, horrifying ways to the creation of prejudice against The Other, but has barely begun the kind of self-examination that would begin to reach a comprehensive understanding of its past and its terrible implications. As Victoria Barnett states, Christianity did not fail in the Holocaust for the simple reason that "it had been too Christian."[34] With its decisive, formative contribution to religious prejudice and racism in a theology of sacred violence, Christianity must face the tragic consequences of its belief structure. Kelsey states a sobering basic point: "The logic of racism is genocide because that which is wrong with an out-race is its fundamental being ... it requires the final solution."[35] Sardar agrees: defining The Other as evil leaves as the only solution their elimination.[36] Forrest G. Wood, who has studied Christianity and racism, makes the somber observation that traditional Christian doctrine was racist, that belief in racial inequality was conspicuous from the beginning. Wood offers the judicious assessment that an actual *weakening* of what he calls "Christian idealism" would have been more effective in eliminating racism.[37] Wood's point, surely one that is highly disturbing to thoughtful people, must also bring us to a deeper consideration of the implications of all aspects of the theology of sacred violence. Rigid adherence to furthering "God's plan," and to the transcendent vision and dogmatic demands of Christianity makes it unlikely or very difficult for the devout adherent to overcome the religion's "idealism" in favor of a moral stance that might prove to be sympathetic to The Other. The weakening of which Wood speaks is perhaps akin to some of the conclusions found in *The Altruistic Personality* by Samuel P. Oliner and Pearl M. Oliner. For instance, rather than an acceptance of the dictates of authority, one is less likely to contribute to dehumanization if one has been raised to reach independent positions involving moral obligations.

As stated several times, many scholars see the Holocaust as a terrible deviation in the supposedly humane context of Western culture and civilization, seeing it as an event that shattered all previously known moral categories. Robert Wistrich, in his crucial study of the Holocaust, has said, for example, that the Holocaust is "a *caesura* in Western civilization."[38] The German theologian Johann Baptist Metz finds that Auschwitz has caused an "'interruption' of theology's stream of ideas."[39] This study, to the contrary, seeks to reveal that the Holocaust, even with its crucially important distinguishing features, is the culminating point of a cultural process that has covered at least seventeen centuries. Western Europe's Christian culture and civilization did not "fail" or take a detour or collapse. Indeed, operating as designed to do for centuries, Christianity achieved an unparalleled peak of efficiency in the genocide of human "gardening" in the Nazi death camps.

Continuity marks the depredations practiced against the various groups constituting The Other from the early centuries of Christianity until today. We see discursive violence and violent actions aimed at the Jews in the fourth century C.E., continued pressures against them through the next several centuries under various synods, full scale warfare against Muslims and Jews during the crusades, an entire bureaucratic apparatus of sacred violence created for the mission of the

Inquisition, military and theological coercion and violence activated against the indigenous peoples of the New World, and scriptural, social, and legal terror directed against Africans to enslave them and strip them of their human rights and dignity. All these are complicated events, discourses, and processes, but crucial, uniform cultural elements remain.

Joshua Trachtenberg observes that in the Middle Ages, "vilification" against Jews became "actuality in the mind of the uncritical." For these people, Satan and the Jews had battled not only against Christ in his lifetime, but also "in the contemporaneous war against the Church and its civilization." Christianity's response was a summons to a "holy war of extermination" against Satan, in the persons of the Jews.[40] Crusaders felt empowered by a moral imperative to take vengeance on their various enemies to the East to set aright God's world in their charge, and, following precedents established earlier, killed "heretics" without fear of sin.[41] They knew they were serving God when they killed the enemies of the church; they were assured by their religious superiors that they were not committing homicide.[42] Raymond Schmandt recalls Robert Lifton's doubling concept when he points out that Christians had to reconcile the mandates of their religious mysticism with the sheer horror of warfare.[43] The niceties of a sacred violence theology could not, however, obscure the fact that "under the cover of righteous Christian outreach, criminal rapaciousness would be sanctioned."[44] This would involve the numerous perpetrators over many centuries, as well as the countless bystanders who did nothing as the atrocities continued unabated. Too many saw fit to rationalize atrocity with the theological dictates of their religion. Victoria Barnett notes that during the Holocaust, many people, but especially the perpetrators, "seemed to be leading two lives."[45] Certainly true under the Nazis, it was a central pattern for much of Christian existence since the beginnings of the Common Era.

We would be hard pressed to detect the differences in the anti-Semitic rhetoric of the Church's saint named Chrysostom, papal declarations, Luther, German sermons and periodicals, and Hitler's pathological fulminations. Racist discourse, originally aimed at Christianity's self-declared nemesis, the Jews, also served as the crucially necessary template for later cultural encounters with a variety of Others. It was effective in involving both the literate and the illiterate, conditioning the behaviors and attitudes of the entire social spectrum. Jews and those who became The Other in subsequent cultural encounters always had protectors and benefactors, but these Christians were typically a distinct minority, often despised and marginalized by the dominant culture, even declared insane. The most humane declarations of Christian scriptures, the Sermon on the Mount, for example, seem to have had precious little influence on the actions and beliefs of the vast majority of believers when The Other was targeted for anathema and destruction. We may wonder, however, what else might have happened to The Other without the possibly restraining effect of certain charitable scriptural sentiments.

Robert P. Ericksen concentrates on three of the elite leaders in Germany's theological circles in the Hitler era—Gerhard Kittel, Paul Althaus, and Emmanuel Hirsch—as representative of the majority of their colleagues in German universities and churches.[46] All three badly compromised their respective positions during the Nazi years. Kittel's defense of his behavior included two significant points. Ericksen notes that Kittel asked: "Could it not be believed that [his] position towards the Jewish question was imposed upon him by God?" Then, the "final question is 'whether in the Christian cultural world it counts as a crime which must be prevented through legal punishment, that one represents a position on the Jewish question based upon the instruction of Jesus and the Apostles?'"[47]

Kittel's anguished questions ring with poignancy and urgency down through more than twenty centuries of Christian existence and seventeen centuries of Christian domination. Chrysostom, many popes, crusaders, inquisitors, and Luther, among many others cited in this study, could have cried out in similar fashion, having made their many contributions, under the powerful influence of their interpretations of Christian scripture, to the immiseration of The Other over those centuries. We should note well Kittel's sense of a lack of autonomy: God imposed his position upon him. In most respects, he had led a devout, pious life. Strictly speaking, to fail to execute a divine wish in the service of sacred violence could be construed as sinful, an offense against God and his plan for the world. Certainly, Kittel's impressive scholarship had revealed for him massive discursive and cultural substantiation for his position. He did not achieve his theological stance unwittingly or in a discursive vacuum. Obviously, he relied on ample precedents. That he was even dimly aware of the possible criminal implications reveals a conscience not entirely devoid of sensitivity. But the key point is that he is also able to connect his personal past with the crucially important and empowering "instruction" of Jesus and the Apostles. For Kittel, as with the vast majority of Christians, there is a personal continuum of perspectives from historical, scriptural figures to his own life and times. Under such circumstances, the Christian conscience is nullified into passivity, or activated into the evils of atrocity or genocide with regard to the welfare of The Other. We must inquire as to the theological and cultural mechanisms whereby otherwise decent human beings find themselves party to the most inhumane actions. Absent ideological critique, what is to stop decent, believing Christians today from behaving as earlier Christians did? We may wonder about attempting to define the precise moment, based on Ericksen's point, when a "sane" Christian effort to exercise dominion over The Other transmutes into something insane, an atrocity, a genocidal bloodbath. Given its terrible track record, Merryl Wyn Davies argues that Christian history "became a steadily lengthening chronicle of mass neurosis."[48]

Adolf Hitler and Heinrich Himmler were morally unfathomable. It is difficult to project ourselves into their mental landscapes and mythical constructs. The overwhelming proportions of their crimes against humanity, the sheer horror, exceed anyone's ability to grasp the deed. Does this make the inquisitor more scrutable, or innocent of similar crimes? Are we able to penetrate the minds of those who devised the Inquisition's torture instruments better than we can the minds of Hitler and Himmler, or the ordinary men and women who executed the Final Solution? Are we better able to understand a pope who wants all Jews burned? Does the fact that his wish did not take place in his lifetime somehow act as a buffering agent for us today? Does it offer protection from the moral and cultural implications of his position?

All the seemingly countless small measures taken toward dehumanizing The Other over the centuries of Christian dominion and power left not a chasm to be crossed but just another small, incremental step to take for perpetrators and bystanders in the Holocaust. The perpetrators and bystanders of the Holocaust proved perfectly capable of taking that step. As stated in my 1995 book, the Holocaust was thinkable because it had been thinkable. Geoffrey Hartman, in his *The Fateful Question of Culture*, reiterates Adorno's point from a half century ago: Auschwitz was there before Auschwitz.[49] As shown, there are clear examples of those in the Christian past who had been capable of having such thoughts, of creating Auschwitz before Himmler's order. The thoughts that go into this are, after all, deeply embedded in Christian discourse and countless millions of the church's faithful have had access to and subscribed to those thoughts for at least seventeen centuries. Over the centuries, the leaders of the Church appealed for destruction of The Other, most often the Jews, and the people who heard those words almost always responded in kind, killing untold numbers of innocent victims in the process. In the Holocaust, the Germans, and their many helpers, did, indeed, take that small step from, say, the rhetorical extravagances of Martin Luther to activating the murderous rhetoric of *Mein Kampf*. The defense lawyer for convicted war criminal Alfred Rosenberg, author of *Myth of the Twentieth Century* and Nazi minister for occupied territories in the Soviet Union, argued that Christian morality demanded above all one's obedience to the established authorities.[50] Such a claim rests on very substantial historical antecedents for evidence. Also exposed is the moral bankruptcy of all cultural and theological matters that contributed to the Holocaust. Perpetrators such as Rosenberg had abundant examples to model themselves upon. In this sense, then, the Holocaust was implicit in the trajectory of development of Western culture and history, once the culture and its agents set out in a certain way, without developing a restraining ideological critique. As stated earlier, the process of cultural dominion continues even after the Holocaust. In the 1948 Darmstadt Declaration, the German Lutherans blamed the Jewish victims for their fate under the Nazis. Southern Baptists made a concerted effort to convert Jews during Rosh Hashanah in 1999. The Holocaust did not present any insurmountable difficulties for the Christians involved in these latter efforts. Theological and cultural mandates to continue implementing the destructive patterns from the past against The Other proved to be powerful indeed. As George Kelsey notes, the adherents of the racist faith that developed over the centuries to destroy countless lives were Christians and citizens within a Christian civilization.[51] In the twenty-first century, overtly racist Christian groups are apparently isolated to the fringes of American society, but this was not the case for the vast majority of the time that Christianity impacted the beliefs of its members. It also was not the case in South Africa as recently as a decade ago. In certain ways, what is now the fringe was at one time, in the not too distant past, a central feature of the religion and the belief structure of its members. A close friend of mine, a member of the Navajo nation, was a child during the Johnson administration years, reputedly the Great Society years. In his boarding school in Arizona, operated by various missionaries, he was not allowed to speak his native language, and was punished severely for doing so. In the course of his youth, he was baptized no less than *eight* times. These inexplicable events took place, as mentioned, in the 1960s. Very few white Christian children would have had such experiences. This personal example illustrates Robert A. Williams's idea that the "mandate for Christian Europe's subjugation of all peoples whose radical divergence from European-derived norms of right conduct signified their need for conquest and remediation."[52] Although key changes in this area in recent memory are perhaps grounds for a careful optimism, a prudent review of Christian discourse will often find that there are vestiges of the past in some of today's statements. For instance, many see other religions as having only a "partial truth" or an "incomplete communion."

One of the driving features of a Christian culture and civilization is that it relies upon or seeks "transcendent" answers to the difficult, baffling problems of life. This kind of reliance often displaces more mundane considerations and explanations. Transcendent explanations are usually keyed to the alleged overarching designs of God. Under these circumstances, it is difficult for the members of a culture to perceive or acknowledge the evil components of its presence in history, as in the case of Gerhard Kittel. All-inclusive, totalizing cultural constructs can also serve to conceal inherent limitations. Alan Davies notes that "individualistic illusions" fostered by Protestantism, for example, cause believers to "underestimate the depth of" problems such as racism.[53] As an ideology making all-encompassing, transcendent claims, good for all times, conditions, and peoples, Christianity provides "a mode of interpretation in which the intrinsic sense of the dominant idea is applied in all possible directions until everything in history and human experience is subsumed under its logic."[54] Thereby it operates as a key component of the larger culture. Ervin Staub contributes to our understanding with another incisive point: "better world" ideologies are often structured so they are open to a more inclusive involvement of Other victims.[55] After all, in the mere effort to create a "better world," it makes little sense for the endeavor to attempt to repair only a mere fragment of the total experience. If this is true, as a principle it might be extended to similar concerns in this study, for instance, the failure to realize what Robert E. Willis perceives as the evil essence of Christianity, or the inability on the part of many people to recognize "the basic flaw in the dominant conception of contemporary civilization."[56]

Victoria Barnett appears to be in agreement with these basic considerations when she argues that the history of this century might well have been different if the churches had taught different messages and if the schools had taught tolerance.[57]

Personal autonomy can triumph over the violent mandates fostered by society, religion, ideology, and the culture. It requires a specific act of the will and a consciousness that external forces threaten to take over the personality. In the terms of this study, this is the issue of coercion. Such coercion can take either the form of coercive pacification or normative pacification. Either one is potentially dangerous once activated and aimed at The Other, but it is the latter form which the individual needs most to defend against. I am not without hope that this can take place. I must refer, for instance, to my deep friendship with the Reverend Charles Busch, a Congregationalist minister in Oregon. Charles came to his calling late in life, after spending decades in the business world and as a writer. Married to a Buddhist, he has led his congregation in a small Oregon coastal town to replace the usual summer Bible camp with what he calls "Peace Village." There, youngsters from the age of six to about thirteen mingle with Native American medicine people, study yoga and meditation, hear about Gandhi, learn to turn off the television set, learn how to play in socially constructive ways, and come to know about peaceful means of resolving the daily conflicts in their lives, among many other activities. Charles spent part of his most recent sabbatical studying the Hindu masters. Two men who can see retirement looming on the horizon, we shared a good lunch recently. Charles spoke with enthusiasm of a Hindu practice as men age. When the grandfather can see the hair on the top of his grandson's head, it is time to put aside the familiar routines to that point in life and "go to the forest" for meditation and contemplation. Charles and I look forward to that time. I interviewed Reverend Busch as I was completing the writing of this book. I know many fine, thoughtful, good, humane Christians, but Charles stands out. After all of the terrible revelations uncovered in my research, I wanted to know how he might handle being involved in a belief structure that could have criminal implications, the crimes against that portion of humanity known as The Other committed since the fourth century C.E. I was not surprised that Charles had a short answer to a complex question: "Before one can be a good Christian, one must first be a good Jew."[58]

Surely, there are believing Christians who have first made the equivalent of this effort to be a good Jew. If more had done so earlier I sense that the culture and the history of Western Christianity would have turned out differently. That is not, unfortunately, the path upon which the religion took its faithful. We cannot change that lamentable fact, but we need not be controlled by it either. I hope that readers will take it upon themselves to try to be the kind of good Christian that Charles Busch is.

It is not an easy path to take, but those who have done so can help provide important guidance and help all people lead lives free of the terrors of sacred violence. Nevertheless, difficulties are encountered when we hear, for instance, Elie Wiesel's view that "nothing is innocent anymore." Or his assertion that "Auschwitz can only be the revelation of something absolute, absolute evil."[59] For example, even an event such as the papal apology offered in March 2000 reveals that the prayer confessing Christian sins and asking for forgiveness is couched in terms relying upon an unmistakable Christian view of history. The pope asked, "Let us pray that our confession and repentance will be inspired by the Holy Spirit." The prayer continues with a discussion of God's "pilgrim Church," which God ever sanctifies "in the blood of your Son." The pope spoke of the Christian "methods not in keeping with the Gospel in the solemn duty of defending the truth." In something of an understatement, the pope reveals his awareness that "Christians have at times given in to intolerance and have not been faithful to the great commandment of love." Later in the prayer, the pope is more specific, using terminology that is familiar from the cultural standpoint under study here. He hopes that "Christians will be able to repent of the words and attitudes caused by pride, and hatred, by the desire to dominate others, by enmity towards members of other religions."[60] This is an important Christian statement, long overdue, but even in its desire to seek forgiveness and to activate repentance, there are references to matters that must seem chilling to The Other. How many of The Other died at the hands of Christians serving the same Holy Spirit? Did that Holy Spirit intervene to stop the sacred violence, or bless those proceedings, thereby empowering the perpetrators and sustaining the bystanders? The reference to the blood of the Son of God stands in a certain hierarchical, rhetorical, and theological relationship to all other blood shed through the last twenty centuries, with Christ's blood being shed as one of the central claims in the Christian *weltanschauung*. The Other blood has, in many cases, been shed due largely to Christian claims about Christ's blood that impelled believers to strike out against The Other. Perhaps the line from the prayer that best reveals the difficulties is the pope's reference to the lamentable "methods" used in the service of "defending the truth." There is virtually no chance that the pope would call into question the nature of the truth being served, or whether that truth claim is itself intimately involved in the devastating practice of sacred violence, or whether any vestiges of truth reside with The Other. Countless devout followers of Christianity would most likely follow this pattern.

We simply must ask how we are to separate the dancer from the dance. I do not doubt the pope's sincerity. It is obvious from the prayer itself how difficult it is to extricate oneself from the theology that sustains one's life, even though that theology can function in a doubling capacity, its claims producing both acts of love and vicious acts of sacred violence in the service of love. Nevertheless, there are individuals who have seen into the heart of the matter. José Aldunate, S.J., in "The Christian Ministry of Reconciliation in Chile," acknowledges that the terror and violence that afflicted Chile in the last half of the twentieth century had "their roots in the Conquest and the domination of the continent by

Spain and Portugal: the usurpation of sovereignty, of the lands and liberty of the indigenous people; exploitation and genocide; a legacy of misery and poverty."[61] Aldunate then notes that a condition of the desired reconciliation "with God is reparation for offenses and injustices committed against one's neighbor."[62] He is acutely aware of the "lack of ethical and theological discernment on the part of certain leaders of our churches" but he chooses instead to focus on acts of reconciliation emerging in recent years.[63] Aldunate's review of the situation places these acts on a plane that is not identical with the theology that sustained the initial atrocities enacted as sacred violence. His admirable approach is quite unlike any seen in a review of the situation surrounding reconciliation between German and Polish churches, in which another author finds that such reconciliation "is the work of the Holy Spirit."[64] Perhaps this formulation is to be expected in efforts between different elements of the Christian world. We can see the difficulties this could present to members of Other communities, unless we are willing to admit that the Holy Spirit also operates on behalf of those whose theology and beliefs are anathema to Christianity. For The Other, is it possible for reconciliation to be conducted under auspices that are independent of the theology and culture that initially created the problems? More to the point, is it possible for Christians and Christianity to operate in this manner? As Johann Baptist Metz notes, it is necessary to do more than "revise the way Christians and Jews [and Others] have related to one another down through history; rather, it calls for a revision of Christian theology."[65] Similarly, even though it is theologian Gregory Baum who speaks of the operation of the Holy Spirit in achieving reconciliation, it is also Baum who calls for "a transformation of cultural consciousness, a repentance of [the] false sense of superiority, a turning away from the stereotyped images, ... a sorrowing over [the] tradition of aggression and conquest, and a new commitment to peace."[66] Baum is speaking of the situation existing between the churches of Poland and Germany, but his list of concerns could easily be expanded to cover many of the cultural and ideological distortions involving The Other examined in this study.

Stuart Hall, the founder of the British culture studies movement, notes that ideology, and I would submit, a culture, does not allow people to "learn *how things are*" but only "*where they fit* into the existing scheme of things."[67] Thus, those people who find themselves situated within the precincts of a dominant culture are not likely to be able to assess, or cannot realize, that they are in the midst of an enormity such as genocide. They can only know that the anathematized group somehow deserves its punishment, that it is justified, and that by virtue of their identification with and membership in the dominant culture, they are executing the necessary provisions of a grand design. Hall's observation helps us understand the creation of the carceral state where sacred violence against The Other best flourishes. The development and use of an ideological critique would permit people to understand "how things are" rather than being limited to knowing only "where they fit."

In sum, then, there is virtual unanimity among scholars that the Holocaust cannot be equated with or usefully compared to any other historical events involving wholesale slaughters or genocides. I understand and sympathize with these positions, but urge that we all stand to gain much by becoming more aware of and examining crucial patterns of behavior over time within our cultural discourse that contributed in large measure to laying the groundwork for the acts of the perpetrators and the bystanders against the victims of the Holocaust and The Other—and have done so for many centuries. The six million Jewish victims of the Nazis, lost to humanity for all time, should have no further additions to this sad number.

Notes

INTRODUCTION

1. Cited in Kiernan Ryan, ed., *New Historicism and Cultural Materialism* (London: Arnold, 1996), 35.

2. David Svaldi, *Sand Creek and the Rhetoric of Extermination: A Case Study in Indian-White Relations* (Lanham, Md.: University Press of America, 1989), 18.

3. Edward Said, "Representing the Colonized: Anthropology's Interlocutors," *Critical Inquiry* 15 (1989): 211.

4. Stanley Aranowitz and Henry Giroux, *Postmodern Education: Politics, Culture, and Social Criticism* (Minneapolis: University of Minnesota Press, 1991), 137.

CHAPTER ONE

1. Victoria J. Barnett, *Bystanders: Conscience and Complicity during the Holocaust* (Westport, Conn.: Greenwood Press, 2000), 11.

2. Peter Berger, *The Sacred Canopy: Elements of a Sociological Theory of Religion* (New York: Doubleday, 1967), 46.

3. Catherine Belsey, "Towards Cultural History," in *New Historicism*, ed. Ryan, 84.

4. François Furet, *Unanswered Questions: Nazi Germany and the Genocide of the Jews* (New York: Schocken Books, 1989), 280.

5. Cited in Robert Wistrich, *Hitler's Apocalypse: Jews and the Nazi Legacy* (London: Weidenfeld and Nicolson, 1985), 119.

6. Roger Bastide, "Color, Racism, and Christianity," *Daedulus* (Spring 1967): 323.

7. Ervin Staub, *The Roots of Evil: The Origins of Genocide and Other Group Violence* (Cambridge: Cambridge University Press, 1992), 17.

8. Hyam Maccoby, *The Sacred Executioner: Human Sacrifice and the Legacy of Guilt* (London: Thames and Hudson, 1982), 171.

9. Lenore A. Stiffarm and Phil Lane Jr., "The Demography of Native North America: A Question of American Indian Survival," in *The State of Native America,* ed. M. Annette Jaimes (Boston: South End Press, 1992), 30.

10. James Axtell, *Beyond 1492: Encounters in Colonial North America* (New York: Oxford University Press, 1992), 231–232.

11. Donald A. Wells, *The War Myth* (New York: Pegasus, 1967), 76.

12. Graeme Turner, *British Cultural Studies: An Introduction* (London: Routledge, 1996), 30.

13. Ibid., 188.

14. Ibid., 14.

15. Berger, *The Sacred Canopy,* 39.

16. Regina M. Schwartz, *The Curse of Cain: The Violent Legacy of Monotheism* (Chicago: University of Chicago Press, 1997), 16.

17. Merryl Wyn Davies, Ashis Nundy, and Ziauddin Sardar, *Barbaric Others: A Manifesto on Western Racism* (London: Pluto Press, 1993), 21.

18. Jim McKay, quoted in Varda Burstyn, "Sport as Secular Sacrament," in *Sport and Contemporary Society,* 6th ed., ed. D. Stanley Eitzen (New York: Worth Publishers, 2001), 13.

19. Thomas Virgil Peterson, *Ham and Japheth: The Mythic World of Whites in the Antebellum South* (Metuchen, N.J.: Scarecrow Press, 1978), xiii.

20. Berger, *The Sacred Canopy,* 11.

21. Staub, *Roots of Evil,* 54.

22. Raul Hilberg, *The Destruction of the European Jews* (New York: Holmes and Meier, 1985), I, 9.

23. Michael Mann, *The Sources of Social Power* (Cambridge: Cambridge University Press, 1986), 381.

24. Stuart Hall, quoted in Simon During, ed., *The Cultural Studies Reader* (London: Routledge, 1993), 366.

25. K. Ryan, *New Historicism,* 95.

26. Turner, *British Cultural Studies,* 26.

27. T. J. Jackson Lears, "The Concept of Cultural Hegemony: Problems and Possibilities," *American Historical Review,* 90:3 (1985): 569.

28. Staub, *Roots of Evil,* 29.

29. Jaime Contreras, "The Impact of Protestantism in Spain," in *Inquisition and Society in Early Modern Europe,* ed. Stephen Haliczer (Totowa, N.J.: Barnes and Noble Books, 1987), 61.

30. Turner, *British Cultural Studies,* 29.

31. Aiban Wagua, "Present Consequences of the European Invasion of America," in Leonardo Boff and Virgil Elizondo, eds., *1492–1992: The Voice of the Victims* (London: SCM Press, 1990), 53.

32. Stephen Greenblatt, "Resonance and Wonder," in *New Historicism,* ed. Ryan, 60.

33. Rupert Costo and Jeannette Henry Costo, *The Missions of California: A Legacy of Genocide* (San Francisco: The Indian Historian Press, 1987), 112, 93.

34. Maccoby, *Sacred Executioner,* 181.

35. Ibid., 182.

36. Cited in Svaldi, *Sand Creek and the Rhetoric of Extermination,* 9.

37. Francis Jennings, *The Invasion of America* (Chapel Hill: University of North Carolina Press, 1975), 14.

38. Costo and Costo, *Missions of California*, 179.

39. Eric Hobsbawm, "Barbarism: A User's Guide," *New Left Review* 206 (1994): 54.

40. Ziauddin Sardar, *Postmodernism and the Other: The New Imperialism of Western Culture* (London: Pluto Press, 1998), 40.

41. Ibid., 68.

42. John Tomlinson, *Cultural Imperialism: A Critical Introduction* (Baltimore: Johns Hopkins University Press, 1991), 146.

43. Ibid., 10.

44. Barnett, *Bystanders*, 41.

45. Staub, *Roots of Evil*, 134.

46. Jennings, *Invasion of America*, ix.

47. Ibid., 4.

48. Raymond Williams, *Keywords* (London: Fontana, 1976), 16.

49. Staub, *Roots of Evil*, 13.

50. Clifford Geertz, *The Interpretation of Cultures* (New York: Basic Books, 1973), 45.

51. Ibid., 50–51.

52. Turner, *British Cultural Studies*, 26.

53. Ibid., 14.

54. Lee Patterson, "Historical Criticism and the Claims of Humanism," in *New Historicism*, ed. Ryan, 93.

55. Stuart Hall, quoted in Dick Hebdige, "From Culture to Hegemony," in *Cultural Studies Reader*, ed. During, 364.

56. Michel Foucault, "The Subject and Power," *Critical Inquiry* 8 (Summer 1982): 781.

57. Geertz, *Interpretation of Cultures*, 126.

58. Suzanne Langer, *Philosophy in a New Key*, 4th ed. (Cambridge: Harvard University Press, 1957), 287.

59. Richard Rubenstein and John K. Roth, *Approaches to Auschwitz: The Holocaust and Its Legacy* (Atlanta: John Knox Press, 1987), 139.

60. Berger, *The Sacred Canopy*, 24.

61. Staub, *Roots of Evil*, 18.

62. Hobsbawm, "Barbarism," 49.

63. Marcel Simon, *Verus Israel: A Study of the Relations Between Christians and Jews in the Roman Empire (135–425)*, trans. H. McKeating (New York: Oxford University Press, 1986), 146.

64. Rubenstein and Roth, *Approaches to Auschwitz*, 59.

65. John Gager, *The Origins of Anti-Semitism* (New York: Oxford University Press, 1985), 22.

66. Samuel P. Oliner and Pearl M. Oliner, *The Altruistic Personality: Rescuers of Jews in Nazi Europe* (New York: Free Press, 1988), 155 and 373 n8.

67. John T. Pawlikowski, "The Teaching of Contempt: Judaism in Christian Education and Liturgy," in *Auschwitz, Beginning of a New Era? Reflections on the Holocaust*, ed. Eva Fleischner (New York: KTAV Publishing House, 1977), 155.

68. Too numerous to detail each instance; see Joshua Trachtenberg, *The Devil and the Jews: The Medieval Conception of the Jew and Its Relation to Modern Anti-Semitism* (Philadelphia: Jewish Publication Society of America, 1943), and Léon Poliakov, *The History of Anti-Semitism*, trans. Richard Howard (New York: Schocken Books, 1974).

69. Pawlikowski, "Teaching of Contempt," 162–165.

70. Michael R. Steele, *Christianity, Tragedy, and Holocaust Literature* (Westport, Conn.: Greenwood Press, 1995), 118.

71. Edward H. Flannery, "Anti-Zionism and the Christian Psyche," in *When God and Man Failed: Non-Jewish Views of the Holocaust,* ed. Harry James Cargas (New York: Macmillan, 1981), 109–110.

72. Robert E. Willis, "Auschwitz and the Nurturing of Conscience," in *When God and Man Failed,* ed. Cargas, 149.

73. Wells, *War Myth,* 152.

74. Gerhard Falk, *The Jew in Christian Theology* (Jefferson, N.C.: McFarland, 1992), 64.

75. Foucault, "Subject and Power," 783.

76. Hermann Doerris, *Constantine and Religious Liberty,* trans. Roland H. Bainton (New Haven: Yale University Press, 1960), 54–55.

77. Foucault, "Subject and Power," 783.

78. Doerris, *Constantine and Religious Liberty,* 55.

79. Ibid., 59.

80. Robert Ian Moore, *The Formation of a Persecuting Society* (Oxford: Blackwell Publishers, 1990), 108.

81. Wells, *War Myth,* 181.

82. Simon, *Verus Israel,* 146.

83. John Westbury-Jones, *Roman and Christian Imperialism* (London: Macmillan, 1939), 1–2.

84. Poliakov, *The History of Anti-Semitism,* 21.

85. Westbury-Jones, *Roman and Christian Imperialism,* 6.

86. Forrest G. Wood, *The Arrogance of Faith: Christianity and Race in America from the Colonial Era to the Twentieth Century* (New York: Alfred A. Knopf, 1990), 33.

87. Simon, *Verus Israel,* 224.

88. Staub, *Roots of Evil,* 13.

89. Ibid., 79.

90. Ibid., 13.

91. Ibid., 121.

92. Cited in Barnett, *Bystanders,* 148.

CHAPTER TWO

1. Zygmunt Bauman, *Modernity and the Holocaust* (Ithaca: Cornell University Press, 1991), 92.

2. Ibid., 13.

3. Ibid., 70.

4. Alan Davies, *Infected Christianity: A Study of Modern Racism* (Kingston: McGill-Queen's University Press, 1988), 120.

5. Hans Kohn, *The Idea of Nationalism: A Study in Its Origins and Background* (New York: Macmillan, 1961), 70, 49.

6. Frederic Cople Jaher, *A Scapegoat in the New Wilderness: The Origins and Rise of Anti-Semitism in America* (Cambridge: Harvard University Press, 1994), 18–19.

7. Lawrence R. Brown, *The Might of the West* (New York: Ivan Obolensky, 1963), 100; Helen Ellerbe, *The Dark Side of Christian History* (San Rafael, Calif.: Morningstar

Books, 1995), 17; John Driver, *How Christians Made Peace with War* (Scottsdale, Pa.: Herald Press, 1988), 72.

8. Jacob Neusner, *Judaism and Christianity in the Age of Constantine* (Chicago: University of Chicago Press, 1987), 15.

9. Moore, *Formation of a Persecuting Society*, 5.

10. Ibid., 12.

11. Y. Baer, "Israel, the Christian Church and the Roman Empire," *Scripta Hierosolymitana* 7 (1960–1961): 79.

12. Falk, *Jew in Christian Theology*, 65.

13. Rosemary Reuther, "Judaism and Christianity: Two Fourth-Century Religions," *Studies in Religion* 2 (1972): 6.

14. Boff and Elizondo, *1492–1992*, 63.

15. Ellerbe, *Dark Side of Christian History*, 12.

16. David M. Olster, *Roman Defeat, Christian Response, and the Literary Construction of the Jew* (Philadelphia: University of Pennsylvania Press, 1994), 30.

17. Reuther, "Judaism and Christianity," 5.

18. Averil Cameron, *Christianity and the Rhetoric of Empire* (Berkeley: University of California Press, 1991), 2–3.

19. Bernhard Blumenkranz, "Anti-Jewish Polemics and Legislation in the Middle Ages: Literary Fiction or Reality?" *Journal of Jewish Studies* 15 (1964): 126.

20. Ramsay Macmullen, *Christianizing the Roman Empire (A.D. 100–400)* (New Haven: Yale University Press, 1984), 66–67.

21. Simon, *Verus Israel*, 106.

22. Falk, *Jew in Christian Theology*, 21–28. See also Amnon Linder, *The Jews in Roman Imperial Legislation* (Detroit: Wayne State University Press, 1987) and James Parkes, *The Conflict of the Church and the Synagogue: A Study in the Origins of Antisemitism* (New York: Atheneum, 1974).

23. Brian Brennan, "The Conversion of the Jews of Clermont in AD 576," *Journal of Theological Studies* 36 (October 1985): 328.

24. Falk, *Jew in Christian Theology*, 28–35.

25. Ibid., 35–36.

26. Ibid., 36.

27. Blumenkranz, "Anti-Jewish Polemics," 129.

28. Linder, *Jews in Roman Imperial Legislation*, 22–23.

29. John Friesen, "War and Peace in the Patristic Age," in *Essays on War and Peace: Bible and Early Church*, ed. Willard Swartley (Elkhart, Ind.: Institute of Mennonite Studies, 1986), 130.

30. Driver, *How Christians Made Peace with War*, 36, 14.

31. William L. Elster, "The New Law of Christ and Early Christian Pacifism," in *Essays on War and Peace*, ed. Swartley, 119.

32. Gerrit Jan Heering, *The Fall of Christianity: A Study of Christianity, the State and War*, trans. J. W. Thompson (New York: Fellowship Publications, 1943), 28.

33. John Helgeland, "Christians and the Roman Army A.D. 173–337," *Church History* 43 (March 1974), 151.

34. Jean-Michel Hornus, *It Is Not Lawful for Me to Fight: Early Christian Attitudes Toward War, Violence, and the State*, trans. Alan Krieder (Scottsdale, Pa.: Herald Press, 1980), 119.

35. Heering, *Fall of Christianity*, 30.

36. Hornus, *It Is Not Lawful*, 167.

37. Ibid., 171.

38. Adolf Harnack, *Militia Christi*, trans. David McInnes Gracie (Philadelphia: Fortress Press, 1981), 99.

39. Friesen, "War and Peace," 144.

40. Driver, *How Christians Made Peace with War*, 77.

41. Neusner, *Judaism and Christianity*, 35.

42. Hornus, *It Is Not Lawful*, 181; Harnack, *Militia Christi*, 101.

43. Macmullen, *Christianizing the Roman Empire*, 65.

44. Reuther, "Judaism and Christianity," 8.

45. Macmullen, "What Difference Did Christianity Make?" *Historia* 35 (1986): 336.

46. Hornus, *It Is Not Lawful*, 161.

47. Ibid., 169.

48. Friesen, "War and Peace," 150–151.

49. Wells, *War Myth*, 259 n12.

50. Hornus, *It Is Not Lawful*, 198, 186.

51. Neusner, *Judaism and Christianity*, 34.

52. Elie Wiesel, "Jewish Values in the Post-Holocaust Future," *Judaism* 16 (1967): 285.

53. Robert Jay Lifton, *Nazi Doctors* (New York: Basic Books, 1986), 418, 422.

54. Ibid., 458.

55. Ibid., 418.

56. Ibid., 442.

57. Ibid., 458.

58. Robert Jay Lifton, "Doubling: The Faustian Bargain," in *The Web of Violence: From Interpersonal to Global*, ed. Jennifer Turpin and Lester R. Kurtz (Urbana: University of Illinois Press, 1997), 38.

59. James E. Waller, "Perpetrators of the Holocaust: Divided and Unitary Self Conceptions of Evildoing," *Holocaust and Genocide Studies* 10:1 (Spring 1996): 16.

60. Ibid., 20 and 31 n50.

61. Ibid., 28.

62. Ibid., 27.

63. Staub, *Roots of Evil*, 146.

64. Hyam Maccoby, "The Origins of Anti-Semitism," in *The Origins of the Holocaust: Christian Anti-Semitism*, ed. Randolph L. Braham (New York: Columbia University Press, 1986), 11.

65. Simon, *Verus Israel*, 222.

66. Robert L. Wilken, *John Chrysostom and the Jews: Rhetoric and Reality in the Late 4th Century* (Berkeley: University of California Press, 1983), 105 and 116.

67. Paul W. Harkins, trans., *Saint John Chrysostom: Discourses Against Judaizing Christians* (Washington, D.C.: Catholic University of America Press, 1979), 147.

68. Brennan, "Conversion of the Jews," 328.

69. Simon, *Verus Israel*, 217–218.

70. Harkins, *Saint John Chrysostom*, 3, 174, 133.

71. Fred Allen Grissom, "Chrysostom and the Jews: Studies in Jewish-Christian Relations in Fourth-Century Antioch," Diss., Southern Baptist Theological Seminary, 1978, 175–180.

72. Maccoby, *Sacred Executioner*, 150.

73. Grissom, "Chrysostom and the Jews," 121.

74. Ibid., 156.

75. Jaher, *Scapegoat in the New Wilderness*, 30.

76. Maccoby, *Sacred Executioner*, 150.

77. Grissom, "Chrysostom and the Jews," 157–158.

78. Simon, *Verus Israel*, 211.

79. Grissom, "Chrysostom and the Jews," 219–220.

80. Robert P. Ericksen, *Theologians under Hitler* (New Haven: Yale University Press, 1985), 41.

81. Harkins, *Saint John Chrysostom*, 74.

82. Maccoby, *Sacred Executioner*, 154.

83. Macmullen, *Christianizing the Roman Empire*, 100.

84. Simon, *Verus Israel*, 226.

85. Ibid., 227.

86. Jaher, 32.

87. Simon, *Verus Israel*, 225.

88. Falk, *Jew in Christian Theology*, 11.

89. Simon, *Verus Israel*, 221.

90. Jean Juster, "The Legal Conditions of the Jews under the Visigothic Kings," *Israel Law Review* 11 (1976): 262–276.

CHAPTER THREE

1. Luis N. Rivera, *A Violent Evangelism: The Political and Religious Conquest of the Americas* (Louisville, Ky.: Westminster/John Knox Press, 1992), 21, 50.

2. Ellerbe, *Dark Side of Christian History*, 38.

3. Davies, *Infected Christianity*, 36.

4. Robert A. Williams, *The American Indian in Western Legal Thought, The Discourses of Conquest* (New York: Oxford University Press, 1990), 13.

5. Davies, *Infected Christianity*, 21.

6. Benzion Netanyahu, *The Origins of the Inquisition in Fifteenth Century Spain* (New York: Random House, 1995), 171.

7. Sardar, *Postmodernism and the Other*, 36.

8. Leonardo Boff, *New Evangelization: Good News to the Poor*, trans. Robert R. Barr (Maryknoll, N.Y.: Orbis Books, 1990), 40.

9. Staub, *Roots of Evil*, 53. Emphasis in the original.

10. R. A. Williams, *American Indian in Western Legal Thought*, 15.

11. Berger, *The Sacred Canopy*, 39.

12. Rivera, *Violent Evangelism*, 22, 25.

13. Sardar, *Postmodernism and the Other*, 68.

14. Henry Giroux, *Theory and Resistance in Education* (South Hadley, Mass.: Bergin and Garvey, 1983), 132.

15. Boff, *New Evangelization*, 7.

16. Giroux, *Theory and Resistance*, 149.

17. Davies, *Infected Christianity*, 9.

18. Ibid., 8; Jonathan Riley-Smith, ed., "The Crusading Movement and Historians," *The Oxford History of the Crusades* (Oxford: Oxford University Press, 1999), 5.

19. Davies, *Infected Christianity*, 37.

20. Zoé Oldenbourg, *Massacre at Montségur: A History of the Albigensian Crusade,* trans. Peter Green (London: Phoenix, 1998), 183.

21. Ibid., 125.

22. Robert Chazan, *In the Year 1096: The First Crusade and the Jews* (Philadelphia: Jewish Publication Society, 1996), 23.

23. Joshua Prawer, *The Crusaders' Kingdom: European Colonialism in the Middle Ages* (New York: Praeger, 1972), 245.

24. James Turner Johnson, *Ideology, Reason, and the Limitations of War* (Princeton: Princeton University Press, 1975), 10.

25. Chazan, *European Jewry and the First Crusade* (Berkeley: University of California Press, 1987), 75.

26. Jennings, *Invasion of America,* 6.

27. Riley-Smith, "An Approach to Crusading Ethics," *Reading Medieval Studies* 6 (1980): 3.

28. Ibid., 3.

29. Riley-Smith, "The Crusading Movement and Historians," *Oxford History of the Crusades,* 3–5.

30. Poliakov, *The History of Anti-Semitism,* 74.

31. Maccoby, *Sacred Executioner,* 173.

32. Poliakov, *The History of Anti-Semitism,* 36.

33. Marcus Bull, "Origins," in *Oxford History of the Crusades,* ed. Riley-Smith, 25.

34. Riley-Smith, "Approach to Crusading Ethics," 1.

35. Harnack, *Militia Christi,* 35.

36. Chazan, *European Jewry,* 25, 36.

37. Chazan, *In the Year 1096,* 53.

38. Poliakov, *The History of Anti-Semitism,* 42, 44, 50.

39. Prawer, *Crusaders' Kingdom,* 239.

40. Malcolm Barber, *Crusaders and Heretics, 12th–14th Centuries* (London: Variorum, 1995), 5, 12–13.

41. Ibid., ix–5.

42. Chazan, *European Jewry,* 59.

43. Allan Cutler, "Innocent III and the Distinctive Clothing of Jews and Muslims," *Studies in Medieval Culture* 3 (1970): 115.

44. Poliakov, *The History of Anti-Semitism,* 123.

45. Karl F. Morrison, *Understanding Conversion* (Charlottesville: University Press of Virginia, 1992), 81.

46. Sander Gilman, *Jewish Self-Hatred: Anti-Semitism and the Hidden Language of Jews* (Baltimore: Johns Hopkins University Press, 1986), 51.

47. Aziz Suryal Atiya, *The Crusade in the Later Middle Ages* (London: Metheum, 1938), 86.

48. Riley-Smith, "The Crusading Movement and Historians," *Oxford History of the Crusades,* 6.

49. John Godfrey, *1204: The Unholy Crusade* (Oxford: Oxford University Press, 1980), 37.

50. Palmer A. Throop, *A Criticism of the Crusade: A Study of Public Opinion and Crusade Propaganda* (Philadelphia: Porcupine Press, 1975), 27.

51. Desmond Seward, *The Monks of War: The Military Religious Orders* (London: Penguin Books, 1972), 36.

52. Throop, *Criticism of the Crusade*, 72.

53. Ibid., 33, 39.

54. Ibid., 132–133.

55. Kohn, *Idea of Nationalism*, 74.

56. Sardar, *Postmodernism and the Other*, 235.

57. Ellerbe, *Dark Side of Christian History*, 65.

58. Hans Siemson, *Hitler Youth* (London: Drummond, 1940), 74.

59. Williams, *The American Indian in Western Legal Thought*, 35.

60. Throop, *Criticism of the Crusade*, 123.

61. James A. Brundage, *The Crusades: A Documentary Survey* (Milwaukee: Marquette University Press, 1962), 17–20.

62. Simon Lloyd, "The Crusading Movement: 1096–1274," in Riley-Smith, *Oxford History of the Crusades*, 42–43.

63. Ibid., 34; Walter Porges, "The Clergy, the Poor, and the Non-Combatants on the First Crusade," *Speculum* 21:1 (1946): 10–13.

64. Lloyd, "The Crusading Movement: 1096–1274," in Riley-Smith, *Oxford History of the Crusades*, 35, 66.

65. Elizabeth Siberry, *Criticism of Crusading: 1095–1274* (Oxford: Clarendon Press, 1985), 197.

66. Prawer, *Crusaders' Kingdom*, 243.

67. Chazan, *European Jewry*, 5.

68. Jaher, *Scapegoat in the New Wilderness*, 50.

69. Chazan, *European Jewry*, 5, 52.

70. Simon Lloyd, "The Crusading Movement: 1096–1274," in Riley-Smith, *Oxford History of the Crusades*, 46.

71. Poliakov, *The History of Anti-Semitism*, 49–52, 60, 99.

72. Godfrey, *Unholy Crusade*, 50.

73. Ibid., 37.

74. Ellerbe, *Dark Side of Christian History*, 65.

75. Seward, *Monks of War*, 35.

76. Ibid., 40.

77. Lifton, "Doubling," 35.

78. Staub, *Roots of Evil*, 108.

79. Oldenbourg, *Massacre at Montségur*, 269.

80. Walter L. Wakefield, *Heresy, Crusade and the Inquisition in Southern France 1100–1250* (London: George Allen and Unwin, 1974), 83.

81. Barnett, *Bystanders*, 23.

82. Ellerbe, *Dark Side of Christian History*, 68.

83. Barnett, *Bystanders*, 41.

84. Sharon Begley, "The Roots of Evil," *Newsweek*, 21 May 2001, 33.

CHAPTER FOUR

1. Angel Alcalá, ed., *The Spanish Inquisition and the Inquisitorial Mind* (Boulder, Colo.: Social Science Monographs, 1987), 17.

2. Moore, *Formation of a Persecuting Society*, 99

3. Ibid., 151.

4. Jean-Pierre DeDieu, "The Inquisition and Popular Culture in New Castile," in *Inquisition and Society in Early Modern Europe,* ed. Haliczer, 143.

5. Virgilio Pinto Crespo, "Thought Control in Spain," in *Inquisition and Society in Early Modern Europe,* ed. Haliczer, 173.

6. Rivera, *Violent Evangelism,* 51.

7. Ellerbe, *Dark Side of Christian History,* 76.

8. Contreras, "Impact of Protestantism in Spain," 61.

9. Mary Elizabeth Perry and Anne J. Cruz, eds., *Cultural Encounters: The Impact of the Inquisition in Spain and the New World* (Berkeley: University of California Press, 1991), 16.

10. Lears, "The Concept of Cultural Hegemony," 569–570.

11. Sardar, *Postmodernism and the Other,* 32.

12. Edward Peters, *Inquisition* (New York: Free Press, 1988), 29.

13. Ibid., 3.

14. Ibid., 47.

15. Moore, *Formation of a Persecuting Society,* 29, 10.

16. Jaher, *Scapegoat in the New Wilderness,* 59.

17. Wakefield, *Heresy, Crusade and the Inquisition,* 133–134.

18. Oldenbourg, *Massacre at Montségur,* 284.

19. Cecil Roth, *The Spanish Inquisition* (New York: W. W. Norton, 1964), 35.

20. Edward Burman, *The Inquisition: The Hammer of Heresy* (Wellingborough, Great Britain: Aquarian Press, 1984), 41.

21. Wakefield, *Heresy, Crusade and the Inquisition,* 135.

22. Elkan Nathan Adler, *Auto De Fé and Jew* (London: Oxford University Press, 1908), 10.

23. DeDieu, "Inquisition and Popular Culture in New Castile," 144.

24. Haliczer, *Inquisition and Society in Early Modern Europe,* 7.

25. Hoffman Nickerson, *The Inquisition: A Political and Military Study of Its Establishment* (1932; reprint, Port Washington, N.Y.: Kennikat Press, 1968), 212.

26. John A. O'Brien, *The Inquisition* (New York: Macmillan, 1973), 101–102.

27. Wakefield, *Heresy, Crusade and the Inquisition,* 175–178.

28. Moore, *Formation of a Persecuting Society,* 5. Italics in the original.

29. Alcalá, *The Spanish Inquisition,* 39.

30. Contreras, "Impact of Protestantism in Spain," 57.

31. Alcalá, *The Spanish Inquisition,* 26; Netanyahu, *Origins of the Inquisition,* 128.

32. Wakefield, *Heresy, Crusade and the Inquisition,* 141.

33. Arthur Stanley Turberville, "Heresies and the Inquisition in the Middle Ages, c. 1000–1305," *Cambridge Medieval History* 6 (1936): 715.

34. Ibid., 715.

35. Angus MacKay, "Popular Movements and Pogroms in Fifteenth-Century Castile," *Past and Present* 55 (1972): 62.

36. Peters, *Inquisition,* 50.

37. Roth, *Spanish Inquisition,* 50.

38. Poliakov, *The History of Anti-Semitism,* 183.

39. George D. Kelsey, *Racism and the Christian Understanding of Man* (New York: Charles Scribner and Sons, 1965), 120.

40. Netanyahu, *Origins of the Inquisition,* 492.

41. Sardar, *Postmodernism and the Other,* 235.

42. Joshua Starr, "The Mass Conversion of Jews in Southern Italy: 1290–1293," *Speculum* 21 (1946): 204–207.

43. Netanyahu, *Origins of the Inquisition,* 505–506.

44. Ibid., 511.

45. Staub, *Roots of Evil,* 61, 83.

46. Christopher G. Ellison and John P. Bartkowski, "Religion and the Legitimation of Violence: Conservative Protestantism and Corporal Punishment," in *Web of Violence,* ed. Turpin and Kurtz, 47.

47. Roth, *Spanish Inquisition,* 123.

48. Ibid., 25.

49. Morrison, *Understanding Conversion,* 7.

50. Roth, *Spanish Inquisition,* 212–213.

51. Adler, *Auto De Fé and Jew,* 65.

52. Alan Lawson Maycock, *The Inquisition: From Its Establishment to the Great Schism* (New York: Harper and Row, 1926), 92, 88.

53. Starr, "Mass Conversion," 295.

54. Ellerbe, *Dark Side of Christian History,* 83.

55. Ibid., 30.

56. Roth, *Spanish Inquisition,* 87.

57. Netanyahu, *Origins of the Inquisition,* 181.

58. Richard Kieckhefer, *Repression of Heresy in Medieval Germany* (Philadelphia: University of Pennsylvania Press, 1979), 14.

59. Alcalá, *The Spanish Inquisition,* 21.

60. Netanyahu, *Origins of the Inquisition,* 1090.

61. Ibid., 149.

62. Ibid., 139.

63. Poliakov, *The History of Anti-Semitism,* 58.

64. Peters, *Inquisition,* 79.

65. Gilman, *Jewish Self-Hatred,* 32.

66. Alcalá, *The Spanish Inquisition,* 26.

67. Henry C. Lea, "Ferrand Martinez and the Massacres of 1391," *American Historical Review* 1:2 (January 1896): 211.

68. Adler, *Auto De Fé and Jew,* 52.

69. John Huxtable Elliott, *Imperial Spain: 1469–1716* (Harmondsworth, England: Penguin Books, 1970), 106.

70. Nicolas Davidson, "The Inquisition and the Italian Jews," in *Inquisition and Society in Early Modern Europe,* ed. Haliczer, 24.

71. Gilman, *Jewish Self-Hatred,* 38.

72. Ibid., 54.

73. Davidson, "Inquisition and the Italian Jews," 30.

74. Poliakov, *The History of Anti-Semitism,* 183.

75. Nickerson, *Inquisition,* 78.

76. Netanyahu, *Origins of the Inquisition,* 129.

77. Ibid., 132–135.

78. Ibid., 134–142.

79. Ibid., 145–147.

80. Roth, *Spanish Inquisition,* 22.

81. Poliakov, *The History of Anti-Semitism,* 146.

82. William A. Clebsch, "Introduction" in Peterson, *Ham and Japheth*, xiii.

83. Richard Kieckhefer, "Radical Tendencies in the Flagellant Movement of the Mid-Fourteenth Century," *Journal of Medieval and Renaissance Studies* 4 (1974): 102, 105.

84. Peters, *Inquisition*, 73.

85. Harry Culverwell Porter, *The Inconstant Savage* (London: Duckworth, 1979), 35.

86. Staub, *Roots of Evil*, 71.

87. Maycock, *Inquisition*, 7.

88. Ibid., 12, 15.

89. Herbert S. Klein, "Anglicanism, Catholicism and the Negro Slave," *Comparative Studies in Society and History* 3:3 (April 1966): 296.

90. Oldenbourg, *Massacre at Montségur*, 291.

91. Staub, *Roots of Evil*, 18, 35.

92. Ibid., 83.

93. Maccoby, *Sacred Executioner*, 8.

94. Maurice Bévenot, "The Inquisition and Its Antecedents: I," *Heythrop Journal* 6 (1966): 258, 260.

95. Nickerson, *Inquisition*, 175.

96. Bévenot, "Inquisition and Its Antecedents," 261.

97. Ibid., 262.

98. Maurice Bévenot, "The Inquisition and Its Antecedents: III," *Heythrop Journal* 8 (1967): 59.

99. Rivera, *Violent Evangelism*, 21, 50.

100. Staub, *Roots of Evil*, 13.

101. Netanyahu, *Origins of the Inquisition*, 1076; Roth, *Spanish Inquisition*, 273.

102. Moore, *Formation of a Persecuting Society*, 153.

103. Staub, *Roots of Evil*, 119, 147.

104. Ibid., 244.

105. Cited in Staub, 71.

CHAPTER FIVE

1. Valentin Y. Mudimbe, "*Romanus Pontifex* and the Expansion of Europe," in *Race, Discourse, and the Origins of the Americas*, ed. Vera Lawrence Hyatt and Rex Nettleford (Washington, D.C.: Smithsonian Institution Press, 1995), 60.

2. David E. Stannard, *American Holocaust: The Conquest of the New World* (Oxford: Oxford University Press, 1992), 22.

3. Jennings, *Invasion of America*, 4.

4. Axtell, *Beyond 1492*, 156.

5. Mudimbe, "*Romanus Pontifex*," 60–61.

6. Kenneth J. Pennington, Jr., "Bartolome de las Casas and the Tradition of Medieval Law," *Church History* 39 (1970): 152.

7. Jennings, *Invasion of America*, 4.

8. R. A. Williams, *American Indian in Western Legal Thought*, 36.

9. Kirkpatrick Sale, *The Conquest of Paradise: Christopher Columbus and the Columbian Legacy* (New York: Penguin Books, 1991), 93, 117.

10. Stannard, *American Holocaust*, 65.

11. Jennings, *Invasion of America*, 43.

12. Daniel Fogel, *Junipero Serra, the Vatican, and Enslavement Theology* (San Francisco: ISM Press, 1988), 9.

13. Rivera, *Violent Evangelism*, 93.

14. Djelal Kadir, *Columbus and the Ends of the Earth: Europe's Prophetic Rhetoric as Conquering Ideology* (Berkeley: University of California Press, 1992), 67.

15. Jennings, *Invasion of America*, 4.

16. Kadir, *Columbus*, 176.

17. Boff, *New Evangelization*, 97, 99.

18. Davies et al., *Barbaric Others*, 2.

19. Ibid., 45.

20. Porter, *Inconstant Savage*, 8, 10.

21. Roy Harvey Pearce, *The Savages of America: A Study of the Indian and the Idea of Civilization* (Baltimore: Johns Hopkins University Press, 1965), 22.

22. Kadir, *Columbus*, x.

23. Ibid., 18.

24. Ibid., 69.

25. Ibid., 96, 99.

26. Porter, *Inconstant Savage*, 480.

27. Rivera, *Violent Evangelism*, 33, 38.

28. Ibid., 33.

29. Ibid., 46.

30. Stannard, *American Holocaust*, 66.

31. Rivera, *Violent Evangelism*, 53.

32. Porter, *Inconstant Savage*, 157.

33. Bartolomé de Las Casas, *The Devastation of the Indies: A Brief Account,* trans. Herma Briffault (New York: Seabury Press, 1974), 43.

34. Beatriz Pastor Bodmer, *The Armature of Conquest: Spanish Accounts of the Discovery of America, 1492–1589,* trans. Lydia Longstreth Hunt (Stanford: Stanford University Press, 1992), 212.

35. Axtell, *Beyond 1492*, 247.

36. Rivera, *Violent Evangelism*, 243.

37. Barnett, *Bystanders*, 150.

38. Anthony Pagden, *The Fall of Natural Man: The American Indian and the Origins of Comparative Ethnology* (Cambridge: Cambridge University Press, 1982), 109.

39. Rivera, *Violent Evangelism*, 237.

40. Stannard, *American Holocaust*, 81.

41. Ibid., 64.

42. Lewis Hanke, *All Mankind Is One* (DeKalb: Northern Illinois University Press, 1974), 69.

43. Juan Friede and Benjamin Keen, *Bartolome de Las Casas in History: Toward an Understanding of the Man and His Work* (DeKalb: Northern Illinois University Press, 1971), 290–291.

44. Hanke, *All Mankind Is One*, 9.

45. George E. Tinker, *Missionary Conquest: The Gospel and Native American Cultural Genocide* (Minneapolis: Fortress Press, 1993), 19.

46. Luis Villoro, "Sahagún, or the Limits of the Discovery of the Other," 1992 Lecture Series, University of Maryland Department of Spanish and Portuguese, 12.

47. Kadir, *Columbus*, 76.

48. de Las Casas, *Devastation of the Indies*, 137.

49. Ibid., 43–49.

50. Ibid., 58, 70, 91.

51. Kadir, *Columbus*, 135.

52. Axtell, *Beyond 1492*, 248.

53. Stannard, *American Holocaust*, 79.

54. Ibid., 80, 83.

55. Jalal Al-I Ahmad, *Occidentosis: A Plague From the West*, trans. R. Campbell (Berkeley, Calif.: Mizan Press, 1984), 40.

56. de Las Casas, *Devastation of the Indies*, 87–88, 104.

57. Sylvia Wynter, "1492: A New World View," in *Race*, ed. Hyatt and Nettleford, 17.

58. Porter, *Inconstant Savage*, 125.

59. Stannard, *American Holocaust*, 179.

60. Sale, *Conquest of Paradise*, 157.

61. Hanna Rosin, "Southern Baptist Campaign Aims to Convert Jews to Christianity," *Oregonian*, 9 September 1999, A3.

62. Cited in David J. Weber, "Blood of Martyrs, Blood of Indians: Toward a More Balanced View of Spanish Missions in Seventeenth-Century North America," in *Columbus, Confrontation, Christianity: The European-American Encounter Revisited*, ed. Timothy J. O'Keefe (Los Gatos, Calif.: Forbes Mill Press, 1994), 145.

63. Porter, *Inconstant Savage*, 95.

64. Ibid., 95.

65. Rivera, *Violent Evangelism*, 230.

66. James Louwen, "Columbus in High School," in *Confronting Columbus*, ed. John Yewell, Chris Dodge, and Jan DeSirey (Jefferson, N.C.: McFarland, 1992), 98.

67. Rivera, *Violent Evangelism*, 214.

68. Tinker, *Missionary Conquest*, 44–45.

69. Stannard, *American Holocaust*, 14.

70. Wynter, "New World View," 31.

71. Villoro, "Sahagún," 5.

72. Wynter, "New World View," 40.

73. Jennings, *Invasion of America*, 6.

74. Jacob Glatstein, Israel Knox, Samuel Margoshes, eds., *Anthology of Holocaust Literature* (Philadelphia: Jewish Publication Society, 1969), 117.

75. Wigberto Jiménez Moreno, "The Indians of America and Christianity," *Americas* 14:4 (April 1958): 418.

76. Porter, *Inconstant Savage*, 157.

77. Boff and Elizondo, *1492–1992*, 41–42, 60.

78. Rivera, *Violent Evangelism*, 260.

79. Sardar, *Postmodernism and the Other*, 31.

80. Edward Hyams and George Ordish, *The Last of the Incas: The Rise and Fall of an American Empire* (New York: Barnes and Noble, 1963), 260–261.

81. Stannard, *American Holocaust*, 216.

82. Kadir, *Columbus*, 75.

83. Tinker, *Missionary Conquest*, 117.

84. Kadir, 169.

85. Stannard, *American Holocaust*, 101.

86. Porter, *Inconstant Savage*, 339.

87. Ibid., 354.

88. R. Pierce Beaver, *Church, State, and the American Indian* (St. Louis: Concordia Publishing House, 1966), 10.

89. Sardar, *Postmodernism and the Other*, 98.

90. Beaver, *Church, State*, 12.

91. F. G. Wood, *Arrogance of Faith*, 21.

92. John Hopkins Kennedy, *Jesuit and Savage in New France* (New Haven: Yale University Press, 1950), 109.

93. Porter, *Inconstant Savage*, 356.

94. Richard Slotkin, *Regeneration Through Violence: The Mythology of the American Frontier* (New York: HarperPerennial, 1996), 84.

95. Tinker, *Missionary Conquest*, 25.

96. Stannard, *American Holocaust*, 107.

97. Axtell, *Beyond 1492*, 58.

98. Tinker, *Missionary Conquest*, 24.

99. Jennings, *Invasion of America*, 221.

100. Slotkin, *Regeneration Through Violence*, 76.

101. Stannard, *American Holocaust*, 114.

102. Slotkin, *Regeneration Through Violence*, 85. Mather's emphasis.

103. Stannard, *American Holocaust*, 136.

104. Ibid., 116.

105. Beaver, *Church, State*, 58.

106. Jennings, *Invasion of America*, 55.

107. Slotkin, *Regeneration Through Violence*, 88, 80.

108. F. G. Wood, *Arrogance of Faith*, 19.

109. Porter, *Inconstant Savage*, 513.

110. Lenore A. Stiffarm and Phil Lane Jr., "The Demography of Native North America: A Question of American Indian Survival," in Jaimes, *State of Native America*, 32.

111. Ward Churchill, *Indians Are Us? Culture and Genocide in Native North America* (Monroe, Maine: Common Courage Press, 1994), 35.

112. F. G. Wood, *Arrogance of Faith*, 35.

113. Kardar, 160.

114. Reginald Horsman, *Race and Manifest Destiny: The Origins of Racial Anglo-Saxonism* (Cambridge: Harvard University Press, 1981), 108.

115. James Treat, ed, *Native and Christian: Indigenous Voices on Religious Identity in the United States and Canada* (New York: Routledge, 1996), 33.

116. Horsman, *Race and Manifest Destiny*, 219.

117. John Fiske, "Manifest Destiny," *Harper's New Monthly Magazine*, 1885, 578.

118. Ibid., 579.

119. Ibid., 580.

120. Ibid., 581. Emphasis in the original.

121. Ibid., 582–583.

122. Ibid., 590.

123. Richard Drinnon, *Facing West: The Metaphysics of Indian-Hating and Empire Building* (Norman: University of Oklahoma Press, 1997), 217.

124. Dee Brown, *Bury My Heart at Wounded Knee* (New York: Holt, Rinehart and Winston, 1970), 184.

125. See D. Brown in *Bury My Heart* for examples of this rhetoric.

126. Pearce, *Savages of America*, 65.

127. Lenore A. Stiffarm and Phil Lane Jr., "The Demography of Native North America: A Question of American Indian Survival," in Jaimes, *State of Native America*, 35–37.

128. D. Brown, *Bury My Heart*, 79.

129. Ibid., 85.

130. Ibid., 400.

131. Jorge Noriega, "American Indian Education in the United States: Indoctrination for Subordination to Colonialism," in *State of Native America*, ed. Jaimes, 374.

132. Stannard, *American Holocaust*, 242.

133. William G. McLaughlin, *The Cherokees and Christianity, 1794–1870* (Athens: University of Georgia Press, 1994), 48.

134. Horsman, *Race and Manifest Destiny*, 166–167.

135. Costo and Costo, *Missions of California*, 55–56, 69.

136. Ibid., 69.

137. Churchill, *Indians Are Us?*, 130. Emphasis added.

138. Tinker, *Missionary Conquest*, 5–6.

139. Costo and Costo, *Missions of California*, 123.

140. Tinker, *Missionary Conquest*, 113.

141. Kadir, *Columbus*, 5.

142. Porter, *Inconstant Savage*, 131.

143. Costo and Costo, *Missions of California*, 113.

144. Horsman, *Race and Manifest Destiny*, 76.

145. Tomlinson, *Cultural Imperialism*, 2.

146. Rivera, *Violent Evangelism*, 161.

147. Boff and Elizondo, *1492–1992*, 118.

148. Hyams and Ordish, *Last of the Incas*, 260.

149. Stannard, *American Holocaust*, 98.

150. Boff and Elizondo, *1492–1992*, 61.

CHAPTER SIX

1. Jack P. Maddex, Jr. "'The Southern Apostasy' Revisited: The Significance of Proslavery Christianity," in *Religion and Slavery*, ed. Paul Finkelman (New York: Garland, 1989), 138.

2. Boff and Elizondo, *1492–1992*, 93.

3. Maddex, "'Southern Apostasy' Revisited," 138.

4. David Brion Davis, *The Problem of Slavery in Western Culture* (New York: Oxford University Press, 1966), 190.

5. Marcus W. Jernegan, "Slavery and Conversion in the American Colonies," *American Historical Review* 21:3 (April 1916): 511.

6. Betty Wood, *The Origins of American Slavery* (New York: Hill and Wang, 1997), 63.

7. Rivera, *Violent Evangelism*, 91.

8. Jaher, *Scapegoat in the New Wilderness*, 61.

9. Netanyahu, *Origins of the Inquisition*, 149–151, 195.

10. Boff and Elizondo, *1492–1992*, 93.

11. Rivera, *Violent Evangelism*, 95.

12. Jennings, *Invasion of America*, 5.

13. Orlando Patterson, *Slavery and Social Death* (Cambridge: Harvard University Press, 1982), 32, 30.

14. Ibid., 37.

15. Larry E. Tise, *Proslavery: A History of the Defense of Slavery in America, 1701–1840* (Athens: The University of Georgia Press, 1987), 116.

16. Patterson, *Slavery and Social Death*, 37.

17. Clebsch, "Introduction," xii–xiii.

18. L. R. Brown, *Might of the West*, 101.

19. Mann, *Sources of Social Power*, 327.

20. William D. Phillips, Jr., *Slavery from Roman Times to the Early Transatlantic Trade* (Minneapolis: University of Minnesota Press, 1985), 35, 49.

21. Kelsey, *Racism*, 28.

22. Winthrop D. Jordan, *White over Black: American Attitudes Toward the Negro, 1550–1812* (New York: W. W. Norton, 1968), 363.

23. Jernegan, "Slavery and Conversion," 519.

24. Richard H. Popkin, "The Philosophical Basis of Eighteenth-Century Racism." in *Racism and the Eighteenth Century*, ed. Harold E. Pagliaro (Cleveland: Case Western Reserve University Press, 1973), 251.

25. B. Wood, *Origins of American Slavery*, 24.

26. Tise, *Proslavery*, 77.

27. Davis, *Problem of Slavery*, 208.

28. John A. Auping, *Religion and Social Justice: The Case of Christianity and the Abolition of Slavery in America* (Mexico, D.F.: Universidad Iberoamericana, Dept. de Ciencias Religiosas, 1994), 26.

29. Jordan, *White over Black*, 20.

30. James Walvin, *Questioning Slavery* (London: Routledge, 1996), 16.

31. B. Wood, *Origins of American Slavery*, 11.

32. Ibid., 12.

33. Walvin, *Questioning Slavery*, 9.

34. Ibid., 76.

35. Tise, *Proslavery*, 294.

36. Davis, *Problem of Slavery*, 208.

37. Maddex, "'Southern Apostasy' Revisited," 139.

38. Phillips, *Slavery*, 34.

39. Fred A. Ross, *Slavery Ordained of God* (1859; reprint, New York: Negro Universities Press, 1969), 47.

40. Phillips, *Slavery*, 186.

41. McLaughlin, *Cherokees and Christianity*, 77.

42. Douglas Ambrose, "Proslavery Christianity in Early National Virginia," in *Religion and the Antebellum Debate over Slavery*, ed. John R. McKivigan and Mitchell Snay (Athens: University of Georgia Press), 47.

43. Peterson, *Ham and Japheth*, 24.

44. Olster, *Roman Defeat*, 122.

45. Peterson, *Ham and Japheth*, 6.

46. Walvin, *Questioning Slavery*, 77.

47. Peterson, *Ham and Japheth*, 83.

48. Ross, *Slavery Ordained of God*, 101.

49. Davis, *Problem of Slavery*, 191.
50. Ross, *Slavery Ordained of God*, 100.
51. Ibid., 144. Emphasis in the original.
52. Tise, *Proslavery*, 17.
53. Peterson, *Ham and Japheth*, 20.
54. Ross, *Slavery Ordained of God*, 42. Emphasis in the original.
55. Ibid., 81. Emphasis in the original.
56. Ibid., 81, 84. Emphasis in the original.
57. Horsman, *Race and Manifest Destiny*, 273.
58. Jennings, *Invasion of America*, 59.
59. Ambrose, "Proslavery Christianity," 43.
60. Westbury-Jones, *Roman and Christian Imperialism*, 352.
61. Davis, *Problem of Slavery*, 194.
62. Ibid., 199.
63. John B. Boles, ed., *Masters and Slaves in the House of the Lord: Race and Religion in the American South* (Lexington: University Press of Kentucky, 1988), 106, 121.
64. Ibid., 122.
65. Ambrose, "Proslavery Christianity," 40.
66. R. Emmett Curran, S.J., "'Splendid Poverty': Jesuit Slaveholding in Maryland, 1805–1838," in *Catholics in the Old South*, ed. Randall M. Miller and Jon L. Wakelyn (Macon, Ga.: Mercer University Press, 1983), 126; and Boles, *Masters and Slaves*, 128.
67. Boles, *Masters and Slaves*, 129.
68. Ibid., 129.
69. Curran, "'Splendid Poverty,'" 129.
70. Ibid., 130.
71. Ibid., 140.
72. Rivera, *Violent Evangelism*, 182.
73. F. G. Wood, *Arrogance of Faith*, 38.
74. Laurence Mordekhai Thomas, *Vessels of Evil: American Slavery and the Holocaust* (Philadelphia: Temple University Press, 1993), 22.
75. Ibid., 36.
76. Ibid., 39.
77. Walvin, *Questioning Slavery*, 61, 70.
78. Davis, *Problem of Slavery*, 172.
79. Ibid., 220.
80. Adam Hochschild, *King Leopold's Ghost* (Boston: Houghton Mifflin, 1998), 165.
81. Ibid., 217.
82. Ibid., 164–166.
83. Ibid., 112.
84. Ibid., 279.
85. Ibid., 299.
86. Ibid., 166.
87. Ibid., 172.
88. Ibid., 279.
89. Popkin, "The Philosophical Basis," 249; also see p. 257 n11.
90. Ross, *Slavery Ordained of God*, 105.
91. Ibid., 105, 107.
92. Jernegan, "Slavery and Conversion," 512.

93. Patterson, *Slavery and Social Death,* 72. See also Colin Palmer, *Slaves of the White God: Blacks in Mexico, 1570–1650* (Cambridge: Harvard University Press, 1976), 113–114.

94. Boles, *Masters and Slaves,* 130, 150.

95. Ambrose, "Proslavery Christianity," 38–39.

96. Jernegan, "Slavery and Conversion," 514.

97. Tise, *Proslavery,* 303.

98. Walvin, *Questioning Slavery,* 25.

CHAPTER SEVEN

1. Falk, *Jew in Christian Theology,* 12.

2. Jaher, *Scapegoat in the New Wilderness,* 69.

3. Egon Schwartz, "Jews and Anti-Semitism in Fin-de-Siècle Vienna," in *Insiders and Outsiders: Jewish and Gentile Culture in Germany and Austria,* ed. Dagmar C. G. Lorenz and Gabriele Weinberger (Detroit: Wayne State University Press, 1994), 50.

4. Falk, *Jew in Christian Theology,* 36.

5. Elisabeth Schussler Fiorenza and David Tracy, eds., *The Holocaust as Interruption* (Edinburgh: T. & T. Clark, 1984), 58.

6. Barnett, *Bystanders,* 88.

7. Norbert Elias, *The Germans* (New York: Columbia University Press, 1996), 305.

8. Jaher, *Scapegoat in the New Wilderness,* 68.

9. Poliakov, *The History of Anti-Semitism,* 112, 49.

10. Barnett, *Bystanders,* 5.

11. Moshe David Herr, "Persecutions and Martyrdoms in Hadrian's Days," *Scripta Hierosolymitana* 23 (1972): 88.

12. Reuther, "Judaism and Christianity," 6.

13. Falk, *Jew in Christian Theology,* 83.

14. Haliczer, *Inquisition and Society in Early Modern Europe,* 7.

15. Staub, *Roots of Evil,* 159.

16. Lifton, "Doubling," 41.

17. David O'Reilly, "Translating 'the Jews,'" *Oregonian,* 18 August 2001, C5.

18. Elias, *Germans,* 329.

19. Barnett, *Bystanders,* 238.

20. Allan Fenigstein, "Reconceptualizing the Obedience of the Perpetrators," paper presented at the Remembering the Future 2000 Conference, Oxford University, July 2000, 5.

21. Barnett, *Bystanders,* 236.

22. Fenigstein, "Reconceptualizing the Obedience," 14.

23. Ibid., 23.

24. James C. Russell, *The Germanization of Early Medieval Christianity* (New York: Oxford University Press, 1994), 40.

25. Ibid., 167.

26. James A. Zabel, *Nazism and the Pastors: A Study of the Ideas of Three Deutsche Christen Groups* (Missoula, Mont.: Scholars Press, 1976), 52.

27. Falk, *Jew in Christian Theology,* 55, 58.

28. Poliakov, *The History of Anti-Semitism,* 225.

29. Contreras, "Impact of Protestantism in Spain," 49.

30. Morton Irving Seiden, *The Paradox of Hate: A Study in Ritual Murder* (New York: South Brunswick, 1967), 166–169.

31. Gilman, *Jewish Self-Hatred*, 60, and a translation of this pamphlet by Jill Neuwelt, based on *D. Martin Luther Werke*, 58 vols. (Weimar: Hermann Böhlau, 1883–1972), 53: 636–637.

32. Poliakov, *The History of Anti-Semitism*, 220.

33. Ibid., 124.

34. Heering, *Fall of Christianity*, 54.

35. Ibid., 53.

36. Ibid., 56.

37. Jacob Katz, *From Prejudice to Destruction, Anti-Semitism, 1700–1933* (Cambridge: Harvard University Press, 1980), 97–101.

38. Ibid., 195–198.

39. Uriel Tal, *Christians and Jews in Germany: Religion, Politics, and Ideology in the Second Reich, 1870–1914*, trans. Noah Jonathan Jacobs (Ithaca: Cornell University Press, 1975), 137.

40. Ibid., 133.

41. Ibid., 139.

42. Katz, *From Prejudice to Destruction*, 304–305.

43. Ibid., 315, and John K. Roth, David Aretha, et al., *Holocaust Chronicle* (Lincolnwood Ill.: Publications International, 2000), 31.

44. Walter Zwi Bacharach, *Anti-Jewish Prejudices in German-Catholic Sermons*, trans. Chaya Galai (Lewiston, N.Y.: Edwin Mellen Press, 1993), 107.

45. Ibid., 53.

46. Ibid., 58–59.

47. Ibid., 60, 70.

48. Ibid., 70.

49. Wistrich, *Hitler's Apocalypse*, 120 n.

50. Bacharach, *Anti-Jewish Prejudices*, 102.

51. Gilman, *Jewish Self-Hatred*, 215.

52. Christina Von Braun, "*Blutschande*: From the Incest Taboo to the Nuremberg Racial Laws," in *Encountering the Other(s): Studies in Literature, History, and Culture*, ed. Gisela Brinker-Gabler (Albany: State University of New York Press, 1995), 127–128.

53. Bacharach, *Anti-Jewish Prejudices*, 110.

54. Wistrich, *Hitler's Apocalypse*, 17–18.

55. Ericksen, *Theologians under Hitler*, 17.

56. Wistrich, *Hitler's Apocalypse*, 139.

57. Kelsey, *Racism*, 64.

58. Tal, *Christians and Jews in Germany*, 277.

59. Wistrich, *Hitler's Apocalypse*, 39.

60. Ibid., 30.

61. Ibid., 69.

62. Ibid., 29.

63. Gerald Reitlinger, *The SS: Alibi of a Nation* (New York: Viking Press, 1957), 66.

64. Wistrich, *Hitler's Apocalypse*, 136, 133.

65. Zabel, *Nazism and the Pastors*, 99.

66. Ibid., 101–102.

67. Ibid., 103.

68. Ibid., 152.

69. John Cornwell, *Hitler's Pope: The Secret History of Pope Pius XII* (New York: Viking, 1999), ix.

70. Ibid., 11.

71. Ibid., 70–71, 75.

72. Ibid., 85.

73. Ibid., 185–186.

74. Ibid., 273.

75. Ibid., 253–254.

76. Ibid., 292, 319.

77. Victor Klemperer, *I Will Bear Witness: 1942–1945*, trans. Martin Chalmers (New York: Modern Library, 2001), 68.

78. Barnett, *Bystanders*, 3.

79. Barnett, *Bystanders*, 8.

80. Victor Klemperer, *I Will Bear Witness: 1933–1941*, trans. Martin Chalmers (New York: Random House, 1998), 10.

81. Ibid., 56.

82. Ibid., 118.

83. Ibid., 186.

84. Wistrich, *Hitler's Apocalypse*, 39.

85. Eric Johnson, *Nazi Terror: The Gestapo, Jews, and Ordinary Germans* (New York: Basic Books, 1999), 204.

86. Staub, *Roots of Evil*, 151.

87. Maccoby, *Sacred Executioner*, 154.

88. Klemperer, *1933–1941*, 139.

89. Ibid., 228–229.

90. Braham, *Origins of the Holocaust*, 13; Maccoby, *Sacred Executioner*, 175.

91. Elias, *Germans*, 316.

92. E. Johnson, *Nazi Terror*, 379.

93. George Victor, *Hitler: The Pathology of Evil* (Dulles, Va.: Brassey's, 1998), 122.

94. Frank Felsenstein, *Anti-Semitic Stereotypes: A Paradigm of Otherness in English Popular Culture, 1660–1830* (Baltimore: Johns Hopkins University Press, 1995), 26.

95. Staub, *Roots of Evil*, 20.

96. Ibid., 117.

97. Netanyahu, *Origins of the Inquisition*, 128.

98. Turpin and Kurtz, *Web of Violence*, 34.

99. Barnett, *Bystanders*, 150.

100. Ellerbe, *Dark Side of Christian History*, 65.

101. E. Johnson, *Nazi Terror*, 221, 257–258.

CONCLUSION

1. Maccoby, *Sacred Executioner*, 181–182.

2. Kelsey, *Racism*, 21.

3. Turner, *British Cultural Studies*, 188.

4. Sardar, *Postmodernism and the Other*, 68.

5. Gilman, *Jewish Self-Hatred*, 14.

6. Poliakov, *The History of Anti-Semitism*, 144.

7. Pearce, *Savages of America*, 105.

8. F. G. Wood, *Arrogance of Faith*, xix.

9. Costo and Costo, *Missions of California*, 116.

10. *The Works of Robert G. Ingersoll* (New York: Ingersoll League, 1929), 2: 273–275.

11. Doerris, *Constantine and Religious Liberty*, 55.

12. José Oscar Beozzo, "Humiliated and Exploited Natives," in *1492–1992*, ed. Boff and Elizondo, 82.

13. Tinker, *Missionary Conquest*, 113.

14. Ibid., 115.

15. Staub, *Roots of Evil*, 51.

16. Netanyahu, *Origins of the Inquisition*, 164, 147.

17. Olster, *Roman Defeat*, 109.

18. Netanyahu, *Origins of the Inquisition*, 994, 997. It is impossible to write of such matters without some thought for the feelings sweeping this nation over the September 11, 2001 attacks on the World Trade Center and the Pentagon. One can see and hear the crystallization of viciously negative attitudes against people thought to share an ethnic or national background with the terrorists. People have been killed or attacked by outraged, perhaps deranged Americans. Innocent people are terrified, living in hiding, unable to lead normal lives. Such attitudes are reflected throughout Victor Klemperer's diary about his life as a Jew under the Nazi reign of terror. As argued throughout this study, both Jews and Others have faced such wrath over many centuries, their lives have been turned into shambles or much worse by the sacred violence that surrounded them.

19. Simon, *Verus Israel*, 32.

20. Ibid., 224.

21. L. R. Brown, *Might of the West*, 31.

22. Turpin and Kurtz, *Web of Violence*, 37.

23. Staub, *Roots of Evil*, 147.

24. James W. Bernauer, "Beyond Life and Death: On Foucault's Post-Auschwitz Ethic," *Philosophy Today* 32:2 (1988): 135.

25. Barnett, *Bystanders*, 19.

26. Staub, *Roots of Evil*, 29. Emphasis in the original.

27. Ibid., 85.

28. L. R. Brown, *Might of the West*, 336, 338.

29. Barnett, *Bystanders*, 41.

30. Poliakov, *The History of Anti-Semitism*, 180.

31. Sardar, *Postmodernism and the Other*, 101.

32. Mario Eidman, personal communication, 16 August 2001.

33. Kelsey, *Racism*, 22.

34. Barnett, *Bystanders*, 139.

35. Kelsey, *Racism*, 32.

36. Sardar, *Postmodernism and the Other*, 236.

37. F. G. Wood, *Arrogance of Faith*, 28, xix.

38. Wistrich, *Hitler's Apocalypse*, 136. Wistrich also says that the Holocaust is the culmination of the "spiritual treason of Christendom" (p. 136). I do not see how it is possible to maintain both positions: the Holocaust as a *caesura* in Western civilization, and the Holocaust as a culmination of spiritual treason. The treason, as it were, has been present and active for a very long time, perhaps from as early as the movement led by Paul

to separate Christianity from its parent religion. Western civilization has been operating on at least a dual track for a very long time: one that allows some people to thrive and prosper in all dimensions of life and one that uses sacred violence to leave Others with blasted hopes and diminished prospects (Bauman's gardening concept), or severely reduced possibilities for fulfillment.

39. Johann Baptist Metz, in Ekkehard Schuster and Reinhold Boschert-Kimmig, eds., *Hope against Hope: Johann Baptist Metz and Elie Wiesel Speak Out on the Holocaust* (New York: Paulist Press, 1999), 13.

40. Trachtenberg, *Devil and the Jews,* 21–22.

41. Raymond H. Schmandt, "The Fourth Crusade and the Just-War Theory," *Catholic Historical Review* 61 (1975): 218–219.

42. Siberry, *Criticism of Crusading,* 210.

43. Schmandt, "Fourth Crusade," 195.

44. Davies, *Infected Christianity,* 41.

45. Barnett, *Bystanders,* 27.

46. Ericksen, *Theologians under Hitler,* 199.

47. Ibid., 41.

48. Davies et al., *Barbaric Others,* 34.

49. Geoffrey H. Hartman, *The Fateful Question of Culture* (New York: Columbia University Press, 1997), 107.

50. Staub, *Roots of Evil,* 109.

51. Kelsey, *Racism,* 134.

52. R. A. Williams, *American Indian in Western Legal Thought,* 59.

53. Davies, *Infected Christianity,* xi.

54. Ibid., 15.

55. Staub, *Roots of Evil,* 121.

56. Willis, in *Largas,* 149.

57. Barnett, *Bystanders,* 44.

58. Reverend Charles Busch, personal interview, 19 September 2001.

59. Elie Wiesel, in *Hope against Hope,* ed. Schuster and Boschert-Kimmig, 72, 76.

60. John Paul II, "Universal Prayer: Confession of Sins and Asking for Forgiveness," *http://www.lafonds.net/pagans/Papal_Apology/PA-apology.htm,* March 12, 2000.

61. José Aldunate, S.J., "The Christian Ministry of Reconciliation in Chile," in *The Reconciliation of Peoples: Challenge to the Churches,* ed. Gregory Baum and Harold Wells (Maryknoll, N.Y.: Orbis Books, 1997), 57.

62. Ibid., 58.

63. Ibid., 59.

64. Gregory Baum, "The Role of the Churches in Polish-German Reconciliation," in *Reconciliation of Peoples,* ed. Baum and Wells, 131.

65. Metz, in *Hope against Hope,* ed. Schuster and Boschert-Kimmig, 16.

66. Baum, "Role of the Churches," 142.

67. Stuart Hall, cited in Dick Hebdige, *Subculture: The Meaning of Style* (London: Metheun & Co. Ltd), 1979.

Selected Bibliography

Adler, Elkan Nathan. *Auto De Fé and Jew*. London: Oxford University Press, 1908.

Ahmad, Jalal Al-I. *Occidentosis: A Plague from the West*. Trans. R. Campbell. Berkeley, Calif.: Mizan Press, 1984.

Alcalá, Angel, ed. *The Spanish Inquisition and the Inquisitorial Mind*. Boulder, Colo.: Social Science Monographs, 1987.

Almog, Samuel. *Antisemitism Through the Ages*. Trans. Nathan H. Reisner. Oxford: Pergamon Press, 1988.

Alvarez, J. "Apostolic Writings and the Roots of Anti-Semitism." *Studia Patristica* 13:2 (1975): 69–76.

Apter, David E. *Ideology and Discontent*. New York: Free Press, 1964.

Aranowitz, Stanley, and Henry A. Giroux. *Postmodern Education: Politics, Culture, and Social Criticism*. Minneapolis: University of Minnesota Press, 1991.

Atiya, Aziz Suryal. *The Crusade in the Later Middle Ages*. London: Metheun, 1938.

Auping, John A. *Religion and Social Justice: The Case of Christianity and the Abolition of Slavery in America*. Mexico, D.F.: Universidad Iberoamericana, Departemento de Ciencias Religiosas, 1994.

Axel, Larry E. "Christian Theology and the Murder of the Jews." *Encounter* 40 (Spring 1979): 121–141.

Axtell, James. *After Columbus: Essays in the Ethnohistory of Colonial North America*. New York: Oxford University Press, 1988.

———. *Beyond 1492: Encounters in Colonial North America*. New York: Oxford University Press, 1992.

———. "Forked Tongues: Moral Judgments in Indian History." *Perspectives: Newsletter of the American Historical Association* 25:2 (1987): 10–13.

Ayres, Lewis, and Gareth Jones, eds. *Christian Origins: Theology, Rhetoric and Community*. London: Routledge, 1998.

Bacharach, Walter Zwi. *Anti-Jewish Prejudices in German-Catholic Sermons*. Trans. Chaya Galai. Lewiston, N.Y.: Edwin Mellen Press, 1993.

Baer, Yitzhak. "Israel, the Christian Church, and the Roman Empire." *Scripta Hierosolymitana* 7 (1960–1961): 79–149.

Banton, Michael. *Anthropological Approaches to the Study of Religion*. New York: Frederick A. Praeger, 1966.

Barber, Malcolm. *Crusaders and Heretics, 12th–14th Centuries*. London: Variorum, 1995.

Barnett, Victoria J. *Bystanders: Conscience and Complicity during the Holocaust*. Westport, Conn.: Greenwood Press, 2000.

Bastide, Roger. "Color, Racism, and Christianity." *Daedalus* (Spring 1967): 312–327.

Bathrick, David. "Cultural Studies." *Introduction to Scholarship in Modern Languages and Literatures*, 2d ed. New York: Modern Language Association of America, 1992.

Bauer, Walter. *Orthodoxy and Heresy in Earliest Christianity*. Philadelphia: Fortress Press, 1971.

Baum, Gregory. *Compassion and Solidarity: The Church for Others*. New York: Paulist Press, 1990.

Baum, Gregory, and John Coleman, eds. *The Church and Racism*. New York: Seabury Press, 1982.

Baum, Gregory, and Harold Wells, eds. *The Reconciliation of Peoples: Challenge to the Churches*. Maryknoll, N.Y.: Orbis Books, 1997.

Bauman, Zygmunt. *Modernity and the Holocaust*. Ithaca: Cornell University Press, 1991.

Beaver, R. Pierce. *Church, State, and the American Indian*. St. Louis, Mo.: Concordia Publishing House, 1966.

Begley, Sharon. "The Roots of Evil." *Newsweek*, 21 May 2001, 30–35.

Bell, Aubrey F. G. *Juan Ginés Sepúlveda*. NP: Oxford University Press, 1925.

Berger, Peter. *The Sacred Canopy: Elements of a Sociological Theory of Religion*. New York: Doubleday, 1967.

Bernauer, James W. "Beyond Life and Death: On Foucault's Post-Auschwitz Ethic." *Philosophy Today* 32:2 (1988): 128–142.

Bévenot, Maurice, S. J. "The Inquisition and Its Antecedents," I, II, III, IV. *Heythrop Journal* 6 (1966): 257–268; 7 (1966): 381–393; 8 (1967): 52–69; 9 (1967): 152–168.

Birney, James Gillespie. *The American Churches: The Bulwarks of American Slavery*. New York: Arno Press, 1969.

Blumenkranz, Bernhard. "Anti-Jewish Polemics and Legislation in the Middle Ages: Literary Fiction or Reality?" *The Journal of Jewish Studies* 15 (1964): 125–140.

Bodmer, Beatriz Pastor. *The Armature of Conquest: Spanish Accounts of the Discovery of America, 1492–1589*. Trans. Lydia Longstreth Hunt. Stanford: Stanford University Press, 1992.

Boff, Leonardo. *New Evangelization: Good News to the Poor*. Trans. Robert R. Barr. Maryknoll, N.Y.: Orbis Books, 1990.

Boff, Leonardo, and Virgil Elizondo, eds. *1492–1992: The Voice of the Victims*. London: SCM Press, 1990.

Boles, John B., ed. *Masters and Slaves in the House of the Lord: Race and Religion in the American South*. Lexington: University Press of Kentucky, 1988.

Bowden, Henry Warner. *American Indians and Christian Missions: Studies in Cultural Conflict*. Chicago: University of Chicago Press, 1981.

Braham, Randolph, ed. *The Origins of the Holocaust: Christian Anti-Semitism*. New York: Columbia University Press, 1986.

Brennan, Brian. "The Conversion of the Jews of Clermont in AD 576." *Journal of Theological Studies* 36 (October 1985): 321–337.

Brinker-Gabler, Gisela, ed. *Encountering the Other(s): Studies in Literature, History, and Culture.* Albany: State University of New York Press, 1995.

Broszat, Martin. "Hitler and the Genesis of the 'Final Solution.'" *Yad Vashem Studies* 13 (1979): 73–125.

Brown, Dee. *Bury My Heart at Wounded Knee.* New York: Holt, Rinehart and Winston, 1970.

Brown, Lawrence R. *The Might of the West.* New York: Ivan Obolensky, 1963.

Brown, Peter. *Religion and Society in the Age of St. Augustine.* New York: Harper and Row, 1972.

Browning, Christopher. *Ordinary Men: Reserve Police Battalion 101 and the Final Solution in Poland.* New York: HarperPerennial, 1993.

Brundage, James A. *The Crusades: A Documentary Survey.* Milwaukee: Marquette University Press, 1962.

———. *The Crusades, Holy War and Canon Law.* Aldershot, England: Variorum, 1991.

———. *Medieval Canon Law and the Crusader.* Madison: University of Wisconsin Press, 1969.

———. "A Transformed Angel (X 3.31.18): The Problem of the Crusading Monk." *Studies in Medieval Cistercian History* 8 (1971): 57–62.

Buczek, Daniel S. "'Pro Defendendis Ordinis'—The French Cistercians and Their Enemies." *Studies in Medieval Cistercian History* 8 (1971): 90–108.

Burman, Edward. *The Inquisition: The Hammer of Heresy.* Wellingborough, Great Britain: Aquarian Press, 1984.

Busch, Reverend Charles. Personal interview, 19 September 2001.

Buswell, James O., III. *Slavery, Segregation, and Scripture.* Grand Rapids, Mich.: William B. Eerdmans, 1964.

Cameron, Averil. *Christianity and the Rhetoric of Empire.* Berkeley: University of California Press, 1991.

Caputo, John, and Mark Yount. *Foucault and the Critique of Institutions.* University Park: Pennsylvania State University Press, 1993.

Cargas, Harry James, ed. *When God and Man Failed: Non-Jewish Views of the Holocaust.* New York: Macmillan, 1981.

Chazan, Robert. *European Jewry and the First Crusade.* Berkeley: University of California Press, 1987.

———. *In the Year 1096: The First Crusade and the Jews.* Philadelphia: Jewish Publication Society, 1996.

Cherry, Conrad. *God's New Israel: Religious Interpretations of American Destiny.* Englewood Cliffs, N.J.: Prentice-Hall, 1971.

Chidester, David. *Savage Systems: Colonialism and Comparative Religion in Southern Africa.* Charlottesville: University Press of Virginia, 1996.

Churchill, Ward. *Indians Are Us? Culture and Genocide in Native North America.* Monroe, Maine: Common Courage Press, 1994.

Coleman-Norton, Paul R., ed. *Studies in Roman Economic and Social History in Honor of Allan Chester Johnson.* Freeport, N.Y.: Books for Libraries Press, 1951.

Cornelius, Janet Duitsman. *"When I Can Read My Title Clear": Literacy, Slavery, and Religion in the Antebellum South.* Columbia: University of South Carolina Press, 1991.

Cornwell, John. *Hitler's Pope: The Secret History of Pope Pius XII.* New York: Viking, 1999.

Costo, Rupert, and Jeannette Henry Costo. *The Missions of California: A Legacy of Geno- cide.* San Francisco: Indian Historian Press, 1987.

Coulton, George G. *The Inquisition.* New York: J. Cape & H. Smith, 1929.

Curran, James, Michael Gurevitch, Janet Woollacott, eds. *Mass Communication and So- ciety.* Beverly Hills: SAGE Publications, 1977.

Cutler, Allan. "Innocent III and the Distinctive Clothing of Jews and Muslims." *Studies in Medieval Culture* 3 (1970): 92–116.

Davies, Alan. *Antisemitism and the Foundations of Christianity.* New York: Paulist Press, 1979.

———. *Infected Christianity: A Study of Modern Racism.* Kingston: McGill-Queen's University Press, 1988.

Davies, Merryl Wyn, Ashis Nundy, and Ziauddin Sardar. *Barbaric Others: A Manifesto on Western Racism.* London: Pluto Press, 1993.

Davis, David Brion. *The Problem of Slavery in Western Culture.* New York: Oxford Uni- versity Press, 1966.

De Certeau, Michel. *Heterologies: Discourse on the Other.* Minneapolis: University of Minnesota Press, 1986.

de Las Casas, Bartolomé. *The Devastation of the Indies: A Brief Account.* Trans. Herma Briffault. New York: Seabury Press, 1974.

Dimont, Max I. *Jews, God, and History.* 1962; reprint, New York: Signet, 1994.

Doerris, Hermann. *Constantine and Religious Liberty.* Trans. Roland H. Bainton. New Haven: Yale University Press, 1960.

Douglass, Frederick. *Narrative of the Life of Frederick Douglass.* New York: Penguin Books, 1968.

Drinnon, Richard. *Facing West: The Metaphysics of Indian-Hating and Empire Build- ing.* Norman: University of Oklahoma Press, 1997.

Driver, John. *How Christians Made Peace with War.* Scottsdale, Pa.: Herald Press, 1988.

During, Simon, ed. *The Cultural Studies Reader.* London: Routledge, 1993.

Eidman, Mario. Personal communication, 16 August 2001.

Eitzen, D. Stanley, ed. *Sport and Contemporary Society,* 6th ed. New York: Worth, 2001.

Elias, Norbert. *The Germans.* New York: Columbia University Press, 1996.

Elison, George. *Deus Destroyed: The Image of Christianity in Early Modern Japan.* Cam- bridge: Harvard University Press, 1973.

Ellerbe, Helen. *The Dark Side of Christian History.* San Rafael, Calif.: Morningstar Books, 1995.

Elliott, John Huxtable. "The Discovery of America and the Discovery of Man." *Proceed- ings of the British Academy* 58 (1972): 101–125.

———. *Imperial Spain: 1469–1716.* Harmondsworth, England: Penguin Books, 1970.

Ericksen, Robert P. *Theologians under Hitler.* New Haven: Yale University Press, 1985.

Falk, Gerhard. *The Jew in Christian Theology.* Jefferson, N.C.: McFarland, 1992.

Faust, Drew Gilpin. *The Ideology of Slavery.* Baton Rouge: Louisiana State University Press, 1981.

Feldman, Louis. *Jew and Gentile in the Ancient World.* Princeton: Princeton University Press, 1993.

Feldman, Stephen M. *Please Don't Wish Me a Merry Christmas: A Critical History of the Separation of Church and State.* New York: New York University Press, 1997.

Felsenstein, Frank. *Anti-Semitic Stereotypes: A Paradigm of Otherness in English Popular Culture, 1660–1830.* Baltimore: Johns Hopkins University Press, 1995.

Fenigstein, Allan. "Reconceptualizing the Obedience of the Perpetrators." Paper presented at the Remembering for the Future 2000 Conference, Oxford University, July 2000.

Finkelman, Paul, ed. *Comparative Issues in Slavery.* New York: Garland, 1989.

———. *Religion and Slavery,* vol. 16. New York: Garland, 1989.

Fiorenza, Elisabeth Schussler, and David Tracy, eds. *The Holocaust as Interruption.* Edinburgh: T. and T. Clark, 1984.

Fischer, Klaus P. *The History of an Obsession: German Judeophobia and the Holocaust.* New York: Continuum, 1998.

Fiske, John. "Manifest Destiny." *Harper's New Monthly Magazine,* 1885, 578–590.

Fitzhugh, George. *Cannibals All! Or Slaves Without Masters.* Ed. C. Vann Woodward. Cambridge: Harvard University Press, 1988.

Fleischner, Eva, ed. *Auschwitz, Beginning of a New Era? Reflections on the Holocaust.* New York: KTAV Publishing House, 1977.

Fogel, Daniel. *Junipero Serra, the Vatican, and Enslavement Theology.* San Francisco: ISM Press, 1988.

Fontaine, Jacques. "Christians and Military Service in the Early Church." *Concilium* 7 (1965): 107–119.

Foucault, Michel. "The Subject and Power." *Critical Inquiry* 8 (Summer 1982): 777–795.

Friede, Juan, and Benjamin Keen. *Bartolome de Las Casas in History: Toward an Understanding of the Man and His Work.* DeKalb: Northern Illinois University Press, 1971.

Friedlander, Henry. *The Origins of Nazi Genocide: From Euthanasia to the Final Solution.* Chapel Hill: University of North Carolina Press, 1995.

Furet, François. *Unanswered Questions: Nazi Germany and the Genocide of the Jews.* New York: Schocken Books, 1989.

Gager, John. *The Origins of Anti-Semitism.* New York: Oxford University Press, 1985.

Galeano, Eduardo. *Open Veins of Latin America.* Trans. Cedric Bellfrage. New York: Monthly Review Press, 1973.

Gallagher, Susan Van Zanten, ed. *Postcolonial Literature and the Biblical Call for Justice.* Jackson: University Press of Mississippi, 1994.

Geertz, Clifford. *The Interpretation of Cultures.* New York: Basic Books, 1973.

Gibson, Charles, ed. *The Spanish Tradition in America.* New York: Harper and Row, 1968.

Gieysztor, Alexander. "The Genesis of the Crusades: The Encyclicals of Sergius IV (1009–1012)." *Medievalia et Humanistica* 5 (1948): 3–23; 6 (1949): 3–34.

Gilman, Sander. *Jewish Self-Hatred: Anti-Semitism and the Hidden Language of Jews.* Baltimore: Johns Hopkins University Press, 1986.

Giroux, Henry. *Education and Cultural Studies.* New York: Routledge, 1997.

———. *Theory and Practice in Education.* South Hadley, Mass.: Bergin and Garvey, 1983.

Glatstein, Jacob, Israel Knox, and Samuel Margoshes, eds. *Anthology of Holocaust Literature.* Philadelphia: Jewish Publication Society, 1969.

Glock, Charles Y., and Rodney Stark. *Christian Beliefs and Anti-Semitism.* New York: Harper and Row, 1966.

Godfrey, John. *1204: The Unholy Crusade.* Oxford: Oxford University Press, 1980.

Goldhagen, Daniel. *Hitler's Willing Executioners.* New York: Alfred A. Knopf, 1996.

Grady, Hugh. "Containment, Subversion—and Postmodernism." *Textual Practice* 7 (1993): 31–49.

Grayzel, Solomon. "The Talmud and the Medieval Papacy." *Essays in Honor of Solomon B. Freehof.* Pittsburgh: Rodef Shalom Congregation, 1964, 220–245.

Grissom, Fred Allen. "Chrysostom and the Jews: Studies in Jewish-Christian Relations in Fourth-Century Antioch." Diss., Southern Baptist Theological Seminary, 1978.

Grossberg, Lawrence, Cary Nelson, and Paula Treichler, eds. *Cultural Studies.* New York: Routledge, 1992.

Haliczer, Stephen, ed. *Inquisition and Society in Early Modern Europe.* Totowa, N.J.: Barnes and Noble Books, 1987.

Hallie, Phillip. *Lest Innocent Blood Be Shed.* New York: Harper and Row, 1979.

Handy, Robert T. "The Protestant Quest for Christian America: 1830–1930." *Church History* 22 (March 1953) 8–20.

Hanke, Lewis. *All Mankind Is One.* DeKalb: Northern Illinois University Press, 1974.

———. "Pope Paul III and the American Indians." *Harvard Theological Review* 30 (1937): 65–102.

Harkins, Paul W., trans. *Saint John Chrysostom: Discourses Against Judaizing Christians.* Washington, D.C.: Catholic University of America Press, 1979.

Harnack, Adolf. *Militia Christi.* Trans. David McInnes Gracie. Philadelphia: Fortress Press, 1981.

Harper, William, James Henry Hammond, William Gilmore Simms, and Thomas Roderick Dew. *The Pro-Slavery Argument.* 1852; reprint, New York: Negro Universities Press, 1968.

Harrill, J. Albert. *The Manumission of Slaves in Early Christianity.* Tübingen, Germany: J.C.B. Mohr, 1995.

Hartman, Geoffrey H. *The Fateful Question of Culture.* New York: Columbia University Press, 1997.

Hawley, John C. *Christian Encounters with the Other.* New York: New York University Press, 1998.

Hayes, Peter, ed. *Lessons and Legacies: The Meaning of the Holocaust in a Changing World.* Evanston: Northwestern University Press, 1991.

Hebdige, Dick. *Subculture: The Meaning of Style.* London: Metheun & Co. Ltd., 1979.

Heering, Gerrit Jan. *The Fall of Christianity: A Study of Christianity, the State and War.* Trans. J. W. Thompson. New York: Fellowship Publications, 1943.

Helgeland, John. "Christians and the Roman Army A.D. 173–337." *Church History* 43:1 (March 1974): 149–161.

Herr, Moshe David. "Persecutions and Martyrdom in Hadrian's Days." *Scripta Hierosolymitana* 23 (1972): 85–125.

Hilberg, Raul. *The Destruction of the European Jews.* New York: Holmes and Meier, 1985.

Hobsbawm, Eric. "Barbarism: A User's Guide." *New Left Review* 206 (1994): 44–54.

Hochhuth, Rolf. *The Deputy.* Trans. Richard and Clara Winston. New York: Grove Press, 1964.

Hochschild, Adam. *King Leopold's Ghost.* Boston: Houghton Mifflin, 1998.

Hornus, Jean-Michel. *It Is Not Lawful for Me to Fight: Early Christian Attitudes Toward War, Violence, and the State.* Trans. Alan Krieder. Scottsdale, Pa.: Herald Press, 1980.

Horsman, Reginald. *Race and Manifest Destiny: The Origins of Racial Anglo-Saxonism.* Cambridge: Harvard University Press, 1981.

Huddleston, Lee Eldridge. *Origins of the American Indians: European Concepts, 1492–1729*. Austin: University of Texas Press, 1967.

Hyams, Edward, and George Ordish. *The Last of the Incas: The Rise and Fall of an American Empire*. New York: Barnes and Noble, 1963.

Hyatt, Vera Lawrence, and Rex Nettleford, eds. *Race, Discourse, and the Origins of the Americas*. Washington, D.C.: Smithsonian University Press, 1995.

Jaher, Frederic Cople. *A Scapegoat in the New Wilderness: The Origins and Rise of Anti-Semitism in America*. Cambridge: Harvard University Press, 1994.

Jaimes, M. Annette, ed. *The State of Native America*. Boston: South End Press, 1992.

Jennings, Francis. *The Invasion of America*. Chapel Hill: University of North Carolina Press, 1975.

Jernegan, Marcus W. "Slavery and Conversion in the American Colonies." *American Historical Review* 21:3 (April 1916): 504–527.

John Paul II. "Universal Prayer: Confession of Sins and Asking for Forgiveness." *http://www.lafonds.net/pagans/Papal_Apology/PA-apology.htm*, March 12, 2000.

Johnson, Eric A. *Nazi Terror: The Gestapo, Jews, and Ordinary Germans*. New York: Basic Books, 1999.

Johnson, James Turner. *Ideology, Reason, and the Limitations of War*. Princeton: Princeton University Press, 1975.

Jordan, Winthrop D. *White over Black: American Attitudes Toward the Negro, 1550–1812*. New York: W. W. Norton, 1968.

Juster, Jean. "The Legal Condition of the Jews under the Visigothic Kings." *Israel Law Review* 11 (1976): 259–286.

Kadir, Djelal. *Columbus and the Ends of the Earth: Europe's Prophetic Rhetoric as Conquering Ideology*. Berkeley: University of California Press, 1992.

Kaplan, Amy, and Donald E. Pease, eds. *Cultures of United States Imperialism*. Durham: Duke University Press, 1993.

Katz, Jacob. *From Prejudice to Destruction: Anti-Semitism, 1700–1933*. Cambridge: Harvard University Press, 1980.

Kee, Alistair. *Constantine Versus Christ: The Triumph of Ideology*. London: SCM Press, 1982.

Keen, Maurice Hugh. *The Laws of War in the Late Middle Ages*. London: Routledge and Kegan Paul, 1965.

Kelsey, George D. *Racism and the Christian Understanding of Man*. New York: Charles Scribner and Sons, 1965.

Kennedy, John Hopkins. *Jesuit and Savage in New France*. New Haven: Yale University Press, 1950.

Kieckhefer, Richard. "Radical Tendencies in the Flagellant Movement of the Mid-Fourteenth Century." *Journal of Medieval and Renaissance Studies* 4 (1974): 157–176.

———. *Repression of Heresy in Medieval Germany*. Philadelphia: University of Pennsylvania Press, 1979.

Klein, Herbert S. "Anglicanism, Catholicism and the Negro Slave." *Comparative Studies in Society and History* 3:3 (April 1966): 295–327.

———. *Slavery in the Americas*. Chicago: University of Chicago Press, 1967.

Klemperer, Victor. *I Will Bear Witness: 1933–1941*. Trans. Martin Chalmers. New York: Random House, 1998.

————. *I Will Bear Witness: 1942–1945.* Trans. Martin Chalmers. New York: Modern Library, 2001.

Kohn, Hans. *The Idea of Nationalism: A Study in Its Origins and Background.* New York: Macmillan, 1961.

La Monte, John L. "The Significance of the Crusaders' States in Medieval History." *Byzantion* 15 (1941): 300–315.

Landau, Ronnie S. *Studying the Holocaust.* New York: Routledge, 1998.

Langer, Suzanne. *Philosophy in a New Key,* 4th ed. Cambridge: Harvard University Press, 1957.

Lea, Henry C. "Ferrand Martinez and the Massacres of 1391." *American Historical Review* 1:2 (January 1896): 209–219.

Lears, T. J. Jackson. "The Concept of Cultural Hegemony: Problems and Possibilities." *American Historical Review* 90:3 (1985): 567–593.

Lerner, Melvin J. and Carolyn H. Simmons. "Observer's Reaction to the 'Innocent Victim': Compassion or Rejection?" *Journal of Personality and Social Psychology* 4:2 (1966): 203–210.

Lewis, Archibald. *Nomads and Crusaders: A.D. 1000–1368.* Bloomington: Indiana University Press, 1988.

Liebeschuetz, J.H.W.G. *Continuity and Change in Roman Religion.* Oxford: Clarendon Press, 1979.

Lifton, Robert Jay. *Nazi Doctors.* New York: Basic Books, 1986.

Linder, Amnon. *The Jews in Roman Imperial Legislation.* Detroit: Wayne State University Press, 1987.

Lorenz, Dagmar C. G., and Gabriele Weinberger, eds. *Insiders and Outsiders: Jewish and Gentile Culture in Germany and Austria.* Detroit: Wayne State University Press, 1994.

Maccoby, Hyam. *The Sacred Executioner: Human Sacrifice and the Legacy of Guilt.* London: Thames and Hudson, 1982.

MacCormack, Sabine. "'The Heart Has Its Reasons': Predicaments of Missionary Christianity in Early Colonial Peru." *Hispanic American Historical Review* 65:3 (1985): 443–466.

MacKay, Angus. "Popular Movements and Pogroms in Fifteenth-Century Castile." *Past and Present* 55 (1972): 33–67.

Macmullen, Ramsay. *Christianizing the Roman Empire: (A.D. 100–400).* New Haven: Yale University Press, 1984.

————. "What Difference Did Christianity Make?" *Historia* 35 (1986): 322–343.

Mann, Michael. *The Sources of Social Power.* Cambridge: Cambridge University Press, 1986.

Matheson, Peter. *The Third Reich and the Christian Churches.* Grand Rapids, Mich.: William B. Eerdmans, 1981.

Maycock, Alan Lawson. *The Inquisition: From Its Establishment to the Great Schism.* New York: Harper and Row, 1926.

McHoul, Alec, and Wendy Grace. *A Foucault Primer: Discourse, Power and the Subject.* New York: New York University Press, 1993.

McKivigan, John R., and Mitchell Snay, eds. *Religion and the Antebellum Debate over Slavery.* Athens: University of Georgia Press, 1998.

McLaughlin, William G. *The Cherokees and Christianity, 1794–1870.* Athens: University of Georgia Press, 1994.

McNeill, William H. *The Pursuit of Power: Technology, Armed Force, and Society since A.D. 1000*. Chicago: University of Chicago Press, 1982.

Miller, Randall M., and Jon L. Wakelyn, eds. *Catholics in the Old South*. Macon, Ga.: Mercer University Press, 1983.

Miller, William Robert. *Nonviolence: A Christian Interpretation*. New York: Schocken Books, 1966.

Moore, Robert Ian. *The Formation of a Persecuting Society*. Oxford: Blackwell, 1990.

———. *The Origins of European Dissent*. London: Penguin Books, 1977.

Moreno, Wigberto Jiménez. "The Indians of America and Christianity." *Americas* 14:4 (April 1958): 411–431.

Morley, David, and Kuan-Hsing Chen. *Stuart Hall: Critical Dialogues in Cultural Studies*. London: Routledge, 1996.

Morley, Sylvanus G. *The Ancient Maya*, 3d ed. Stanford: Stanford University Press, 1956.

Morrison, Karl F. *Understanding Conversion*. Charlottesville: University Press of Virginia, 1992.

Nash, Gary B., and Richard Weiss. *The Great Fear: Race in the Mind of America*. New York: Holt, Rinehart and Winston, 1970.

Netanyahu, Benzion. *The Origins of the Inquisition in Fifteenth Century Spain*. New York: Random House, 1995.

Neusner, Jacob. *Judaism and Christianity in the Age of Constantine*. Chicago: University of Chicago Press, 1987.

Nickerson, Hoffman. *The Inquisition: A Political and Military Study of Its Establishment*. 1932; reprint, Port Washington, N.Y.: Kennikat Press, 1968.

Oakes, James. *The Ruling Race*. New York: Vintage Books, 1983.

O'Brien, John A. *The Inquisition*. New York: Macmillan, 1973.

O'Connell, Robert L. *Ride of the Second Horseman: The Birth and Death of War*. New York: Oxford University Press, 1995.

O'Keefe, Timothy J., ed. *Columbus, Confrontation, Christianity: The European-American Encounter Revisited*. Los Gatos, Calif.: Forbes Mill Press, 1994.

Oldenbourg, Zoé. *Massacre at Montségur: A History of the Albigensian Crusade*. Trans. Peter Green. London: Phoenix, 1998.

Oliner, Samuel P., and Pearl M. Oliner. *The Altruistic Personality: Rescuers of Jews in Nazi Europe*. New York: Free Press, 1988.

Olster, David M. *Roman Defeat, Christian Response, and the Literary Construction of the Jew*. Philadelphia: University of Pennsylvania Press, 1994.

O'Reilly, David. "Translating 'the Jews.'" *Oregonian*, 18 August 2001, C5.

Pagden, Anthony. *The Fall of Natural Man: The American Indian and the Origins of Comparative Ethnology*. Cambridge: Cambridge University Press, 1982.

Pagliaro, Harold E., ed. *Racism and the Eighteenth Century*. Cleveland: Case Western Reserve University Press, 1973.

Palmer, Colin. *Slaves of the White God: Blacks in Mexico, 1570–1650*. Cambridge: Harvard University Press, 1976.

Parkes, James. *The Conflict of the Church and the Synagogue: A Study in the Origins of Antisemitism*. New York: Atheneum, 1974.

Patterson, Orlando. *Slavery and Social Death*. Cambridge: Harvard University Press, 1982.

Pearce, Roy Harvey. *The Savages of America: A Study of the Indian and the Idea of Civilization*. Baltimore: Johns Hopkins University Press, 1965.

Pennington, Kenneth J., Jr. "Bartolome de las Casas and the Tradition of Medieval Law." *Church History* 39 (1970): 149–161.

Perry, Mary Elizabeth, and Anne J. Cruz, eds. *Cultural Encounters: The Impact of the Inquisition in Spain and the New World.* Berkeley: University of California Press, 1991.

Peters, Edward. *Inquisition.* New York: Free Press, 1988.

Peterson, Thomas Virgil. *Ham and Japheth: The Mythic World of Whites in the Antebellum South.* Metuchen, N.J.: Scarecrow Press, 1978.

Phillips, William D., Jr. *Slavery from Roman Times to the Early Transatlantic Trade.* Minneapolis: University of Minnesota Press, 1985.

Poliakov, Léon. *The Aryan Myth: A History of Racist and Nationalistic Ideas in Europe.* Trans. Edmund Howard. New York: Barnes and Noble, 1974.

———. *The History of Anti-Semitism.* Trans. Richard Howard. New York: Schocken Books, 1974.

Poole, Stafford. "War by Fire and Blood: The Church of the Chichemacas, 1585." *Americas* 22 (1965): 116–137.

Porges, Walter. "The Clergy, the Poor, and the Non-Combatants on the First Crusade." *Speculum* 21:1 (1946): 1–23.

Porter, Harry Culverwell. *The Inconstant Savage.* London: Duckworth, 1979.

Prawer, Joshua. *The Crusaders' Kingdom: European Colonialism in the Middle Ages.* New York: Praeger, 1972.

Prucha, Francis Paul. *American Indian Policy in Crisis.* Norman: University of Oklahoma Press, 1976.

———. "The Image of the Indian in Pre-Civil War America." In *Lectures: 1970–1971.* Indianapolis: Indiana Historical Society, 1971.

Pullan, Brian. *The Jews of Europe and the Inquisition of Venice, 1550–1670.* New York: Barnes and Noble, 1983.

Redding, Saunders. *They Came in Chains.* Philadelphia: J. B. Lippincott, 1950.

Reitlinger, Gerald. *The SS: Alibi of a Nation.* New York: Viking Press, 1957.

Reuther, Rosemary. *Faith and Fratricide.* New York: Seabury Press, 1979.

———. "Judaism and Christianity: Two Fourth-Century Religions." *Studies in Religion* 2 (1972): 1–10.

Riley-Smith, Jonathan. "An Approach to Crusading Ethics." *Reading Medieval Studies* 6 (1980): 3–20.

———, ed. *The Oxford History of the Crusades.* Oxford: Oxford University Press, 1999.

Rivera, Luis N. *A Violent Evangelism: The Political and Religious Conquest of the Americas.* Louisville, Ky.: Westminster/John Knox Press, 1992.

Rogers, Mary F. *Multicultural Experiences, Multicultural Theories.* New York: McGraw-Hill 1996.

Rosaldo, Renato. *Culture and Truth: The Remaking of Social Analysis.* 1989; reprint, Boston: Beacon Press, 1993.

Rosenbaum, Alan S., ed. *Is the Holocaust Unique? Perspectives of Comparative Genocide.* Boulder, Colo.: Westview Press, 1996.

Rosin, Hanna. "Southern Baptist Campaign Aims to Convert Jews to Christianity." *Oregonian,* 9 September 1999, A3.

Ross, Fred A. *Slavery Ordained of God.* 1859; reprint, New York: Negro Universities Press, 1969.

Roth, Cecil. *The Spanish Inquisition.* New York: W. W. Norton, 1964.

Roth, John K., Marilyn Harran, Dieter Kuntz, Russell Lemmons, Robert Ashley Michael, Keith Pickus, contributors. *Holocaust Chronicle.* Lincolnwood, Ill.: Publications International, 2000.

Roth, John K., and Michael Berenbaum, eds. *Holocaust: Religious and Philosophical Implications.* New York: Paragon House, 1989.

Rubenstein, Richard, and John K. Roth. *Approaches to Auschwitz: The Holocaust and Its Legacy.* Atlanta: John Knox Press, 1987.

Russell, James C. *The Germanization of Early Medieval Christianity.* New York: Oxford University Press, 1994.

Russell, Jeffrey. "Interpretations of the Origins of Medieval History." *Medieval Studies* 25 (1963): 26–53.

Ryan, Edward A., S.J. "The Rejection of Military Service by the Early Christians." *Theological Studies* 13 (March 1952) 1–29.

Ryan, Kiernan, ed. *New Historicism and Cultural Materialism.* London: Arnold, 1996.

Said, Edward. *Culture and Imperialism.* London: Chatto and Windus, 1993.

———. "Representing the Colonized: Anthropology's Interlocutors." *Critical Inquiry* 15 (1989): 205–225.

Sale, Kirkpatrick. *The Conquest of Paradise: Christopher Columbus and the Colombian Legacy.* New York: Penguin Books, 1991.

Salisbury, Neal Emerson. "Conquest of the 'Savage': Puritans, Puritan Missionaries, and Indians, 1620–1680." Diss., UCLA, 1972.

Sardar, Ziauddin. "Lies, Damned Lies and Colombus: The Dynamics of Constructed Ignorance." *Third Text* 21 (1992–1993): 47–56.

———. *Postmodernism and the Other: The New Imperialism of Western Culture.* London: Pluto Press, 1998.

Schmandt, Raymond H. "The Fourth Crusade and the Just-War Theory." *Catholic Historical Review* 61 (1975): 191–221.

Schoedel, William R., and Robert L. Wilken, eds. *Early Christian Literature and the Classical Intellectual Tradition.* Paris: Editions Beauchesne, 1979.

Schuster, Ekkehard, and Reinhold Boschert-Kimmig, eds. *Hope against Hope: Johann Baptist Metz and Elie Wiesel Speak Out on the Holocaust.* Trans. J. Matthew Ashley. New York: Paulist Press, 1999.

Schwartz, Regina. *The Curse of Cain: The Violent Legacy of Monotheism.* Chicago: University of Chicago Press, 1997.

Scott, James C. *Domination and the Arts of Resistance.* New Haven: Yale University Press, 1990.

Seiden, Morton Irving. *The Paradox of Hate: A Study in Ritual Murder.* New York: South Brunswick, 1967.

Seward, Desmond. *The Monks of War: The Military Religious Orders.* London: Penguin Books, 1972.

Shay, Johnathan. *Achilles in Vietnam: Combat Trauma and the Undoing of Character.* New York: Simon and Schuster, 1995.

———. Private correspondence, January 1998.

Siberry, Elizabeth. *Criticism of Crusading: 1095–1274.* Oxford: Clarendon Press, 1985.

Sider, Ronald J., and Richard K. Taylor. *Nuclear Holocaust and Christian Hope.* New York: Paulist Press, 1982.

Siemson, Hans. *Hitler Youth.* London: Drummond, 1940.

Simon, Marcel. *Verus Israel: A Study of the Relations Between Christians and Jews in the Roman Empire (135–425)*. Trans. H. McKeating. New York: Oxford University Press, 1986.

Slotkin, Richard. *Regeneration Through Violence: The Mythology of the American Frontier*. New York: HarperPerennial, 1996.

Snowden, Frank M., Jr. *Before Color Prejudice: The Ancient View of Blacks*. Cambridge: Harvard University Press, 1991.

Stampp, Kenneth M. *The Peculiar Institution: Slavery in the Ante-Bellum South*. New York: Vintage Press, 1956.

Stannard, David E. *American Holocaust: The Conquest of the New World*. Oxford: Oxford University Press, 1992.

Starr, Joshua. "The Mass Conversion of Jews in Southern Italy: 1290–1293." *Speculum* 21 (1946): 203–211.

Staub, Ervin. *The Roots of Evil: The Origins of Genocide and Other Group Violence*. Cambridge: Cambridge University Press, 1992.

Steele, Michael R. *Christianity, Tragedy, and Holocaust Literature*. Westport, Conn.: Greenwood Press, 1995.

Stocking, George W., Jr. *Race, Culture, and Evolution*. New York: Free Press, 1968.

Sumption, Jonathan. *The Albigensian Crusade*. London: Faber and Faber, 1978.

Svaldi, David. *Sand Creek and the Rhetoric of Extermination: A Case Study in Indian-White Relations*. Lanham, Md.: University Press of America, 1989.

Swartley, Willard, ed. *Essays on War and Peace: Bible and the Early Church*. Elkhart, Ind: Institute of Mennonite Studies, 1986.

Tal, Uriel. *Christians and Jews in Germany: Religion, Politics, and Ideology in the Second Reich, 1870–1914*. Trans. Noah Jonathan Jacobs. Ithaca: Cornell University Press, 1975.

Theissen, Gerd. *Social Reality and the Early Christians*. Trans. Margaret Kohl. Minneapolis: Fortress Press, 1992.

Thomas, Laurence Mordekhai. *Vessels of Evil: American Slavery and the Holocaust*. Philadelphia: Temple University Press, 1993.

Throop, Palmer A. *Criticism of the Crusade: A Study of Public Opinion and Crusade Propaganda*. Philadelphia: Porcupine Press, 1975.

———. "Criticism of Papal Crusade Policy in Old French and Provençal." *Speculum* 23:4 (1938): 379–412.

Tinker, George E. *Missionary Conquest: The Gospel and Native American Cultural Genocide*. Minneapolis: Fortress Press, 1993.

Tise, Larry E. *Proslavery: A History of the Defense of Slavery in America, 1701–1840*. Athens: University of Georgia Press, 1987.

Tomlinson, John. *Cultural Imperialism: A Critical Introduction*. Baltimore: Johns Hopkins University Press, 1991.

Toynbee, Arnold. *War and Civilization*. New York: Oxford University Press, 1950.

Trachtenberg, Joshua. *The Devil and the Jews: The Medieval Conception of the Jew and Its Relation to Modern Anti-Semitism*. Philadelphia: Jewish Publication Society of America, 1943.

Treat, James, ed. *Native and Christian: Indigenous Voices on Religious Identity in the United States and Canada*. New York: Routledge, 1996.

Turberville, Arthur Stanley. "Heresies and the Inquisition in the Middle Ages, c. 1000–1305." *Cambridge Medieval History* 6 (1936): 699–726.

Turner, Graeme. *British Cultural Studies: An Introduction*. London: Routledge, 1996.

Turpin, Jennifer, and Lester R. Kurtz, eds. *The Web of Violence: From Interpersonal to Global*. Urbana: University of Illinois Press, 1997.

Victor, George. *Hitler: The Pathology of Evil*. Dulles, Va.: Brassey's, 1998.

Villoro, Luis. "Sahagún, or the Limits of the Discovery of the Other." 1992 Lecture Series, University of Maryland Department of Spanish and Portuguese.

Wakefield, Walter L. *Heresy, Crusade and the Inquisition in Southern France 1100–1250*. London: George Allen and Unwin, 1974.

Waller, James E. *Children of Cain: How Ordinary People Commit Extraordinary Evil*. New York: Oxford University Press, 2001.

———. "Ordinary People, Extraordinary Evil: Understanding the Institutional Frameworks of Evildoing." *Proteus* 21 (1995): 12–16.

———. "Perpetrators of the Holocaust: Divided and Unitary Self Conceptions of Evildoing." *Holocaust and Genocide Studies* 10:1 (Spring 1996): 11–33.

Walvin, James. *Questioning Slavery*. London: Routledge, 1996.

Waring, Luther Hess. *The Political Theories of Martin Luther*. 1910; reprint, Port Washington, N.Y.: Kennikat Press, 1968.

Waugh, Scott L., and Peter D. Diehl, eds. *Christendom and Its Discontents: Exclusion, Persecution, and Rebellion, 1000–1500*. Cambridge: Cambridge University Press, 1996.

Weinstein, Allen, and Frank Otto Gatell. *American Negro Slavery*. New York: Oxford University Press, 1968.

Weiss, John. *Ideology of Death*. Chicago: Ivan R. Dee, 1996.

Wells, Donald A. *The War Myth*. New York: Pegasus, 1967.

Westbury-Jones, John. *Roman and Christian Imperialism*. London: Macmillan, 1939.

Whittaker, John. "Christianity and Morality in the Roman Empire." *Vigiliae Christianae* 33 (1979): 209–225.

Wiesel, Elie. "Jewish Values in the Post-Holocaust Future." *Judaism* 16 (1967): 281–299.

Wilken, Robert L. *John Chrysostom and the Jews: Rhetoric and Reality in the Late 4th Century*. Berkeley: University of California Press, 1983.

Williams, A. Lukyn. *Adversus Judaeos*. Cambridge: University Press, 1935.

Williams, Raymond. *Keywords*. London: Fontana, 1976.

Williams, Robert A. *The American Indian in Western Legal Thought, The Discourses of Conquest*. New York: Oxford University Press, 1990.

Wish, Harvey. *Slavery in the South*. New York: Noonday Press, 1964.

Wistrich, Robert. *Hitler's Apocalypse: Jews and the Nazi Legacy*. London: Weidenfeld and Nicolson, 1985.

Wood, Betty. *The Origins of American Slavery*. New York: Hill and Wang, 1997.

Wood, Forrest G. *The Arrogance of Faith: Christianity and Race in America from the Colonial Era to the Twentieth Century*. New York: Alfred A. Knopf, 1990.

The Works of Robert G. Ingersoll, vol. 2. New York: Ingersoll League, 1929.

Wright, Quincy. *A Study of War*. Chicago: University of Chicago Press, 1964.

Yerushalmi, Yosef Hayim. "The Inquisition and the Jews of France in the Times of Bernard Gui." *Harvard Theological Review* 63:3 (1970): 317–376.

Yewell, John, Chris Dodge, and Jan DeSirey, eds. *Confronting Columbus*. Jefferson, N.C.: McFarland, 1992.

Zabel, James A. *Nazism and the Pastors: A Study of the Ideas of Three Deutsche Christen Groups*. Missoula, Mont.: Scholars Press, 1976

Index

184   INDEX

About the Author

MICHAEL R. STEELE is Distinguished Professor of English at Pacific University. He has taught there, devoting much of his time to teaching Holocaust Literature, since 1975. He has served as the president and executive director of the Oregon Holocaust Resource Center and currently serves as the director of Holocaust Education at Pacific University. He is the author of *Christianity, Tragedy, and the Holocaust* (Greenwood, 1995).

Recent Titles in
Contributions to the Study of Religion